DIAMONDS IN THE SKY

Those who travel watch the sail and the stars
They hear the wind they hear the other sea beyond the wind
Near them like a closed shell, they don't hear
Anything else, don't look among the cypress shadows
For a lost face, a coin, don't ask,
Seeing a raven on a dry branch, what it remembers.

GEORGE SEFERIS

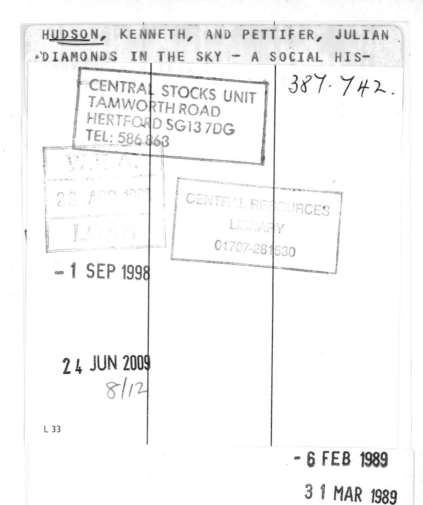

Kenneth Hudson and Julian Pettifer

DIAMONDS IN THE SKY

A Social History of Air Travel

THE BODLEY HEAD
London Sydney Toronto

BRITISH BROADCASTING CORPORATION

© Kenneth Hudson and Julian Pettifer 1979

Published by
The Bodley Head Ltd
9 Bow Street
London WC2E 7AL
and the
British Broadcasting Corporation
35 Marylebone High Street
London W1M 4AA

First published 1979

British Library Cataloguing in Publication Data
Hudson, Kenneth
  Diamonds in the sky.
  1. Air travel – History
  2. Air travel – Social aspects
  I. Title II. Pettifer, Julian
  III. British Broadcasting Corporation
  387.7′42′0904 HE9787
ISBN 0–370–30162–5
ISBN 0–563–17749–7 (British Broadcasting Corporation)

Printed in England by Jolly & Barber Ltd, Rugby

Contents

Preface

This book is primarily about passengers, not aeroplanes. There are many technical experts in the field of aviation history, and the present authors make no claim to be among them, although we are grateful for the existence of their scholarly writings on the finer points of designing, making and operating aircraft.

We are, in fact, something of an oddity among aviation historians, people whose experience of airlines and aeroplanes has been entirely as passengers. Nearly all books about the history of flying have been written either by pilots or by people who have what can best be described as a train spotter's interest in aeroplanes, a connoisseur's passion for the technical minutiae. We ourselves have never even dreamt of flying an aeroplane, we have never worked for an airline in any capacity whatever and our technical awareness of aeroplanes could be described, somewhat flatteringly perhaps, as informed general knowledge. But, on the other side of the scales, we can place with some pride the fact that we are both very experienced air travellers. We have been at it for many years and in many countries and we know what it is really like, as distinct from what the publicity people tell us it is like. We have flown Concorde, we have savoured the pleasures of First Class, and we have spent thousands of tedious, cramped hours in Economy. We have taken off from and landed at big airports and little airports, we have prepared several times for crash landings but, fortunately, never yet had one. We have learnt to defend ourselves, so far as one can, against the manifold inconveniences of going by air, we have marvelled many a time at the astonishing and terrifying shrinking of distances that the aeroplane makes possible. We have come to understand, by looking out of aeroplane windows, what the world's geography is all about. Millions of people must have had exactly the same experiences as we have, and in this book we are simply trying to act as their spokesmen and, as historians and observers, to show them where they come in. We have tried, in words and pictures, to make the point as strongly as we can that the history of aviation is not only or chiefly about aeroplanes. It concerns people, too, the people who, in their many different jobs, have made the airlines work and the people who, for sixty years, have taken their courage in both hands and decided to fly. In the pages which follow, what the reader will find amounts to a social history of aviation, an account of the ways in which flying has ministered to human needs, whims and follies.

Every attempt has been made to present a fair and balanced picture and, despite the very uneven nature of the evidence, to look at the world as a whole. The story is not one of unqualified admiration. Progress in aviation has been patchy and, although remarkable things have been accomplished, a great deal of improvement is still possible. The most reliable, comfortable and safe methods of travel so far invented by man have been the train and the engine-driven ship. The aeroplane, although probably superior to the motor car, is still a long way behind both of them. All it has to offer – although this is a great deal – is speed. Its accommodation is cramped, its operations are easily disrupted by bad weather, especially fog, and airports become steadily more tedious and uncomfortable every year.

Passengers have to put up with massive and exhausting delays at both ends of their flights, their baggage is damaged, lost and looted with a frequency that yesterday's travellers by boat and train could never have imagined, and they are required to walk very long distances before they actually reach their aircraft. To go by air today, it is as well to be young and strong.

This book has a great deal to say about achievements but, always remembering that our main allegiance is to the travelling public and not to the airlines or the manufacturers, we have pulled no punches in showing the stages by which what started as an adventure and status symbol for the privileged few has become a trial of fortitude and patience for millions.

And, weaving its way remorselessly through all the hazards, comes the steady stream of ever faster and bigger aeroplanes, making sure that each year eight per cent more people will fly. Before the Second World War, there was virtually no consumers' movement among air travellers. The feeling was always, or nearly always, that the company was doing its best and that it was a good best. Those days are long past. With air travel, as with many other things, more has certainly meant worse, and the natives are beginning to get restless.

Diamonds in the Sky is very much a co-operative effort. The authors have pooled their philosophy, knowledge and experience, in the confident belief that the result is a better and more comprehensive book than either would have been capable of writing separately.

Its publication coincides with the first transmission of the BBC's television series, also called *Diamonds in the Sky*, which is presented by Julian Pettifer and for which Kenneth Hudson has given historical advice. The close link between the book and the television programmes has made it possible to make use of the considerable body of BBC material which has accumulated during the course of research and production.

ONE

The First Generation of Passengers

It would not be too much of an exaggeration to say that the American airlines learned their trade by flying letters and parcels, in contrast to the Europeans, who used human beings as experimental material from the beginning. Passenger flying developed to a different rhythm on the two continents and under quite different conditions. In Europe, distances between major cities were relatively short, but there had always been the unpleasant obstacle of the English Channel, and after the 1914–18 war railway communications on the Continent were in a poor state. There were also governments willing to subsidise the infant airlines in various ways, some well publicised, some not. In the United States, distances were long and the transcontinental mail services correspondingly slow, but the railway system had not been worn out and disrupted by a long, exhausting war. Moreover, there was, in the early 1920s, a powerful railway lobby but no equivalent pressure from the aviation side. Government subsidies to encourage passenger flying were not available, whereas the advantages of a rapid mail service were obvious and public money could be produced without too much difficulty to help it to get established and to grow. In the years immediately following the war, the pioneers in America were the pilots of the US Post Office Department. It was this Department's Air Mail Service which, in 1924, inaugurated the first scheduled night flights along a lighted railway, marked first by bonfires lit by public-spirited citizens and then by a chain of inland lighthouses. There was nothing comparable in Europe, and it was done in the interests of the mail, not of passengers.

The American contribution to the development of passenger-carrying airlines came relatively late, in the middle and late 1920s, rather than in the first half of the decade, when the French, the British, the Dutch and the Germans were discovering the opportunities and the pitfalls of what was soon proved to be a very peculiar industry. Once the Americans did really begin, they quickly left the rest of the world a long way behind. But for some years the story has to be told almost entirely in European terms.

On 16 November 1909 the first aviation enterprise in the world had been

Mrs Caroline Rogers of North Andover, Massachusetts, travels Handley Page from Paris to London, 1920.

9

founded by the Deutsche Luftschiffahrts AG, usually known as DELAG. The company had its headquarters in Frankfurt and the shareholders were the Luftschiffbau Zeppelin, which built the airships, and the Hamburg–Amerika Reederei, HAPAG, a shipping company. The passenger-carrying airship, LZ7, the 'Deutschland', with a cabin accommodating twenty-four passengers, was wrecked on its first flight on 28 June 1910, on a circular route from the main base at Friedrichshafen, via Baden-Baden, Frankfurt-am-Main, Düsseldorf, Hamburg, Potsdam, Leipzig and Gotha. But by the outbreak of war in 1914, seven Zeppelins had carried 33,722 passengers and crew without accident or injury. The Zeppelins operating in 1915 cruised at 75/80 kilometres an hour, and could remain in the air for about forty hours.

During the war, civilian passenger flying came to a halt in Germany, as elsewhere, but there were important developments in the carriage of mail by air. In the area of Russia occupied by German troops, an airmail network extending from St Petersburg to the Crimea was established by the German military organisation. Later, in 1918, there was a regular airmail service from Berlin to Hanover and Cologne, in collaboration with the German Post Office. The first German airline was founded on 13 December 1917. This airline, Deutsche Luft Reederei, was the forerunner of Lufthansa. It began scheduled airmail services between Berlin and Weimar in February 1919.

A few passengers were also carried. The main reason for starting the service was the catastrophic state of the railways, caused by strikes, shortage of coal, and worn-out locomotives and rolling stock. A second service, from Berlin to Hamburg, started on 14 March 1919, and a third, Berlin–Brunswick–Hanover–Gelsenkirchen–Rothausen, on 15 April. In June the services had to be severely curtailed, owing to shortage of fuel.

These pioneering Deutsche Luft Reederei services used the symbol of a dark blue crane on a yellow background. This became very well known after 1926, when Deutsche Luft Hansa came into being, and is still, of course, to be seen on Lufthansa planes today.

Before the First World War, airmindedness had been encouraged in several countries, the United States among them, by a different kind of commercial enterprise, known as joy-riding. This consisted of finding one's way to a field on the outskirts of a city, probably on foot or on a bicycle, but with luck by tram, and there taking one's turn to get into a very small, frail-looking aeroplane and be flown a few times round the airfield.

It was by no means a safe pursuit. In the Museum of Aviation History at Dublin Airport is a printed document headed 'Agreement relieving the Company from liability when carrying a passenger', which continues:

To the Grahame-White Aviation Co Ltd.

In consideration of your agreeing to allow me to accompany (as a Passenger) one of your Pilot Aviators on one of your Aeroplanes or Hydro-aeroplanes I declare that I am fully aware of all the risks attending the same and I agree that I accompany such Pilot Aviator at my own risk and peril and that in the event of any accident injury or

Alan Cobham's joy-riding
Avro at Reading, 1919,
with two passengers in its
open cockpit.

damage resulting neither I nor my executors or administrators shall have or be entitled to make any claim whatever whether such accident injury or damage be caused by the negligence of the pilot or of any other person in your employ or otherwise.

Dated this 1st day of June 1912.

In 1912 'the risks attending the same' were very real. 'Accident injury and damage' were not infrequent and none but the adventurous and foolhardy were likely to want to experience the excitement of flying for themselves. The opportunities for doing so were, in any case, few and far between. Dozens rather than hundreds of people would have been required to sign the Grahame-White Aviation indemnity in a year. But, of those hardy passengers who did go joy-riding in this way, a high proportion went on to become wartime pilots with the Royal Flying Corps and ended their lives fairly quickly as a result.

Once the war had ended, the pent-up demand for joy-rides in aeroplanes was soon apparent. C. G. Grey, the editor of *The Aeroplane*, immediately noted its significance, and on 6 September 1919, *The Illustrated London News*, which had a good nose for social trends, published an article by him called 'Joy-Riding and Commercial Aviation'. There was no doubt in Grey's mind that the more people went joy-riding in the air, the easier it was going to be to recruit the passengers for the scheduled services that the aviation industry was pressing the government to allow. He wrote:

Some considerable time ago, one expressed the opinion in this paper that commercial aviation would eventually grow out of joy-riding. On that occasion one estimated in some detail that out of the total population of this country some two million people would want the experience of having been up in an aeroplane, that a number of these would want to try it a second time, and that a very large proportion of the total number would go on joy-riding as often as they had the opportunity or could afford it; so that ultimately one might reckon that there would be some five million joy-rides to be given before the pleasure-flying market began to decline. The estimate was based simply on a knowledge of human nature, and not on any figures of any kind. Now, however, figures are to some extent available, and they seem to bear out the original estimate to a quite surprising degree.

Non-military flying had been allowed in Britain since May of that year, but only the Avro Company seems to have realised straight away that joy-riding provided a wonderful opportunity to make use of wartime aircraft and war-time pilots, both of which were in plentiful supply. Avro had made two-seat trainers for what was by that time the Royal Air Force, and converted some of them to carry four passengers and a pilot. The Air Ministry, however, was prepared to license them for only two passengers to begin with, although it later relented and permitted the full load, provided the aircraft were fitted with larger engines.

Even with the earlier restriction, however, remarkable success was achieved, particularly at Blackpool, where holidaymakers provided a wonderful market during the summer months. 10,000 passengers were carried during June and July and Grey was not alone in finding this impressive.

It is true that the workpeople in the North of England are notoriously free-handed with their money when they have any, and that Blackpool is a wonderful pleasure resort for these people; but even the most sanguine believer in joy-riding would scarcely have believed that it was possible to induce over 1200 people a week to go flying at one seaside resort, considering the cheapest trip is a guinea a head. Yet, in spite of the enormous number actually carried, one is told that never at any time during the day have the machines been waiting for passengers. On the contrary, there has always been a queue of passengers waiting for the machines.

In August, it became legal to take four passengers, and as a result three pilots at Blackpool took up a total of 500 people a day on quarter-hour trips.

One of the most interesting features of the experiment, Grey observed, was that, although people were a little chary to start with, 'having read so much about the heroism of aviators and the perils of aviation in the Press', they soon lost their fears.

As the machines continued to operate day after day without an accident, and not only made the usual circular trips of a few minutes' duration round Blackpool, but actually flew regularly on a daily service between Blackpool and Manchester, the people began to realise that flying was nothing like as dangerous as they thought it

was. There was just a sufficient spice of danger about it to make people brag about their flying experiences, and yet it was obviously safe enough for anybody to take the risk once for the sake of saying they had flown. Consequently, today flying is rapidly becoming one of the popular pastimes of Lancashire, and, of course, everyone knows the proverb: 'What Lancashire thinks today, England thinks tomorrow.'

A de Havilland DH4A converted bomber, similar to the one used on the Hounslow–Le Bourget service, 1919.

This is as may be, but there can be no doubt that, in all countries where there was a supply of wartime pilots and aircraft, joy-riding did a great deal to prepare the public for scheduled services. Its main service, perhaps, was to convey the idea that flying was basically safe, since during the war the emphasis of newspapers and magazines had always been on the perils of flying and on the heroism of the men who flew. There was a certain irony in the situation, however, since the great majority of the joy-riders belonged to the lower-income groups while the early passengers on scheduled flights and charters came from much further up the social scale.

Flying to the Continent from Britain was not permitted until 14 July 1919. A commercial London–Paris flight, run by Aircraft Transport and Travel Ltd, took place on the following day. This company was a subsidiary of the Aircraft Manufacturing Co, usually known as Airco. It had been formed in 1916 by George Holt Thomas, to run scheduled air services as soon as peace returned. Thomas's Aircraft Manufacturing Company, the predecessor of de Havilland, became the largest firm in the British aircraft industry. In 1919 it bought and converted surplus RAF planes, and Aircraft Transport and Travel operated them. One board of directors controlled both companies, and it included George Holt Thomas as Chairman, General Sefton Brancker as Managing Director, General Festing as Commercial Director and Captain Donald Grey as General Manager. Airco's chief pilot was Captain H. ('Jerry') Shaw, who continued to delight listeners with his reminiscences right up to the time of his death in 1977. Captain Shaw first flew, as a passenger, on a joy-ride flight from Manchester racecourse in 1912 in a Blériot monoplane. After qualifying as a pilot during the winter of 1915–16, he went to France, 'where I flew everything'.[1] After the war he spent a period flying VIPs from Hendon to the Peace Conference. He left the RAF in a hurry, in order to avoid a court martial as a result of cutting-in tactics calculated to annoy General Ludlow-Hewitt, who was trying to land at Kenley.

On 14 July 1919, Mr W. H. Pilkington, of the St Helens glass firm, noticed a small paragraph in the London *Evening News* saying that commercial air services between Britain and the Continent were at last permitted. He telephoned Airco at Hendon immediately, telling the company that he had an important meeting to attend in Paris the following day and that he had missed the boat-train. He could keep his appointment only by flying. Airco agreed to take him from Hounslow, the only place where Customs facilities were provided, at 7.30 the next morning, and charged him £50 for the single journey. The aircraft was an Airco DH9, a converted civil version of the RAF DH9 light bomber. Both the pilot and the passenger sat in open cockpits. The weather on 15 July was bad. 'My log book records that there were low clouds and rain the whole way,' Captain Shaw recalled. 'When we reached the line of hills near Beauvais, the clouds were right down on the ground and we spent twenty minutes flying up and down before finding a break to get through. We took 2 hours 45 minutes for the whole flight, in spite of the wasted time, and that was slow in those days. Not bad when you remember twelve years later Imperial Airways liners were scheduled to take 2 hours 30 minutes.'[2] Mr Pilkington returned to London the next day, highly satisfied. After the scheduled daily services had begun on 25 August, he became a regular customer. He was influential and well known in the industrial world and his enthusiasm must certainly have helped to persuade other businessmen to fly, in the days when every convert counted.

The first scheduled London–Paris flight in a DH16 took place on 25 August 1919. It was piloted by Captain Cyril Patteson and the starting point was the first London airport on Hounslow Heath, close to the south-east corner of what is now Heathrow. Aircraft landed at Hounslow in order to clear Customs, but the London terminal was at Handley Page's factory aerodrome at Cricklewood, in north-west London. In March 1920 Hounslow Heath ceased to be used for passenger traffic and Croydon became the London terminal. It was customary in cases of headwinds or bad weather in the early days for the

---

[1] This, and later quotations and references, are, unless otherwise stated, from a conversation with Kenneth Hudson, 18 May 1970.

[2] Captain H. Shaw, 'The first London–Paris Service', *The Aeroplane*, 14 July 1944.

planes bound for Paris or Brussels to make an intermediate stop at Lympne, on the Kent coast, for refuelling. The pioneering flight is rumoured to have carried, in addition to passengers, newspapers, jars of Devonshire cream, several brace of grouse and a consignment of leather. In the first week there were twenty passengers. Two of them, an American and an Irish priest, returned from Paris on 28 August in 1 hour 45 minutes, with the help of a 100-mph hurricane. The pilot on that occasion was Captain Shaw, and when they landed in England his passengers, who drank a bottle of brandy between Paris and London, told him they thought the unusual amount of movement during the flight had been caused by stunt-flying.

The American's bowler hat had completely disintegrated; its brim was wedged around his chin, and damage to the cabin roof bore witness to the strength of his skull. The pilot's knuckles were raw where his hands had been smacked against the sides of the cockpit. The machine itself had to be completely re-rigged. [3]

One of the passengers on the first flight was Captain Bruce Ingram, travelling on behalf of *The Illustrated London News*. [4] He was the archetypal business passenger, the kind of person treasured and wooed by the world's airlines for sixty years. His account of the trip is an early classic of passenger flying. Captain Ingram had some urgent business to transact in Paris and he wanted to spend the minimum length of time away from London.

The proposed seat in the first passenger aeroplane on the new service provided a perfect solution to the problem. The novelty of this form of transport also had charms which made the prospect doubly alluring and it was with a glow of satisfaction at being able to combine business with pleasure that I wended my way to the aerodrome at Hounslow.

He went to the aerodrome by District Railway and tram, a tedious system which was soon replaced by a motor car service. Aboard the Airco DH16, he found:

. . . four arm-chairs placed side by side in such a manner that, if you were sitting with your back to the engine, your neighbour faced the opposite way. The whole of the carriage (sic) before starting was roofed in by a sliding cover, with windows that could be opened or shut as desired. The result was that, though all the passengers were in very close quarters, there was nevertheless no discomfort, and, above all, one could keep dry and warm whatever the weather.

The plane landed at Lympne for refuelling, and from then on 'the steadiness of the plane came to an end, although nobody was actually sick'. Two hours and twenty minutes after leaving Hounslow, they were on the ground at Le Bourget. A car was waiting and half an hour later this very enthusiastic passenger was carrying out his engagement in the centre of Paris.

On the return journey the next day, Captain Ingram was not so fortunate. The weather was very rough and the flight took three hours. Although 'at no

---

[3] Captain H. Shaw, 'Pioneering without Politics', *The Aeroplane*, 18 August 1944.
[4] Published in *The Illustrated London News*, 6 September 1919.

The actress, Mistinguet, at the end of an Air Union London–Paris flight.

time, whether in squall or cloud, was it possible to feel uneasiness, such a sense of security is given by the reliable machines and fine pilots', one can well understand that 'it was with a feeling of relief that the passengers landed on terra firma once more'.

In France, too, the first post-war airlines were run by the manufacturers – Farman, Potez, Breguet, Latécoère. In December 1918 the Société Latécoère began its Toulouse–Barcelona run, and on 16 September 1919, the first French cross-Channel service was inaugurated by Cie des Messageries Aériennes.

Wing Commander McIntosh was one of the pioneering London–Paris pilots. He flew a Handley Page O400, a converted bomber with an open cockpit. The pilot sat on the right, the flight engineer on his left. The front gun had been taken out and two passengers could be taken in the gunner's cockpit, with helmets and goggles. The cabin could take up to twelve.

Wing Commander McIntosh soon found that passenger flying was much harder work than military flying. The flights were much longer – London–Paris could take four hours, depending on the wind, and for the whole of this time the pilot had physically to wrestle with the aircraft. At the end of the journey, he recalled:

We were very, very tired. It was all taken on the stomach muscles. There were no balanced controls and the height we flew over the ground was governed by the height of the cloud. If the cloud was 200 feet, we flew at 150. Consequently, a lot of our flying was done down valleys and railway lines. In fact, the person who could fly the lowest over the lowest country was the man who got through. [5]

The pilots always carried chewing gum, insulation tape, and a small bottle of ether. If the oil gauge showed the engine was overheated:

We would land in the nearest field, switch off the motor, find the leak, and then stick chewing gum over the hole and bind it with insulation tape. Then we would scrounge some water from a house and fill up the radiator. Now the problem was to start the engine again, especially in winter. So what we used to do was to take out a couple of plugs, put in a teaspoonful of ether, put the plugs back, and then churn round and wait for the bang. It was quite successful.

To avoid the worst of the weather, pilots often used to cross the Channel at no more than forty feet above the water. Forced landings were common.

I remember on one occasion I had Charlie Chaplin aboard and, owing to bad weather, we landed on Boulogne sands. He was immaculately dressed with a blue suit and a blue Melton coat and crowds gathered round, with quite a lot of children. Eventually it got out who he was, and he was amused at the people who were running up and down doing his famous walk.

If we had a forced landing, we always used to take care of our passengers. Later on, the company gave us sealed envelopes. In each envelope were five £1 notes and 500 French francs, which enabled us to put our passengers on the train, if necessary. Eventually, the company arranged with the railways that the tickets were interchangeable.

Incidentally, about 75% of the passengers were American, mostly film stars. We had quite a number of actresses, boxers, jockeys and so on.

By modern standards, flying in the early 1920s was not exactly a speedy affair, especially with a strong wind. On more than one occasion, Captain McIntosh remembered taking off from Cricklewood and watching the No. 16 buses overtaking the plane, which was somewhat humiliating.

The enterprising Aircraft Transport and Travel Ltd soon acquired two Continental associates, one French, and one Dutch. The French concern, the Compagnie Générale Transaérienne, began in November 1919, operated single-seaters and carried only mail. The Dutch company, KLM, opened a London–Amsterdam service on 17 May 1920 jointly with Aircraft Transport and Travel. At that time KLM had no suitable aircraft of its own and rented them from Airco. Of the passengers on both the London–Paris and London–Amsterdam services twenty-five per cent were, as Captain Shaw remembers them, businessmen. They included a mysterious Mr Weinberg, who went to Paris every Thursday. The remainder were 'Americans or holiday-makers', with a men/women ratio of about four to one. Children were

[5] Conversation with Julian Pettifer, 7 May 1978.

very rare as passengers. One particularly good American customer was a Mr Simpson of Marshall Field. One evening Simpson received a message in Paris saying that his wife had been taken ill in London. Shaw agreed to take him back on a charter flight the next morning, despite the bad weather. They were, however, compelled to land near Beauvais and to wait there until conditions improved, with Shaw paying no attention to Simpson's protests. In the early days, passengers of the 'I've-bought-the-plane-haven't-I?' type were not infrequent, especially on charter flights. They had to be told firmly that the pilot was in complete control, no matter how much the passenger might have paid for his ticket or how large a bribe he was offering. On the other hand, some part of a pilot's reputation was made by his ability to take off and land under conditions which grounded less skilful and less daring men. There was certainly a financial incentive to fly whenever possible, because a pilot received extra money when he was actually in the air. Shaw, for instance, had £700 a year while he was with Aircraft Transport and Travel, together with 10s. (50p) an hour flying pay.

But too much credit should not be given to the companies which pioneered the cross-Channel routes, important and potentially highly profitable as these were. The Germans at that time were a long way ahead of them.

Insurance for aircraft was certainly available in 1908,[6] and possibly earlier. To begin with, cover was provided only against fire, since the early aeroplane engines were very liable to burst into flames. Third-party cover was being widely sought by 1911, partly because most flying at that time was at exhibitions and meetings, where there was considerable danger to spectators, and partly because aeroplanes not infrequently had to land in unexpected places, with a consequent risk of damage to property, especially to crops and livestock. Animals were liable to stampede when an aeroplane was flying overhead and this resulted in many claims against pilots.

After 1918 the establishment of regular passenger flights brought about far-reaching changes in the aviation insurance market. Companies had to provide for the insurance of more expensive aircraft and for heavier personal accident losses. By the early 1920s, however, it had become common, if not normal, to include passenger coverage in the terms of the policy. An endorsement to a policy issued in 1922 agreed to 'cover all passengers carried by Messrs Daimler Hire Ltd, against Legal Liability to Passengers as per Section I of the attached policy, limited to £1000 any one passenger, excess £5 each & every claim, at a premium of 3s.5d. per passenger per flight, all passengers to be declared'. For some years there seems to have been no demand by airlines to insure against their liabilities to passengers on scheduled flights. Passengers consequently spent a good deal of money on insuring themselves. The people using air transport were generally well-to-do and

---

[6] For the beginnings and development of this type of insurance, see *A Short History of Aviation Insurance in the United Kingdom*, 2nd ed., 1968. This is Report H.R. 10 of the Historic Records Working Party of the Insurance Institute of London.

therefore wished to insure themselves for fairly large sums, usually between £5000 and £10,000, but sometimes as much as £100,000 or more. The rate for a passenger travelling between London and the Continent was £1 a thousand, roughly ten times the present rate.

In order to protect themselves against unreasonable losses, a number of insurers grouped together in 1920 to set up Lloyd's Aviation Record, on similar lines to Lloyd's Register of Shipping. This provided for a register of aircraft and pilots and for a worldwide system of aircraft surveyors. The surveyors were required to inspect and classify aircraft, provide reports on aerodromes and routes and investigate accidents. It is interesting to notice that flying over sea was regarded as particularly hazardous and in the early 1920s policies were often endorsed to the effect that the shortest sea-crossings between Britain and France were to be undertaken, irrespective of the final destination. Night flying by scheduled airlines also became subject to special consideration by underwriters, with additional premiums being charged, the amount of which depended on the pilots and the routes taken.

In 1924 the British Aviation Insurance Group was established. It was a merger of two rather unlikely partners, the Union Insurance Society of Canton and the White Cross Aviation Insurance Association, sole survivors of the many firms which had lost heavily by dabbling in aviation insurance during the pioneering years, despite premiums of thirty per cent. The new company, by using discriminating tariffs, could virtually control civil aviation, and it was an even more powerful disciplinary force than the Air Navigation Consolidation Order 1923, which defined strict licensing requirements for both aircraft and personnel.

Contrary to popular legend, aircraft never at any time carried parachutes, either for the pilot or his passengers. Few of the latter showed any signs of fear. The airlines' explanation of this was a simple one: 'If you were frightened of flying, you didn't fly. You went by train and boat.'

From the beginning, pilots were well treated in the matter of accommodation and expenses. They were mostly put up in hotels, good hotels, but in Paris KLM provided what Captain Shaw remembers as 'a sumptuous flat, with a resident housekeeper'.

Throughout its short existence – it went out of business at the end of 1920 – Aircraft Transport and Travel used a mixed collection of de Havilland aircraft. The DH9 conversion provided for one passenger in front of the pilot and another behind him. In the opinion of the pilot:

. . . there was nothing to choose between these two passengers' seats, because they were both extremely uncomfortable. Each necessitated the use of Sidcot suits, flying helmets and goggles – use of which was included in the fare of twenty guineas single. Only a contortionist could get into the front seat, and once there he could not move, whilst the comparative roominess of the back seat was offset by the gale of wind rushing around the whole time.[7]

[7] Captain H. Shaw, 'Pioneering without Politics', *The Aeroplane*, 18 August 1944.

Diamonds in The Sky

The DH4A, which accommodated two passengers sitting face to face, was closed in and rather more comfortable, but the first really commercial aircraft was Airco's DH16, introduced on 25 August 1919. There was a four-seat cabin, with the passengers facing one another in pairs. The DH18, which came into service in March 1920, was an eight-passenger cabin machine, with the pilot placed behind the passenger cabin.

In November 1919, Mary Hayman,[8] then a schoolgirl of fifteen, flew with her father from the Handley Page aerodrome at Cricklewood to Brussels. They were met at King's Cross and taken to Cricklewood in a chauffeur-driven car. At the aerodrome they waited in a hut with two other passengers and were eventually told there would be a delay, owing to fog. Three-quarters of an hour later the other passengers had left to catch the boat-train, but Mrs Hayman's father was determined to fly – he liked anything new and was the sort of person to try flying as soon as he could. When it was eventually decided that they should go, the pilot showed them the route on a map. They were to follow the railway lines to the coast and then take the shortest route across the Channel to Calais. Inside the plane were four wicker seats. On the two unused chairs there were piles of mailbags.

The return flight, the following day, was more eventful. As the plane flew over France it met strong headwinds and the pilot decided to land in a field. As it touched down, the plane tipped to one side. Nobody was hurt, but Mrs Hayman twisted her knee climbing out. They were approached almost immediately by a French policeman on a bicycle. His first words to them were, 'May I see your papers?' The pilot had papers authorising him to land in France, but Mrs Hayman had a visa only for Belgium. On seeing this the policeman told her, 'You have no business to land here. You must leave as soon as possible.' Fortunately the plane was undamaged. The farmer was paid to help them right it and the remainder of the journey to London was uneventful.

Forced landings in foreign countries were a constant hazard. In 1922 Mrs M. Fitzrandolph, a member of the Friends' Relief Service, made her first flight, from Warsaw to Prague. With storms ahead, the pilot decided to land at Breslau to take on more fuel. He told his passengers not to get out of the aircraft, because they had no papers, and not to talk while the plane was on the ground.

Another first-time passenger in 1922 was the author Freya Stark, later to become a very experienced air traveller indeed. Her father gave her the ticket for a London to Paris flight as a Christmas present. On arrival at Croydon, she was given the choice of flying inside or outside. She chose outside, for the sheer excitement of it, and then came the problem of getting into the open cockpit. It was simply and efficiently arranged. 'Two men lifted me. One took the head, the other the feet, and lifted me up over the engine.'[9]

[8] Conversation with Kenneth Hudson, 15 June 1970.
[9] Interviewed for BBC-TV, 6 August 1978.

The First Generation of Passengers

Once airborne, 'we flew very low. I remember a fox running below me, so it shows how very low we were.' It was a straightforward, but inevitably windy flight, and at Le Bourget she was 'very dishevelled'. The airport amenities were minimal, 'so I appealed to the nice French Customs officer and said, "Look, I must have a mirror before I go into Paris," and he said, "It's only too reasonable, mademoiselle," and a little mirror was produced and placed on the Customs bench, and I was able to go tidily into Paris.'

Paris–London was the glamorous route, the one with the biggest potential of rich, famous and influential people and the one which, more than any other, helped the European airlines to learn about the economics of passenger flying. But the publicity it received tended to obscure the immensely valuable pioneering being carried out on other routes during the same period, particularly by the French. In the autumn of 1919, there was a regular postal service between Toulouse and Rabat, in Morocco, and between then and 1925 passenger routes were established to Corsica, Morocco, Tunisia and Algeria.

The early passengers expected and received very little in the way of com-

Horse-drawn recovery of a French passenger plane near Warsaw after a breakdown in 1925.

21

The Lignes Aériennes
Farman bus at Le
Bourget.

fort or amenities. On the London–Paris service, after the first few months, they were taken from city centre to city centre. They registered at the office of the company, or of an agent, and were then driven to the aerodrome in a hire-car. Luggage was carried to and from the aircraft by mechanics, whom it was forbidden to tip. There was a 40 lb weight-limit for luggage, but it was not strictly enforced. The habit of weighing the passengers themselves was introduced during the mid-1920s.[10] The weighing-machine at the office counter had its face politely turned inwards, so that only the clerk on duty could see it. The maximum weight allowance was for a passenger and his luggage together, so that a small, thin man could take a lot more luggage than a large, fat man. The name of one's next-of-kin was included with the facts about one's weight. The distribution of weight in the plane has always been almost as

[10] Nowadays the Air Navigation (General) Regulations permit that, provided an aircraft has seats for twelve or more people, the passengers and crew need not be weighed. The following standard weights are assumed:
Males over 12 years   165 pounds
Females over 12 years   143 pounds
Children 2–12 years   85 pounds
Babies under 2 years   17 pounds

22

important as the total weight itself. The airport authorities would work out the aircraft's centre of gravity and ask some of the passengers to move to other seats during take-off. The pilot shepherded his own passengers through the Customs on arrival and he was personally responsible for them until they and their baggage had been cleared.

There were no refreshment facilities at Hounslow, but this airfield was used only until March 1920. Croydon, which then became London's civil airport, had a hotel, which had been an RAF mess, and a restaurant of sorts. Le Bourget and Amsterdam both had restaurants, which were used mainly by visitors, not passengers, and did good business.

Until 1921 no reliable meteorological information was available. Pilots had to trust their own experience and judgement. Broadly speaking, the only way of discovering what the weather ahead was like was to take off and find out. During 1919 weather forecasts began to appear on the noticeboard at Hounslow, but they were of a type which pilots found difficult to take very seriously. Expressions like 'bolsons in the Channel' and 'squaggy around Beauvais' appeared at intervals and at the end of one bulletin was a note saying, 'The cloud height given in yesterday's forecast as 3000 metres should read 300 feet.'[11]

Aircraft Transport and Travel soon ran into difficulties, as a result of inadequate capital, insufficient passengers, especially for charters, and unsuitable planes. No government support was forthcoming and the company closed down at the end of 1920.

It is interesting to notice, in view of later developments, the conditions for a successful London–Paris service which were put forward by George Holt Thomas in the paper, 'Commercial Aeronautics', which he read to the Royal Aeronautical Society on 30 May 1918. In his opinion this route could be run profitably, at a single fare of £5 and with a 75-per-cent holding, if there were forty passengers a day in each direction. Thomas, however, assumed the availability of twelve-passenger aircraft, which his own company never, in fact, had. Using twelve-seater planes, he estimated the total operating cost per seat-mile at three (old) pence, but the actual cost of running the two- and four-seater de Havillands, which were all Aircraft Transport and Travel could get, ranged from 23 to 36 (old) pence. The fares charged therefore had to be very high and the traffic potential was correspondingly reduced.

In February 1921, a short time after Aircraft Transport and Travel vanished from the scene, the other two British companies with international interests, Handley Page and Instone, were also compelled to withdraw their Continental services. The French, Dutch, Belgian and German governments were more realistic and saw from the beginning that civil aviation was going to need official nursing through its early stages. Subsidies of one kind and another were seen as worthwhile investments, which would later produce

---

[11] Captain H. Shaw, 'Pioneering without Politics', *The Aeroplane*, 18 August 1944.

Two Handley Page
HP–42s outside the
terminal buildings at
Croydon.

dividends in the form of increased national prestige, encouragement to aircraft manufacturers and commercial convenience.

In March 1921 the British government gave way to pressure and common
sense and announced a small subsidy to Handley Page and then one to
Instone, who restarted their Paris service immediately. In 1922 they were
joined by a third company, Daimler Airways. The first effect of this was to
produce over-capacity on the London–Paris route, with five companies, two
French and three British, chasing a total volume of traffic which was as yet
too small to allow any of them to make an adequate profit.

In September 1922 the British operators agreed to specialise: Instone
taking London–Brussels–Cologne, Daimler Manchester–London–Amsterdam, Handley Page, which had the largest aircraft, London–Paris, and British
Marine Air Navigation Southampton–Channel Islands–Cherbourg. The
three Handley Page V.8b 12–14-seaters, *Princess Mary*, *Prince George* and
Prince Henry, went into service during the early summer of 1922. Handley
Page made great efforts to promote these new aeroplanes and to persuade
those who had not yet tried air travel that a pleasant new experience awaited
them. The approach, presented in a Handley Page booklet of 1922, was, 'Once
you have flown to Paris, you will never go by boat again.'

Before the war, the hardier type of traveller went from London to Paris through the
night, arriving at about 5 am in an (at that hour) anything but gay city. It took a few
hours to recover from the journey. Nowadays, unless you spend a night and half a day
on the move from Waterloo, through Southampton–Havre you must at any rate use up
nearly all the daylight hours. You must start after a very early breakfast, make sure of
securing a seat, change from train to boat, and from boat to train with incessant
distraction of Passport and Customs formalities, and, thoroughly bored and weary,

24

arrive in Paris in time for dinner. Your day has been spoilt, and your evening is ruined.

It stands to reason that a means by which you can gain a useful morning in London, and arrive unjaded in Paris rather early for afternoon tea, in time, may be, to pay an important business call, or with leisure to do a little sightseeing before dinner, is worthy of some consideration. And especially if by this means you are saved from the confusion and irritation of changing from railway to steamer and back again, and are given, instead of a dull and uncomfortable railway journey with only an hour on the water (and that a torture to many) a glorious panorama of England and France, a short journey by motor car at each end, and a beautifully simple and peaceful Customs office to go through, you will be wise to choose it. If your object be business it will save you valuable time, and probably a night's hotel expenses; if your object be pleasure you achieve it from the very start.

The French schedules were arranged to allow passengers arriving in Paris by the night trains from the Mediterranean, Switzerland and the Near East to get to Le Bourget in good time to catch their plane to London. The services from London permitted a leisurely lunch or dinner in Paris before proceeding south or east to the sunshine. It was a considerate and humane system.

By 1924, when the British airlines were merging to form a single national airline, Imperial Airways,[12] the European and North African network of routes had expanded to a point where international timetables were being published. This was a French venture, the series being called *Guides des Voyages Aériens*. Each of the four booklets was of about sixty pages. The timetables centred on Paris: Paris–London; Paris–Brussels–Amsterdam; Paris–Lausanne–Geneva; and Paris–Prague–Warsaw. The London–Paris timetable had two different introductions; one in French and the other in English.

The London–Paris route taught the airline operators a number of useful and well-publicised lessons. The first and most important was that there was a market for regular, dependable services among people to whom time mattered and that such people were prepared to pay a good deal in order to avoid the tedium and unpleasantness of a long train and boat journey, with all the changing, carrying, waiting and contact with officials this involved. The second discovery was that, in running an airline, economics counted quite as much as enthusiasm. Large aircraft, able to carry at least twelve passengers, were essential if fares were to be kept down to a figure which would allow the market to expand. Even with suitable aircraft, however, a government subsidy was essential and some means had to be found of planning services so that there were not too many operators chasing too little traffic and going

[12] The Air Council's agreement, setting up Imperial Airways, was with a 'Heavier-Than-Air Transport Company to be called Imperial Air Transport Company'. It was required to use only British-made aircraft and engines, and provided it flew a specified number of miles each year, it was to get an initial subsidy of £1 million and a further £1 million over a period of ten years. Imperial Airways lasted until April 1940, when the British Overseas Airways Corporation took over operations from Imperial Airways and the smaller, privately owned, British Airways.

Making the Americans
air-minded. Daisy
Lukens, member of the
Great American Flying
Circus, before a
demonstration at Vinton,
Iowa, in 1921.

bankrupt in the process. The subsidy usually took the form of a mail contract,
which assured the airline of a regular income and made it possible, in many
cases, to think of passengers as a bonus, rather than a necessity.

The Americans, as we have already said, flew letters first and passengers
later, although the world's first scheduled service flew briefly from Tampa in
Florida to St Petersburg in 1914. But, even before the scheduled passenger
services had been developed, pressure was building up in the United States to
prepare the facilities for them. Much of the credit for this was due to a body
called the National Aeronautics Association, set up late in 1923 primarily as
a pressure group to persuade local communities to construct airfields which
the mail planes could use. Once the infrastructure was there, in the name of
letters and parcels, it could be used for what was obviously coming very soon,
a network of passenger-carrying routes.

The real work of the Association was carried out by local voluntary bodies,
the groups of interested citizens which the Americans organise so well and so
enthusiastically, known as Chapters. They had their own publication, the
Aeronautical Review, to support and publicise their efforts.

'It should be the aim of every Chapter,' proclaimed the *Review*, 'to obtain improved landing and supply facilities for airplanes and airships in its community and to encourage inter-city flying as a business enterprise.'[13] The Association had a simple creed: 'If we all pull together we can accomplish a wonderful work. The people are now impressed with the coming importance of airlines, both heavier than air and lighter than air. Businessmen are beginning to see the great benefit of the air mail, and we hope that they will also seek to utilise the advantages of the transportation of merchandise and passengers.'[14]

It would not be unfair to say that the Americans profited by the experiments and mistakes of the European companies. They were cautious to begin with but, once they were convinced, they moved very fast indeed. In April 1925 the *Aeronautical Review* told its readers that 'a total of 121,496 passengers have been transported by airlines throughout the world'. On British and Dutch airlines during the three years 1921–24, '7,990,000 passenger miles were flown. For two years no fatal accident occurred, while in 1923 there was one accident involving three deaths. Hence the passenger air miles per passenger fatality for this period were 2,663,300.' The statistics were reassuring, since for the New York Central Railroad in 1923 the number of passenger-train miles per passenger casualty (killed or injured) was 4,400,000.

'Before the American public, or rather that section of it which was likely to travel by air, could become confident about air transport it had to be convinced that it could be carried out not only in perfect safety but also with reasonable assurance of comfort and punctuality.'[15] That point appears to have been reached by the mid-1920s, although long before that there had been much activity in the conveyance of freight by air. Businessmen, one might say, used their goods as guinea-pigs, to discover if air travel was safe.

Before this point, however, the Americans had certainly not lagged behind the Europeans in interest and curiosity. Consider, for example, the early happenings in Louisville, Kentucky. The first airfield in Louisville was opened on 21 September 1918. The opening day brought 5000 people to the fifty-acre field, where the local paper, the *Courier Journal*, reported that '216 autos were parked'. In July of that year the *Courier Journal*, anxious to appear forward-looking, had delivered thousands of free newspapers from the air in Louisville and other towns in Kentucky. Its enterprise was not an isolated case. Chewing gum was dropped from a plane to advertise the product. The Chief of Police was offered a plane with a machine gun mounted on it, to be kept instantly available in case of riots. The suggestion was, however, declined.

Equally notable events were taking place elsewhere in North America, during the immediate post-war years. One of the earliest commercial uses

[13] December 1924.
[14] Ibid.
[15] *Aeronautical Review*, 26 October.

made of aviation was on 4 July 1919, when several pilots transported themselves in old JN-4Ds from Godman Field, Fort Knox, to Toledo, in order to see the Dempsey-Willard fight. A newspaper photographer who knew one of the pilots asked him to take pictures of the fight to Buffalo, New York. The pilot delivered the plates and 'scored a clean beat for the photographer'.

The American aviation industry was entirely realistic. It realised that human beings are heavy to transport and that, with the small planes available in the early 1920s, it was much more profitable to carry letters and parcels than people – one medium-sized man equals a great many letters. Until 1925 the US Post Office operated the airmail services on its own account, but in that year the first Air Mail Act, the Kelly Act, was passed, and the carriage of airmail was turned over to private contractors on a tendering basis. More than five thousand applications were received to carry the mail. Five contracts were awarded, among them Western Air Express, the parent company of TWA. What the 1925 Act did, in a country which disliked the idea of state-run airlines, was to subsidise air transport by making payments based on the space available in the aircraft for mail. This made it economic for the operating companies to buy bigger planes, carrying both passengers and mail. The more mail was transported, the more passenger accommodation could be provided. This in turn encouraged manufacturers to build larger and better aeroplanes, so that by the early 1930s the United States had not only caught up with Europe, but left it far behind.

14 August 1929. *Punch* is still unable to take air travel seriously.

Granddaughter. "DON'T YOU WISH YOU WERE GOING BACK BY AEROPLANE, GRANNIE?"

Grannie. "NO, MY DEAR, CERTAINLY NOT. I DON'T HOLD WITH THEM. I ALWAYS KEEP TO THE GOOD OLD-FASHIONED RAILWAYS, AS NATURE INTENDED US TO, MY DEAR."

TWO

The Twenties

Almost from the beginning, the development of civil aviation followed two quite different patterns. In the industrialised, prosperous parts of the world, the task was to persuade people who normally travelled by rail and sea to transfer their custom to the airlines. Elsewhere, as in South America, Australia and most of Africa, the need was for air services of a very basic kind, which would move people and goods quickly across difficult country where no transport facilities apart from rivers and jungle paths previously existed. Europeans and Americans who were normally railway travellers demanded a standard of comfort which compared with that of a first-class railway coach. The people of Central Asia, Brazil or the Congo, on the other hand, expected no frills and were grateful for anything better than a horse, a river boat or their own legs.

Passenger flying in Australia in the 1920s was certainly basic. It was started, as in Europe and America, by ex-wartime pilots who needed to earn a living, and who saw a promising future in commercial aviation. One of these pilots was Lieutenant Hudson Fysh,[1] founder of Q.A.N.T.A.S. (subsequently Qantas Airways) and later knighted for his great services to aviation. In 1920 Fysh, with four partners, formed Queensland and Northern Territory Aerial Services Ltd. The company's first head office was at Winton, Western Queensland, and operations began with two war-surplus biplanes, one a BE 2E and the other an Avro 504K. The BE 2E took one passenger, the Avro two and each had an average ground speed of just over sixty mph.

To attract customers and financial backers Fysh set out the airline's potential in a document called *Advantages Offered to an Aerial Company in North West Queensland*. In it he pointed out that, in this region, 'almost every day of the year should be a flying day'. There was the added advantage that 'during wet weather the Company's machines will be able to operate between the railheads when all car traffic is held up owing to the boggy, unmetalled roads', causing serious problems in 'a country in which much big business in

[1] Sir Hudson Fysh died in 1974.

Pilot Hudson Fysh.
3.10.22

QUEENSLAND'S FIRST AERIAL MAIL WELCOMED
AT WINTON NOV. 1922.

The first airmail plane arrives at Winton, Queensland, October/November 1922, depending on which date on the picture you believe. The pilot was Hudson Fysh, later Chairman of Qantas.

the way of stock inspecting, buying and general transactions are carried on, often of an urgent nature'.

One of the founders of Q.A.N.T.A.S., and its first Chairman, was a doctor. His daughter, Margery Marlay, felt that he did more to help establish Q.A.N.T.A.S. than any other person, 'because he was aviation-minded and he could see the great benefit in introducing it to our way of life'.[2]

'If your son were kicked by a horse and had concussion,' she said, 'you could ring up on the telephone and say what had happened. The doctor could leave Longreach by plane and fly out and, if necessary, operate on the kitchen table and save your son's life.' Flying was no easy matter for her father, however. He weighed sixteen stone and had to be hoisted into the plane with a block and tackle.

A curious feature of the pioneering days of aviation in Australia was that everybody put on their best clothes to go flying, because, Margery Marlay felt compelled to remind a more sophisticated age,' 'after all, it was a very big event. You didn't turn up in any old thing.'

In 1921 the company bought two more aircraft, both Avro 504K biplanes, and moved its headquarters to Longreach, advertising joy-rides at £2.50 a time and, for those requiring extra thrills, looping the loop at £5. Within two years 871 joy-riders had been taken up and a good deal of other work undertaken as well. Fysh carried Australia's first maternity case to go to hospital by air, and organised the first aerial shoot of wild bush turkeys. He had also

[2] Conversation with Julian Pettifer, 8 September 1978.

carried a corpse from Longreach to Brisbane, after taking out the aircraft's second seat to make room for the coffin.

A letter from Fysh, written on 7 March 1921, describes a typical week's activities at the time:

Yesterday I returned from a week's trip with the BE. We carried 75 paying passengers and gave two complimentary flights, one to an aboriginal at Blackall who thoroughly enjoyed it, and I think he is the first abo to go up. At Wellshot twelve passengers were carried, and Mr Murray shot two turkeys from the machine, thus opening up a new use for aviation in Australia. We had an excellent morning's sport, and I wish for nothing more fascinating. Not the slightest trouble was experienced in recognising stations passed over. Although I got many enquiries regarding the machines, the people are 'cold' when it comes to taking shares.

A major problem facing Q.A.N.T.A.S., and all other pioneering companies operating to remote places, was the preparation and maintenance of a suitable landing strip. Local communities and individual landowners were sent a printed leaflet telling them what was required. It tells us a lot about the circumstances of the time.

1 The minimum area for safety is 300 feet × 300 feet, with no trees, fences, Telegraph or Telephone wire round the edges. If high trees or the other obstructions mentioned are round the edges, 450 feet × 450 feet is required.

2 If a square is not available, an oblong or L-shaped ground with the greater length in the direction of the prevailing wind will do.

3 The area should be level if possible, but a slight slope may be permitted.

4 The surface of the landing place should be free from all obstructions such as holes, stones, depressions, stumps, bushes, ruts, loose wire, tins, bottles or broken glass.

5 Do not choose a flat or low-lying ground, get away as much as possible from country that is likely to be exceptionally boggy in wet weather. The ideal position is a firm sand, or gravel rise.

6 Remember it is better to have THE BEST LANDING GROUND, even if it is a distance from your Homestead or Town, rather than an inferior or dangerous Landing Ground right beside your Homestead or Town.

7 The centre of the Landing Place should be marked by some white mark on the ground. The best way to do this is to remove the surface soil, to a depth of 3 or 4 inches, and then fill up with white ashes, refuse carbide, or light white-wash gravel, or very small stones white-washed. Most Homesteads or Shearing Sheds or Scouring Sheds have white ashes or refuse carbide. A couple of dray loads would be sufficient, or a dray-load of Gidyea burned on the spot would do.

8 The best mark to place on the centre of your Landing Ground is in the shape of a T or X. Total length of T, between ten and twelve feet, and the width three or four feet, as per sketch attached.

9 After having put down your T or X, send full particulars and a rough sketch of your Homestead to the nearest Office of the Company. The sketch should show all your buildings, yards, haystacks, or anything noticeable or peculiar to your Homestead,

or Landing Ground. Also give compass position of your Landing Ground, as near as possible to your buildings. Immediately you send this sketch your Landing Ground will be placed on a district map, and will be used as a guide for the Pilots. If you help in this way it will be a big help along to safe and efficient Aviation in our district. Remember that Aviation is now established in your district, and that both in Longreach and Winton Aviation is getting the support of the Doctors. Remember that a Pilot at a height of 5000 feet can see all the Homesteads within a radius of fifty miles, which is necessary in case of sickness, accident or urgent business. When wishing a machine to land at your Homestead that you have a good distinctive mark that the Pilot can recognise, helps him to make a good landing, both for your sake and the interests of Aviation.

How to Receive an Aeroplane

1 On the approach of the machine a smoke fire should be lit, on or near the Landing Ground. This enables the Aviator to judge the direction of the wind, which is necessary for a good landing.

2 See the Landing Ground is free from Stock or any temporary obstruction, and keep people from rushing across in front of the landing machine. Remember the landing speed is at the rate of forty miles an hour.

On 2 November 1922, Q.A.N.T.A.S. opened its first regular service, between Charleville and Cloncurry. The 577 miles were flown in two stages, with an overnight stop. Fysh and his wife lived at Longreach, the half-way point, in a wooden house with a corrugated roof. Mrs Fysh had a variety of duties in connection with the airline. Once she was asked on the telephone by one of the pilots to put on her high-heeled shoes, go to the airfield and find out how far the heels sank in after the rain, 'so I'll know if it's safe to land'.

At this time Australia had railways linking the towns and cities along the southern part of the continent and an important part of the airline's task was to provide feeder services from the remote inland areas to the nearest rail-head. Q.A.N.T.A.S. also saw itself, however, as a competitor of the railways and its early sales literature emphasises this. The cover of a booklet issued in 1928 says: 'Save days of travel by using Q.A.N.T.A.S. mail and taxi-planes,' and money savings were important too. 'Flights on any section of the route', it said, 'show a large saving over other means of transport, this being partic-ularly valuable to travellers in Western Queensland, where the distances are great and the rail services are slow and disconnected. Road travel by car is good in dry weather, but is completely suspended following heavy falls of rain. Air travel is, therefore, the most speedy and also the most reliable means of transport.'

Figures were given to show the advantages of air over rail travel:

INSTANCES OF SAVINGS

	Rail	*By Air Connection*
Charleville–Longreach	4½ days	4 hours
Longreach–Cloncurry	3 days	4 hrs 30 mins

Cloncurry–Camooweal	3	days	3 hrs 30 mins
Longreach–Sydney	76	hours	52 hours
Camooweal–Sydney	9	days	4 days
Brisbane–Normanton	11	days	2 days 20 hrs

Cost – Passenger fares on the regular route range from 7d. to 9d. per mile, according to the distance travelled. These charges in instances compare favourably with rail fares, owing to the direct air line flown from point to point and to the travelling expenses [i.e. the cost of hotels and meals *en route*] saved by taking the direct route.

The same booklet gives advice to 'Passengers making their First Trip'.

Only those who have flown on an air route know what an ordinary everyday procedure this is.

Clothing – Wear your ordinary travelling clothes, with a rug and overcoat in winter time. Do not forget a book or magazine.

Deportment – Flying caps and goggles are unnecessary. Sit at ease in the machine; your movements cannot possibly affect its balance.

'Bumps' – When flying in calm air the machine is without motion, except for the slowly moving earth, which appears away below the wing tip. If the machine takes on a slight movement you know that an uneven and gusty patch of air is being encountered. These movements of the machine only become unpleasant when flying in the very roughest weather, such as is rarely encountered. Owing to the speed of the aeroplane, it is almost impossible to be caught in a heavy storm.

Q.A.N.T.A.S. set great store by its aerial taxi service. During 1926–8, 450 passengers were carried at two shillings a mile. Most of these trips were 'of an urgent nature' and the company offered to fly to and from any landing grounds 'which have been certified as suitable'. One such journey was described many years later by Mr N. A. Parker. His mother, then living with him at Aldington Winton, became seriously ill with abscesses in the gall duct and had to be transferred urgently to hospital in Sydney.

The plane to seat six had four seats removed and replaced with a stretcher leaving a seat for my sister and myself.

The plane, flown by pilot Stewart, landed on a claypan close to Aldingham house, in the evening, and next morning we started off early. Landed at Longreach and Charleville to re-fuel and stayed overnight at Bourke. Our mother stayed in the plane overnight. Next morning the plane was hard to start and the writer pulled the propeller round for over an hour before it started. We landed at Dubbo, then Mascot, where an ambulance met us to take the patient to Eastwood. The only part of the trip that in any way distressed her was in the ambulance.

The agreement was that any back passengers would be credited to me. We got only one passenger as far as Dubbo. The cost of the flight was four hundred pounds.[3]

A somewhat different aspect of flying in Australia at that time is provided by one of the early Q.A.N.T.A.S. pilots, Captain Lester Brain. He was rather

[3] Letter to Kenneth Hudson dated 16 January 1970.

less enthusiastic about Australian flying conditions than Hudson Fysh had felt it necessary to be when launching the new company. He pointed out:

Turbulence in flying was worse inland in Australia than in any other part of the world. The temperature out in the far west in Queensland would go up as high as 125° F in the shade. There mightn't be much wind, but there would be little whirlwinds. Dust-storms, of course, were common. The early morning wasn't bad shortly after the dawn, but any time after noon the turbulence would really rocket. If they didn't wear their seat belts, they'd finish up in the open air.[4]

Captain Brain's passengers were consequently air-sick, almost as a matter of course. The only ones who never got sick, he found, were very old people and these, not unnaturally, were his favourite passengers. The pilot had to clean up the aircraft afterwards – there was no one else to do it – and look after the passengers to the best of his ability. His tasks were never-ending:

[4] Conversation with Julian Pettifer, 9 September 1978.

He had to mend his own punctures and refuel from four-gallon benzine tins. He had to punch a hole in these, climb up on the cockpit, pour the petrol in through a funnel with a shammy on it to take the water out. Of course, the passengers would do their part. They'd hand the tins up to him where he could reach them, and, if he had a flat tyre, they'd help with pulling the jack or tyre levers.

It was necessary for the Q.A.N.T.A.S. pilots to be highly adaptable and resourceful. The planes took children from the outback to school in Toowoomba or Brisbane, and it was Captain Brain and his colleagues who bought them comics out of their own pockets. The pilots also carried out shopping errands in town for people.

On one occasion Captain Brain had to take a body in a coffin. It was too long for the aircraft, so the undertaker 'foreshortened it to fit in a smaller coffin. I managed to get that in. I had to take the bracing wires out of the wings while I juggled it into the cabin and put them back afterwards.'

Arthur Affleck flew Q.A.N.T.A.S. aircraft for a number of years in the 1920s. The conditions, as he remembered them, were far from luxurious:

At no one of the hotels where we stayed overnight did the publican consider it worthwhile to supply early breakfast to passengers or crew, and the pilot, in addition to flying aircraft and, in many instances, refuelling and servicing it, was required to wake his passengers, rush down to the hotel kitchen and make a cup of tea and toast for them, help to handle their baggage, collect mails from the local post office and freight from the agent's office, pick up any other passengers from their homes or other hotels, and then get out to the aerodrome in time to open up the hangar, push the aircraft out with the assistance of any of the passengers who felt strong enough to help at that hour of the day, start up, load up and take off at the first crack of dawn.[5]

On the service from Cloncurry to Normanton, passengers

. . . were required to make themselves as comfortable as possible jammed into a cabin with, amongst other items, three or four large cornsacks full of wriggling and twitching fish. Our normal weekly fishy load weighed in the vicinity of 500–600 lbs. and when, in addition to this, there were two or three passengers, suitcases, swags, saddles, rifles, mailbags, sundry items of freight and a couple of savage cattle dogs travelling with their drover master, all to be fitted into a small four-seater cabin, the resultant congestion needed to be seen to be believed.[6]

Very similar conditions still prevail in parts of the world where the interior of an aircraft has much the same appearance and atmosphere as a rural bus, with people, animals, chickens and baskets all packed tightly together.

The passengers using Q.A.N.T.A.S. services in the 1920s included graziers, sheep men, cattle men, drovers (who would bring back their saddles and their dog as their only luggage), doctors, sick people needing medical or hospital treatment, local lawyers, magistrates, sheep and cattle dealers, some commercial travellers and itinerant salesmen, and, with the discovery of the big silver mines at Mt Isa, an increasing number of mining and technical en-

[5] A. H. Affleck, *The Wandering Years*, 1962, p. 29.
[6] Ibid, pp. 29–30.

Sophisticated hoist
for repairing an early
Qantas plane.

gineering people. From the outset womenfolk travelled (many with babies) to avoid the three-day primitive railway journey, and comprised perhaps twenty per cent of travellers. Throughout the 1920s a sprinkling of children travelled unaccompanied to or from their boarding schools, since their parents often lived on sheep or cattle properties remote from even country townships.

There are few countries in the world in which the rapid introduction of air transport was as desirable as in the Soviet Union, but initial development there was very slow, mainly because the government was the only agency involved. By the political accident of Lenin taking power at exactly the same time as civil aviation was beginning, private enterprise has never played the slightest part in establishing commercial aviation in the USSR. The Permanent Council on Civil Aviation was set up on 9 February 1923, and this date is usually reckoned to mark the beginnings of Soviet passenger flying. Regular flights on the first route, Moscow–Gorki (Nizhni Novgorod) began on 15 July 1923. The initial results on this 420-kilometre stretch can hardly be described as spectacular. Only 229 passengers, less than one a day, and 1900 kilos of freight were carried in the first year. The reasons for this slow start are not difficult to find. The route, unlike London–Paris or London–Amsterdam, was not one which already conveyed larger numbers of busy, important people by train and boat – what airlines call its quality-potential was low – and it was not over the kind of territory which made other forms of travel extremely tedious or perilous. It fell into neither of the two categories which made air travel immediately popular. As a laboratory for testing and developing civil aviation, Moscow–Gorki was not a particularly brilliant choice. Moscow–Leningrad would almost certainly have yielded more useful and more immediate results.

Over the Soviet Union as a whole, however, the inadequate road and rail communications provided ample reason for the success of air travel. Punctuality and regularity of services were never considered particularly important and were in any case difficult, if not impossible, to achieve under Russian conditions. The winter climate caused great problems, the aircraft and their maintenance were not of the best, and organisation often left a good deal to be desired. The services were certainly not speedy by the European standards of the time. Even as late as the mid-1930s, an average point-to-point speed of just over fifty miles an hour on the internal routes was considered normal and acceptable.

Speed, however, always has to be valued comparatively. In areas where aeroplanes had to compete with an efficient railway system, which allowed passengers to travel at, say, sixty miles an hour, the air service had to achieve at least 150 miles an hour to make the extra cost seem worthwhile, bearing in mind that at that time aeroplanes, unlike trains, could not operate after dark. What mattered then, and still does, is the total time taken to complete one's journey. In the conditions of 1925, twenty-four hours in a train would almost certainly produce overall results which were as good, if not better, than two flights in a slow aeroplane with an overnight stop in between.

If, on the other hand, an air service is competing with horse-drawn vehicles or water transport, moving at six or seven miles an hour, which was the case in much of the Soviet-administered territory, a speed of seventy or ninety miles an hour offered just as great relative advantages as 150 miles an hour in the United States or France. Another important factor to be kept in mind is that slow planes are cheaper to run than fast planes. In these circumstances, one has to be cautious when accusing the Russians of inefficiency in their pioneering days.

The Ukrainian Air Transport Company, founded in 1923, developed an interesting system, well suited to local needs. The aim was to provide rapid passenger and parcel services between Moscow, Kharkov, Odessa, the Donbass and the most important centres of the Ukraine. At railway stations and at river ports, people who wanted to fly simply had to provide themselves with railway and boat tickets covering the route. If they then decided to fly instead, for all or some of the journey, they could. The possession of a ticket gave passengers the right to take with them five kilos of baggage. A ticket also served as an insurance policy. Every passenger was automatically insured for 5000 roubles. If a plane had to make a forced landing and it proved impossible to continue the flight, passengers were given the cost of a rail ticket to their ultimate destination.

After some short-lived experiments just after the 1914–18 war, air services in China began later than in the USSR, at the end of the 1920s. The pioneer was the China National Aviation Corporation, which was financed largely by American capital. It was founded in 1929, with the intention of operating three key services – Shanghai–Chengtu; Shanghai–Peiping; and Shanghai–Canton. The first part of the system, Shanghai–Hankow, was opened in October 1929, and the remaining sections between then and 1934. It is significant that much the best patronised service was between Chunking and Kweiyang, a point-to-point distance of about two hundred miles. This is hardly surprising, since the journey by air took only an hour and a half against fifteen days by any other form of transport. There were rivers and hills to cross and the roads were wretchedly poor.

If one is faced with the straight question 'Which country did most to develop civil aviation during the 1920s?' the answer has to be 'Either the Dutch or the Germans or the French,' with very little to choose between them.

The Dutch achievement was due almost entirely to the extraordinary drive and single-mindedness of one man, Albert Plesman. He established Koninklijke Luchtvaart Maatschappij (KLM–Royal Dutch Airlines) in October 1919 with three ideas firmly in his mind: to make KLM, or any other airline, successful, one needed adequate capital, aeroplanes designed specifically for carrying passengers, and an air-minded public. Plesman set about obtaining all three.

In August and September 1919 he organised an aviation exhibition and flying demonstrations in Amsterdam. Half a million people visited it and 4000 of them paid forty guilders each for a flight. Largely as a result of the publicity from this exhibition, Royal Dutch Airlines (KLM) was founded the following month as a limited company with a reasonable capital and valuable support from the banks and other commercial institutions. While it was waiting for new aircraft to be designed and manufactured, KLM gathered experience by hiring crews and planes from other operators, including the British company, Aircraft Transport and Travel. On the Amsterdam–London service, inaugurated on 17 May 1920, the water-cooled engine and instruments (compass, air-speed indicator, tachometer and petrol gauge) were not considered safe for long journeys over water, so the flights were routed down the Dutch and Belgian coast and then up to London via Folkestone and Tonbridge. Another experimental service, from Amsterdam to Bremen and Hamburg, was started in September 1920, with aircraft and pilots from the German company, Deutsche Luft Reederei.

In April 1921 KLM opened regular services over these routes with its own

crews and its own German-built[7] Fokker F.11 monoplanes. These had a closed
cabin for four or five passengers and were much more comfortable to travel in
than the borrowed German planes. Three passengers sat on a bench seat and
two in easy chairs. They cruised at nearly eighty mph. The Fokker F.111,
introduced in November of the same year, had a separate freight compartment, so that passengers, baggage and freight were no longer mixed together.
The eight-seater Fokker F.VII, which entered service in 1924, included two
important developments, plane-to-ground radio-telephone and a lavatory. An
improved version of the F.VII, in service from May 1925 onwards, had air-
cooled radial engines, metal propellers, a heated cabin and sponge-rubber
seating.

With the new aircraft the speed went up from eighty to 120 mph and the
number of passengers per aircraft from two to eight. Until 1922, however,
there were no flights during the winter months, that is, from the end of
October until the end of March. When KLM first operated winter services, in
November 1922, passengers were provided with rugs and foot-muffs, since
there was no form of heating in the aircraft cabin.

Until the 1930s, KLM operated scheduled services only within Europe, but
a few passengers were carried earlier on colonial experimental services to
Indonesia. The first flight from Amsterdam to Jakarta, in October–November

Interior of a Fokker
F.VIIA in service with
KLM, 1925–40.

[7] At Schwerin, where Fokker had established a wartime factory for supplying the German
air force.

ROYAL DUTCH KLM AIR LINES

SEE TWICE AS MUCH OF
EUROPE
IN HALF THE TIME

KLM in 1928. A very
similar example of the
F.VIII is preserved in
the museum at
Schiphol Airport.

1924, took fifty-five days to cover the 9500 miles. The actual flying time was a
little over 127 hours, and the average speed of the Fokker F.VII was 75 mph.
The second flight, and also the first return flight, was in 1927 and was a great
improvement on the first. The outward journey lasted from 15 June to
30 June and the return from 6 July to 23 July. The passengers on this trip, for
which the aeroplane had been specially chartered, were the American mil-
lionaire W. van Lear Black and his secretary.

After further proving and mail flights in 1928 and 1929, KLM inaugurated,
on 12 September 1929, a fortnightly service from Amsterdam to Jakarta,
using the three-engined Fokker F.VIIb-3M. Until 1940 this was the longest
scheduled air route in the world, 9500 miles. The aircraft, PH-AEZ, took
twelve days for the journey. It stopped at eighteen places, including Istanbul,
Baghdad, Karachi, Calcutta and Bangkok. The experience gained was in-

valuable, not only for KLM but for long-distance aviation in general. At this time there were no reliable maps of the route, no weather reports, no hangars, no radio stations, no lighting at airfields and no fuel pumps – petrol had to be manhandled into the aircraft from four-gallon drums. Not infrequently, local holidays meant a complete absence of ground personnel when the aircraft took off and landed.

Civil aviation in Germany was in the hands of several companies until the formation of Deutsche Luft Hansa[8] in 1926. For some years it was difficult to get suitable aircraft. After the London Declaration of May 1921 Germany was forbidden to manufacture aeroplanes of any kind, military or civil. Junkers, however, found ways of overcoming the difficulty. Their F13 aircraft, designed and built immediately after the war, was certainly the most advanced in the world at that time. It had a cantilever wing – the struts and wires which conventionally held the wings to the fuselage had been eliminated – the whole aircraft was covered with corrugated sheet-metal skin, and the passengers eventually travelled in a closed, heated cabin. The four seats were fitted with safety belts and the F13 was the first commercial aircraft to be equipped with dual controls, so that two pilots could take turns on long flights.

In 1920, the Americans bought a number of F13s, mainly for use on the New York–Omaha and New York–San Francisco mail routes, and were enthusiastic about it. It was also extensively flown in South America. This robust aeroplane was aviation's first workhorse, operating with equal success in the tropics and the Arctic. Production of it had to continue and, despite the Allied regulations, it did. Until the ban was lifted in 1926, Junkers manufactured in Danzig, Reval and even in Moscow, where the young Russian engineer, Tupolev, helped to build it, and learned a lot in the process. The F13, known in America as the JL 6, was the first big success in the manufacture of commercial aircraft anywhere, despite, ironically, Allied determination to prevent the resurgence of a German aircraft industry. Two other German aircraft firms, it should be noted, also survived and prospered by transferring their factories abroad, Dornier to Italy and Rohrbach to Denmark.

Luft Hansa got off the mark very quickly, once the decision to establish the company had been taken. On 1 May 1926, one of the world's first passenger night routes, guided by both main-line and auxiliary beacons, was opened from Berlin to Königsberg. A flying-boat service from Stettin to Stockholm was begun in May 1926. On the Berlin–Paris route the first Sunday service started operating on 29 April 1928. Until then Luft Hansa, like nearly all other airlines, had not flown on Sundays and public holidays. Soon afterwards, on 21 May, an enterprising new facility allowed passengers sailing from New York to Bremen on the *Columbus* to catch immediate air connections to Berlin, Frankfurt and Munich.

[8] Written as one word, 'Lufthansa', from 1 January 1934.

Cleaners at work on a
Junkers F13 belonging to
Luft Hansa, 1926.

Of all Luft Hansa's technical achievements during the 1920s, those connected with night flying and instrument flying were probably, from the passenger's point of view, the most important. When the plane left Tempelhof, Berlin, on its way to Königsberg, the factory chimneys around the airport were lit up by spotlights. Church spires, masts and any other tall structures were marked with red lamps, and from then on a trail of lights, visible even in bad weather, showed the pilot his route to the north-east. There was a revolving spotlight and every four or five kilometres in between there were lamps on masts or on rooftops. The aircraft itself was fitted with spotlights and with electrically-triggered magnesium flares on the wings. The instruments in the cockpit were illuminated.

The flights were a complete success. During 1926–8 Luft Hansa planes flew nearly a million kilometres on night services, mainly to Königsberg. Other countries, notably the United States, began experiments soon afterwards, and in 1930 the first international conference to discuss uniform airport and route lighting was held in Berlin, a choice which commemorated the pioneering work carried out by Luft Hansa in this field.

The company began training its pilots in instrument flying in 1927 and by 1930 its experience in this field had gained such a reputation that foreign airlines sent their pilots to Germany for Luft Hansa training. Radio communication was also developed as a safety factor, especially in darkness. Luft Hansa began to fit its larger aircraft with radio in 1926 and the first radio operators joined the flight crews in that year. The methods developed in the late 1920s in order to use radio to guide a plane down through cloud cover seem primitive by modern standards, but they represented a great advance, since for the first time the pilot did not have to find a cloud break in order to get his plane down safely.

The system was that the air traffic controller allowed pilots to find their own way down to about 200 metres and then brought them down to a safe landing simply by listening to the engine noise of the plane and then relaying its position to the pilots by radio. It demanded a sensitive ear and great accuracy of judgement, but it worked.

The Alps, with mountains rising to three and four thousand metres, remained a blank on the civil aviation map until the late 1920s, for the existing planes were unable to reach a sufficient altitude to clear these peaks with safety. The breakthrough came with the development of the three-engined Rohrbach Roland, which could climb to 5000 metres. At this height there were problems with frozen fuel lines – the temperature went down as low as −30°C – but these were gradually solved and in 1928 Luft Hansa was able to begin an experimental airmail service across the Alps, in co-operation with the Italian airline, Avio Linee Italiane. Four years later, with the Junkers Ju 52/3m, passenger services began on the Munich–Milan–Rome route.

In 1925, just before the mergers which produced Luft Hansa, a new aviation periodical, *Ikarus*, began to appear in Germany. One article, by Dr Heinz Orlovius, was called 'Six people fly to Copenhagen'. The flight was from Tempelhof, Berlin, and the author describes the group and makes certain deductions from their appearance and their manner of speaking. One appears to be a businessman, thinking only about the timetable and whether the plane will be punctual. The second, a man with an artistic look about him, seems to be asking, 'Is the plane safe? What happens if we come down over the water? I must get there in time. My concert's at eight o'clock.' It is extraordinary, says Dr Orlovius, to see how used the people at the airport seem to be to these sorts of questions – 'Everybody's questions are answered'. Another one of the party seems to be a farmer, and it doesn't need a Sherlock Holmes to know what he is going to Copenhagen for. There is a catalogue of a big cattle sale and show in Copenhagen sticking out of his pocket. Numbers four and five are pretty easy to guess, too. They are a young couple with shiny new rings on their fingers, saying, 'It is wonderful to be Icarus and to know that the Sun God cannot destroy our wings, because our wings are made of aluminium.' Inside, Dr Orlovius remarks, 'there is nothing to distinguish your surroundings from those of a luxury express train,' a comparison frequently made by every airline during the 1920s and 1930s.

Another German periodical[9] investigated the air-travel market in the same year that the observant Dr Orlovius flew from Berlin to Copenhagen. In its leading article it put the question, 'Why not travel by air?' and supplied the most frequently heard answers. Air travel was commonly thought to be 'Uncomfortable. Dear. Dangerous.' The magazine denied all three criticisms. 'The objection that you buy saving of time and the romantic journey at the cost of danger to your own life', it declared, 'is an argument more appropriate to our grandfathers than to ourselves.' It then went on to give a list of what it called 'people suitable as passengers'. Air travel, it felt, was the most appropriate way of transporting 'exceptional businessmen, clever tourists, romantic honeymoon couples, fast-moving directors, modern lawyers, anxious motorists, attractive mannequins, fresh oysters and crabs, expensive silks and perfumes, breakable electric bulbs and sensitive furs and chemicals.'

No European or American airline would have disagreed with this list of desirable passengers, and considerable ingenuity was devoted to securing as many of them as possible. The British and German companies became particularly good at the snob approach, never failing to draw public attention to the statesmen, titled people, film stars and millionaires who travelled on their aircraft and who had presumably found everything to their satisfaction. In 1927 Imperial Airways reported[10] that 'on June 20th, HRH Prince George, who travelled incognito, made a trip from Paris to London; unlike HRH the Prince of Wales, who flew from Paris to London last spring in a "Special", Prince George travelled by the regular "Paris Shopping Service".' Prince George seems to have enjoyed flying. A few weeks later it was reported that 'Imperial Airways have been honoured by HRH Prince George travelling as a passenger on the Paris route. On this occasion he travelled in one of the aircraft operating the "Silver Wing" Service de Luxe.'[11] The Silver Wing Service was Imperial Airways' appeal to the élite. In 1931–2 their London–Paris service was in two parts: Service A was usually operated by the Argosy three-engined twenty-seater aeroplane and Service B, the Silver Wing, used Heracles 38-seaters. Service A cost £4 4s. single, £7 19s. 6d. return, and Service B £4 12s. 6d. single, £8 15s. return. These fares were about fifty per cent higher than those then charged for travel by sea and rail. Service A left Croydon at 8.30 am and Service B at 12.30 pm. Each had a flying time of two and a quarter hours.

Air fares showed no tendency to fall during the 1920s and early 1930s, even though more passengers could be carried on each flight. In 1928 Imperial Airways charged, for example, £4 single to Amsterdam and £9 10s. to Berlin, with no reduction for a return ticket. By 1932 these rates had gone up to £5 and £10 respectively.

Royalty, no matter what their nationality, were invaluable to the airlines

[9] *Die Luftreise*, No. 1, May 1925.
[10] *Imperial Airways Monthly Bulletin*, June 1927.
[11] Ibid, September 1927.

and their patronage rarely went unmentioned. In August 1927 Imperial Airways, who by this time were running services in the Middle East, noted that:

. . . we had the distinction of carrying on the Cairo–Basra service HM King Feisal and the Emir Ghazi of Iraq. Earlier in the month, the heir to the throne of Iraq, who was returning from Harrow accompanied by his tutor, travelled in the 'City of Baghdad' between Cairo and Baghdad. HM King Feisal, attended by Tashin Bey Khadri and other members of his suite, flew from Baghdad to Gaza. During the flight the King sent out by wireless a message of brotherly greeting for the Emir Abdulla of Transjordania.[12]

This, however, was outdone by a later item,[13] from the same airline:

We shall in future, publish each month a list of the most distinguished and interesting passengers who have travelled on our London–Paris services since our last issue. Below we give a list for the first three weeks in March:

> Lord Londonderry, Secretary of State for Air
> Lady Carlisle
> Marqués Bonneval
> Prince and Princess Walkonsky
> Baron Rothschild
> Lord Lymington
> Count Spezia
> Baroness Doiney
> Marquis Traeontal
> Mr Edward Marjoribanks, MP for Eastbourne
> M. René Clair, French film producer
> Mr Eyston, Racing motorist
> Mr Kaye Don, Racing motorist
> Mr Jeff Dickson, Boxing promoter
> Primo Carnera, Italian boxer

The implication was twofold. On the one hand the ordinary citizen could be expected to feel that what was good enough for Prince George, Princess Walkonsky and Primo Carnera must be good enough for him, and, on the other, one princess was reckoned to be attractive bait for another princess.

Film stars, Middle Eastern princes and visiting American Senators may have provided the airlines with their glamour and box-office appeal, but, over the twelve months, businessmen were their bread and butter. In trying to win them over from the railways, the emphasis during the 1920s was always on

---

[12] Ibid.

[13] Ibid, March 1932. It was eventually discovered, however, that publicity about the passenger had its disadvantages. For some years, Imperial Airways was in the habit of giving the Press its passenger lists, as a matter of routine. On one unfortunate occasion, however, the papers printed the fact that a certain Mr and Mrs X had travelled to Paris together for the weekend. The real Mrs X read this item in the paper with considerable interest and, having disentangled itself from the ensuing quarrel with some difficulty, Imperial Airways was not thereafter as free with this kind of information.

speed, very rarely on comfort. In 1928 Imperial Airways drew attention to the enterprise of a party of American businessmen. Travelling in a fourteen-seater Handley Page airliner, they visited Paris, Cologne, Hanover, Berlin, Prague, Vienna, Budapest, Basle and London, all in fourteen days, 'a trip impossible by any other form of transport'.[14]

Not only businessmen were attracted by the speed of air travel. One day during the summer of 1927:

Mr S. Donoghue, the famous jockey, rode in the 2 o'clock race at Windsor, and in a race at 4.30 at Ostend on the same day. After the Windsor race he was rowed across the river to a meadow where a fast aeroplane awaited him. Although a stop was made at Croydon Aerodrome for Customs formalities, Mr Donoghue reached Ostend at 3.45, where a motor-car was waiting to take him to the race course. He actually arrived at the race course with half an hour to spare.[15]

There were other ways of obtaining privileged treatment. On the London–Paris service there were early attempts to sort out the passengers into two classes, so that the famous and influential might have an opportunity to avoid the company of their social inferiors. The separation into sheep and goats could not be guaranteed, but by making some aeroplanes more expensive than others there was a good possibility of achieving the desired results, especially since the first-class services departed at more convenient times and used more up-to-date aircraft.

Immigration officers were exceptionally well placed to observe the type of person who travelled by air, but few people outside service and government departments have had the opportunity or perhaps the inclination to read the annual reports of the Chief Inspectors. They are full of interesting information about the habits and characteristics of the travelling public. In 1924, for instance – the year of the Wembley Exhibition – the British Chief Inspector noted that 'the fares on the different airlines remained fairly high and as a result nearly all the passengers are "of good type" – Americans predominate and indeed they appear to regard at least one flight as essential to "do Europe" properly'.

The contrast with the passengers who arrived by ship was very marked. Many of them were certainly not of good type at all. The ships brought everybody with a need to travel, first, second and third class, the rich and the poor, the elegant and the ragged, the highly respectable and the criminal. The aeroplanes, because fares were high, sorted their passengers out and took only those, the 'good type', who were able to pay the bill.

There were certain consequences of this, which no European or American airline could afford to disregard. The more money a person has and the more socially exalted he is, the more valuable he considers his life to be, and the better treatment he expects. He is unwilling to travel dangerously or uncomfortably and assumes that he will be treated with the deference to which he is

[14] Ibid, April 1928.
[15] Ibid, August 1927.

accustomed. Having said this, it is necessary to add that everyone, however wealthy or famous, has to accept the best that can be provided at the time. The travelling standards and possibilities of 1928 were not those of 1978. In some ways they were worse, in others better. One always has to ask, 'Considering what I am paying, is what I am being given reasonable now, in 1928, 1938, 1978, or whatever the date may be?' and at any date there are, alas, plenty of unreasonable people who make a habit of crying for the moon.

But one should beware of transferring today's expectations into yesterday's environment. A good example of this is the degree of warmth which is taken for granted today, but which was not demanded in the 1920s and 1930s. In the 1970s people reckon to be warm, and complain if they are not – warm in rooms, warm in cars, warm in public places, warm in all forms of public transport. Before the Second World War this was not so. Clothes and shoes were heavier, motoring in the winter months was a spartan affair, and only Americans and the exceptionally well-to-do enjoyed the delights of central heating. During the past thirty years, the West has got soft, although, with the rapidly approaching energy crisis, it may soon have to learn to get hardy again.

On the other hand, the pre-war airlines could not afford to offer their passengers a standard of comfort and service inferior to what was provided

Meal service on Luft Hansa's Junkers G31, 1928. The resemblance to a railway dining car is remarkably close.

for the same people in other fields of life. What the railways and the shipping companies gave their first-class passengers in the way of cleanliness, genteel surroundings and servility, the airlines could not fail to give either. But, until well into the 1930s, it was no good pretending that travelling by air all the year round and in all weathers was as safe or as punctual as travelling by boat and train. Mishaps and hold-ups continued to occur, although the airlines naturally did their best to play them down, reckoning, with excellent judgement, that people will put up with a surprising amount of discomfort, provided such discomfort is not available to their social inferiors.

The grass landing areas were apt to cause problems. Sometimes a plane would skid or have a heavy landing and buckle the undercarriage. On such occasions, as one veteran Imperial Airways employee recalled, 'we had a pot of paint and we used to paint out our name, *Imperial Airways*, in case the Press happened to get hold of the picture and publish it overseas'.[16]

The coming of larger and more comfortable aircraft certainly did not mean the end of aviation's adventurous days. One of Imperial Airways' secretarial staff at Croydon[17] between 1926 and 1929 recalls a number of unpublished

Opposite: The best people fly. Air Union poster of the Twenties.

[16] Eric Wheatley, interviewed for BBC TV on 3 March 1978. Mr Wheatley worked at Croydon in the 1930s.
[17] Mrs Mary Hayman: conversation with Kenneth Hudson, 15 June 1970.

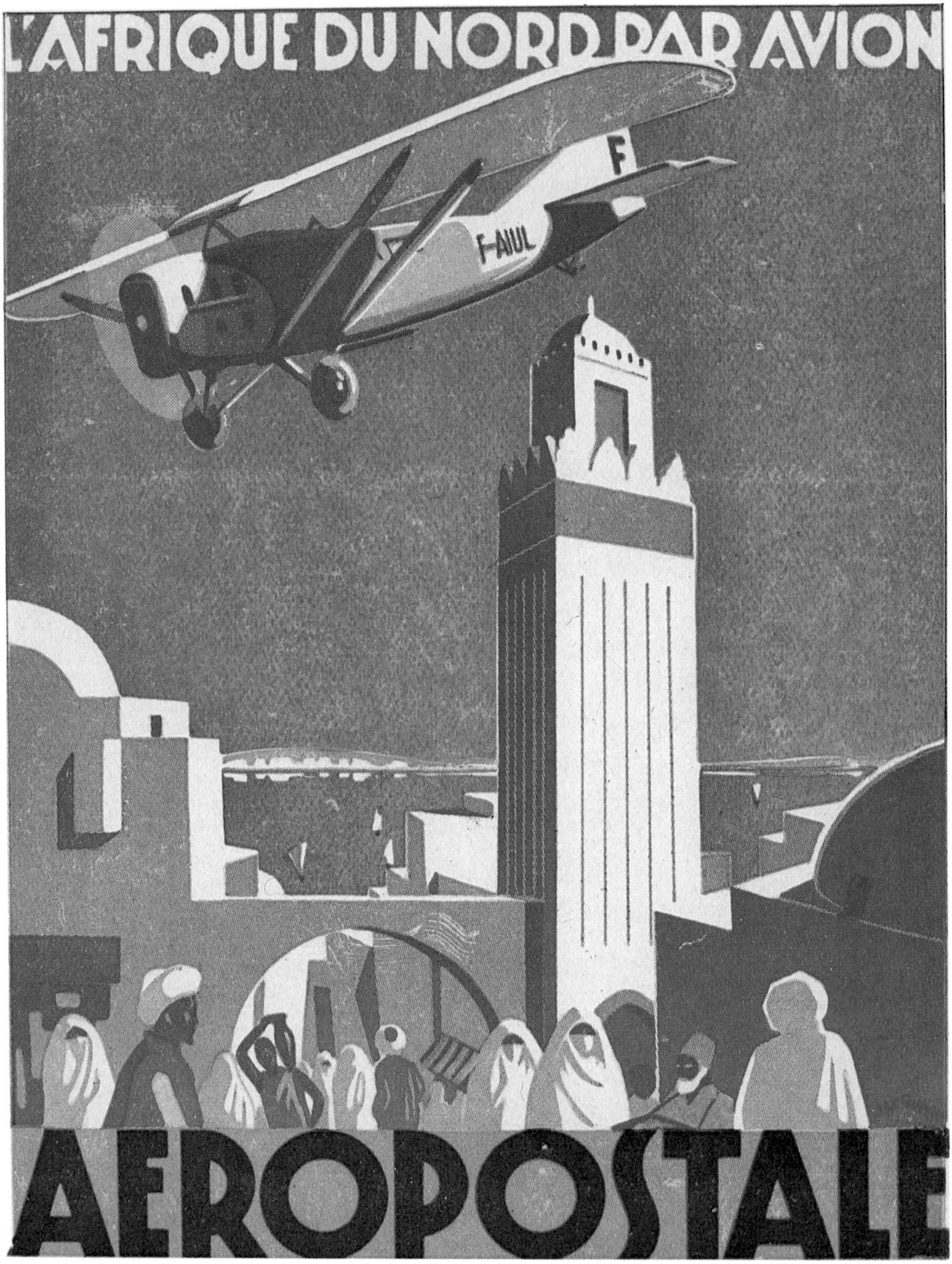
L'AFRIQUE DU NORD PAR AVION
F
F-AIUL
AEROPOSTALE

facts from this period, at a time when the public was being assured daily that flying was as safe as travelling by train.

Once, when she was acting as a relief telephonist, she heard a distress call from a pilot over the Channel: 'I am coming down in the ditch.' He landed in the sea seven miles north-west of the Varne lightship, with a dozen passengers on board, including women and children, and a Pekinese dog. They managed to get out of the plane and sat on the wings, waiting to be picked up. They all remained calm, except for a Greek, who, as soon as he saw the lifeboat was approaching, took off his boots, dived into the sea and started swimming towards the boat, determined at all costs to be saved. To the delight of the other passengers, the lifeboat circled round him, collected all the other passengers first, and then picked him up on the way back. He later sued the company for the loss of his boots.

Such incidents fortunately became steadily less common. As the airlines gained experience, the public expected and usually got steadily improving standards of service. On the whole, aircraft broke down less frequently, arrived more punctually and were warmer and less noisy to travel in. The terminal facilities also improved rapidly. In 1919, with a World War only recently ended and passenger flying a great novelty, a wooden hut might be acceptable as a terminal building, but by 1925 it was not acceptable. Passengers at the principal airports were beginning to take it for granted that there would be a suitable building in which they could pass the time before boarding their plane or while they were waiting for their friends to arrive. In Berlin, Paris, Amsterdam and London they were offered, by the end of the 1920s, something fully comparable to a major railway station, in quality, if not in size. As early as 1923, KLM had its own hotel, with café and restaurant, at Schiphol Airport. At Le Bourget in 1926 there was a waiting room, *bureau de change*, post and telegraph office and a battery of telephone kiosks. In addition, 'as at railway stations', there was a bookstall.[18] The new building at Croydon Airport opened on 30 January 1928. From that date, it was announced:

All services will start from the fine expanse of paving which takes the place of the 'tarmac' of the old aerodrome. On entering the domed Booking Hall, one realises that air services have now taken their place in the civilised world as a recognised means of transport, no longer limited to a few adventurous spirits, but daily used by business men as well as those travelling for pleasure.[19]

At this time, however, it was not altogether easy to define 'the civilised world', at least in airline terms. At the end of the 1920s, a flight might begin in a 'civilised' place, say London or Amsterdam, and a day later its civilised passengers might well find themselves landing or spending the night at a place which did not appear civilised at all. What the airlines have in fact done over the past half-century is to provide their passengers with at least the

[18] *Guide de l'Aéroport du Bourget*, 1926.
[19] *Imperial Airways Monthly Bulletin*, January 1927.

Opposite: The French link with Africa. Passengers and mail in the Twenties.

The restaurant at
Schiphol in the late
Twenties.

trappings of Western civilisation wherever they begin and end their flight. Everywhere now there are terminal buildings, hotels, restaurants and reservation offices which bear some resemblance, although frequently in a minor key, to the facilities offered in Chicago, Copenhagen or Cape Town. What happens in the hinterland, away from the airport, is another matter, but at least at international airports evidence of the civilised world exists, in so far as 'civilised' can be equated with 'Western'.

Airlines and politics have always been inseparable. Consider, for example, the German activities in South America during the 1920s. South America was of great commercial importance to the Germans. They had considerable investments there and industrial exports were on a large scale, while many Germans had settled there and continued to do so throughout the Nazi period. On 5 December 1919, at Barranquilla, in Colombia, the Sociedad Colombo-Alemaña de Transportes Aéreos (SCADTA) was founded with German participation and German pilots. It used F13 sea-planes brought by ship from Germany and within a year there were regular services between Barranquilla and Girardot, a river port near the capital, Bogotá. In 1924 Deutsche Aero Lloyd, one of Luft Hansa's forbears, and SCADTA established the Condor Syndicate, to develop South American operations. The Syndicate bought two Dornier Wal flying boats, 'Atlantico' and 'Pacifico', and in 1927,

50

after an extensive programme of exploratory flights, obtained a concession to operate passenger and airmail services in Brazil. Later in the same year the Brazilian national airline VARIG (Empresa de Viacao Aerea Rio Grandense) was founded, with the Condor Syndicate as its biggest shareholder. With the creation of Luft Hansa, the Condor Syndicate ceased to exist and its concession was transferred to a new Brazilian subsidiary of Luft Hansa, the Syndicato Condor Ltda.

This is only one example of the political, economic and technical network which the major aviation concerns were developing around the world during the 1920s, a package of activity which allowed European and later American airlines and aircraft manufacturers to find profitable markets in what are now called the developing countries. The Germans were particularly enterprising, their ultimate goal being regular direct passenger services between Europe and South America across the South Atlantic. Their success in achieving this is described in the next chapter. Meanwhile, it may perhaps be emphasised that the main impetus behind the development of the long-distance intercontinental routes during the late 1920s was not so much a commercial urge to transport passengers as to speed up the mail. Unless one understands the economic potential of airmail at this time, conveying eight or ten passengers from Cape Town to London or from Jakarta to Amsterdam, with all the capital outlay and running costs involved, makes no sense. The mail subsidised the passengers and made it worthwhile to bother with them.

At a press conference in 1926, a Luft Hansa representative put the point neatly when he said, in reference to the new company's great efforts to link Europe and America by air: 'The quantity of mail which is transported across the Atlantic is so great that it would be a simple matter to pick out the urgent mail and fill a few planes with it every day. Here lies a chance to become self-supporting.' The matter, unfortunately, was not quite as simple as that, mainly because the Atlantic, both for passengers and for mail, was a special case. Everywhere, operators were grateful for plenty of nice, profitable airmail, which always helped the budget, but with the small planes available in the 1920s, airmail alone was not usually sufficient to balance what the aircraft cost to run and what passengers could be persuaded to pay. A direct government contribution, a military contract or some other form of subsidy was very likely to be required if the airline was to survive and prosper, and the proper financing of civil aviation is an important thread running through the history of airline operation in the 1930s.

The story of Western Airlines in the United States illustrates the 'mail or passengers' problem in the 1920s particularly well, because the airline became involved in a sponsored experiment to discover if and how passengers-only flying could be made to pay. Western was incorporated as Western Air Express on 18 July 1925, and flew its first mail between Los Angeles and Salt Lake City on 17 April 1926. The service, using open-cockpit Douglas M-2 aircraft, was profitable from the beginning. Passengers were carried, at ninety dollars for the one-way trip, but under very primitive conditions, as one of the first Western pilots, Alva R. DeGarno, recalled:

I was a passenger myself a time or two in our DM-2 and I didn't like the noise of that engine in my ear any more than when I was in the back cockpit. Six hours of that and you couldn't hear for two days. We put two little folding seats in the mail compartment. It was like riding on a board. The mail went anywhere you could stack it. Some passengers carried mail on their laps and some had sacks draped round their necks. We would often pass notes back and forth commenting about the scenery all along the way.[20]

Another of Western's first group of pilots, Fred Kelly, recalls the method of navigation. 'We followed the railroad track. When the weather was bad, we were very careful to follow the right-hand side of the track bed to avoid collision with the mail plane coming the other way.'[21]

And one or two further details come from Maude Campbell, almost certainly the first woman to travel on an American airline as a fare-paying passenger. In 1926 she bought a return ticket from Salt Lake City to Los Angeles. 'When I arrived at the airport,' she remembered, 'a hangar in the middle of the field, I was given a flying-suit which I pulled on over a pair of plus fours I was wearing for warmth. I was given a parachute to wear and told to jump if there was trouble – then count to ten and pull the rip cord.'[22]

A much-treasured example of Western's Douglas M-2s, resplendent in its red livery, now hangs from the ceiling of the National Air and Space Museum, in Washington. It is a most valuable memento of the pioneer days of American civil aviation.

At that time the US Post Office still ran its own transcontinental mail flights on the trunk route between San Francisco and New York. Western provided the link with Los Angeles, Salt Lake City being the interchange point. The Post Office had inaugurated the first stages of the US airmail service in 1919. In 1925 the Kelly Act turned the airmail business over to private operators, except for the San Francisco–New York route, which remained in Government hands until 1927.

Great efforts were made to keep the airmail service going in all weathers and to speed up the point-to-point times by making it possible for the mail-planes to fly at night. By 1927 there were lighted airways from New York to Los Angeles, from New York to Boston, from Chicago to Dallas, and from Boston to Atlanta, Georgia. The method was to set up 500,000-candlepower revolving beacons, visible for up to a hundred miles, on high ground and to supplement these with smaller acetylene beacons placed every three miles along the route.

In 1928 the Guggenheim Foundation for the Promotion of Aeronautics lent Western $180,000 to launch what was called a 'model airway' between Los

[20] *Oh How We Flew*, published by Western Airlines on their fortieth anniversary, 1966, p. 3.
[21] Ibid, p. 3.
[22] Ibid, p. 8.

The short way by
Western Air Express
in the mid-Twenties.

Angeles and San Francisco. The purpose of the experiment was to discover if
an airline could make money by carrying only passengers. Harris Hanshue,
Western's President, spent the whole of the $180,000 on three new Fokker
F.10 tri-motors, a ten-passenger aircraft which, in 1928, was the last word in
air travel. The cabin was finished in mahogany and in panels of a light pile
fabric. There was 'a completely appointed lavatory' in the rear of the cabin,
reading lights, and 'full cabin length windows' which could be opened in
flight, in case the ventilation seemed inadequate.

The model airway served what were probably the first really palatable in-
flight meals. These were thick and specially succulent sandwiches, prepared
by a Los Angeles restaurant called 'The Pig 'n Whistle'. Each passenger was
given a brochure called *The Log of My Flight between Los Angeles and San
Francisco via Western Air Express*. It was bound in birchwood parchment

53

covered in transparent vellum and included space for writing down data about the flight, a detailed route-map and aerial views of Los Angeles and San Francisco. Stewards – the first in America – were employed to serve the meals, hand out newspapers, answer questions and comfort the passengers if required. Passengers had free rides in a Cadillac to and from the airports. The fare for the three-hour flight was $50.

Safety was a much-advertised feature of the model airway, for the F.10s gave the safety margin that could come only from a multi-engined plane. To help the project, the Guggenheim Foundation employed a prominent meteorologist to establish a chain of thirty-seven weather stations between Los Angeles and San Francisco. The pilot was offered a choice of three routes and selected the one which seemed to provide the best weather conditions.

Western ran the model airway for a year. It was not the financial success the Guggenheim backers hoped, serving mainly to prove that the airlines could not make money without mail contracts. Even with the Cadillac, the $50 fare, the sandwiches and *The Log of My Flight*, Western could not fill the seats. On the other hand, as a piece of customer research, the experiment had been very valuable. Passengers, not surprisingly, were in no doubt that the combination of safety, comfort and speed appealed to them.

Looking back, it is clear that the most important events in American aviation during the 1920s were Charles Lindbergh's solo flight across the Atlantic in 1927, Western's model airway, and the coast-to-coast air and rail link, inaugurated in 1929. The first did more than anything else to get the average American interested in the possibilities of flying, the second introduced new standards of comfort and safety, and the third shrank distances on the American continent in a dramatic and unmistakable way.

The Atlantic–Pacific service was organised by Transcontinental Air Transport (TAT), one of the ancestors of Trans World Airlines (TWA). The route had been surveyed by Lindbergh, who flew the last two sectors at the Los Angeles end. The 110-mph Ford Tri-motor was safe and reliable, but noisy. Passengers stuffed cotton wool in their ears to get a little peace from the roar of the engines, but they could do nothing about the vibration, which shook their glasses off their noses and caused the wicker chairs to slide about. The cabin was distinctly cold, but the food, which sometimes included hot soup, served by the steward (he was called a courier at this time), helped to make the journey tolerable. If the landing fields were wet, as they often were, mud was sucked in through the air vent and distributed itself over the passengers. For all this, they paid $351.94, for a one-way trip.

The coast-to-coast journey took almost forty-eight hours. Night flying was still not considered sufficiently safe or reliable for commercial passenger services, so for some time people travelled by night in rail-Pullman berths. Going East–West, the stages were:

1 New York–Columbus, Ohio, by rail, on 'The Airway Limited'.

2 Columbus–Waynoka, Oklahoma, by air.
3 Waynoka–Clovis, New Mexico, by rail, on the Santa Fé's 'Missionary'.
4 Clovis–Los Angeles by air.

In November 1930 the transcontinental travel time was cut to thirty-six hours, with no rail travel. There were ten stops, with an overnight rest at Kansas City. By 1932, night flying had been mastered, the stopover eliminated, and the journey cut to twenty-four hours.

Joseph S. Edgerton went to Los Angeles this way soon after the service began, and wrote an article describing his experiences.[23] Before embarking:

Courier Canfield hands us our tickets and seat assignments on the plane and requests that we go on board. I draw Seat No. 8. 'Strap your belts, please, and close the windows,' he requests, indicating light safety belts attached to each seat.

Once they were airborne:

The courier comes down the aisle, smiling cheerfully, and tells us we can remove the belts and open the windows. The belts, he explains, are used more to keep the passengers in their seats during landings and take-offs than for safety purposes. The windows are to be closed while on the ground to keep out cinders, mud or water.

On his way back down the aisle, the courier hands each of us a letter of welcome from the TAT officials, a small folder containing facts about the plane and the line, a small oiled paper containing cotton for the ears, and a package of chewing gum.

After leaving St Louis:

Canfield brings out light aluminium trays which are supported by brackets on the fuselage wall and a leg in the aisle, so as to rest firmly in front of each passenger. He produces the box lunches, which are found to include chicken salad, cheese and egg salad sandwiches, a pickle, salt and sugar, coffee, cream, cake, and an apple and banana.

It was a memorable trip.

No account of what happened in the 1920s is complete, or even adequate, without at least a brief reference to the body which, almost single-handed, did so much to persuade individual airlines to co-operate for their common good in a period which was characterised by more than a little buccaneering and devil-take-the-hindmost philosophy.

IATA – the initials then stood for International Air Traffic Association, and later International Air Transport Association – was established at a meeting at The Hague on 25 August 1919. Six companies were represented, of which two had started operations, three had only just been organised, and one was about to be formed. The delegates had little experience to guide them – 3500 passengers, 47,000 kilos of cargo and 178 kilos of mail during the first year – but, even at that early date, they could see that air traffic was an international question and they decided to form IATA as a free union of

[23] 'Seeing America from the TAT', *Aeronautical Review*, August 1929.

One of Yukon Southern Air Transport's early flights. This line eventually became part of Canadian Pacific Airlines.

interested companies, 'with a view to co-operate to mutual advantage in preparing and organising international aerial traffic'.

The problems discussed by IATA during its early days included the relations between airlines and third parties – the public, governments, insurance companies, other forms of transport – timetables, agents, navigation – signs were painted on roofs along major routes and markers were put on the beaches on both sides of the English Channel – and weather reports. IATA's first Technical Committee was set up in 1930 and concerned itself immediately with problems of standardisation – direction of propeller rotation, aerodrome lighting, procedures for aircraft in distress and the provision of life-jackets for passengers when the aircraft was flying over water.

Getting agreement on such matters was often a slow business. It took two years of long and sometimes passionate discussion before the airlines accepted the proposal that all throttles should move forwards to increase power and backwards to reduce it. Later, but equally protracted, was the argument as to how large an aircraft should be before it was no longer considered necessary to weigh the passengers.

The logical ending of this chapter, which describes the years in which the airlines really began to understand the problems and opportunities facing them, is a league table. Here, rated in terms of the number of passengers carried, are the world's leading air transport nations in 1929.

Country	Number of passengers
United States	162,000
Germany	120,000
Canada	95,000
United Kingdom	29,000
France	25,000
Italy	24,000
Netherlands	15,000
Poland	10,000

The ranking order in 1928 had been the same, except that the United States had then been in third place. In one year, from 1928 to 1929, the number of passengers carried by American airlines nearly trebled, a rate of growth which has never occurred in any country since.

The position of Canada in the 1929 list is particularly interesting. At that time, and still today, Canada had a railway system which provided an adequate if slow coast-to-coast service, both for passengers and freight, and good links with the United States. However, the East–West railways ran through the southern part of the country and, although there were one or two lines going a little way north, most of Canada had no railways at all, an entirely different situation from that of the United States, which was well supplied with railway services at this time.

The priority task for passenger-carrying aeroplanes in Canada was consequently to transport people to and from the areas north of the trunk railways and to act as local carriers within large areas where population was sparse. The railway companies themselves were involved from the beginning in setting up and operating these services, which needed only a small capital investment and which supplemented rather than competed with what they were already providing. Canada's 95,000 air passengers in 1929 were mostly conveyed in aeroplanes carrying half a dozen people or less, frequently in daunting weather conditions. Few countries in the world have appreciated this amenity more.

THREE

The Airlines Go Worldwide

The 1930s were the decade in which long-distance passenger flying really came into its own. It is natural to think first of Pan American, the airline which more than any other has always concentrated on long-haul flights. The first Pan Am passenger flight was on 18 January 1928. By the end of 1930 there was a continuous Pan Am route encircling the Caribbean, with connections to Texas via Mexico, and one could fly in the company's planes almost round the coast of South America, beginning at Panama and proceeding by way of Lima, Santiago, Buenos Aires, Montevideo, Rio de Janeiro, Natal, Paramaribo and so back home to the Pan American base at Miami. By 1935 San Francisco–Hawaii–Manila was operating and two years later Auckland and Hong Kong had been added to the list. Seattle–Fairbanks was there by 1933 and, as a last gesture before the outbreak of the Second World War, both the North and South Atlantic routes were operating in 1939.

Meanwhile, the Dutch and the British were opening up the world from the opposite direction, taking passengers from London and Amsterdam to the Middle East, Far East, India, the East Indies, Australia and South Africa, the routes to their imperial territories. The French had pushed down into Mauritania, Senegal and Central Africa, were beginning to compete with the British and the Dutch on the Far Eastern routes, and had established services in the Caribbean and over a large part of South America. And, providing a different class of comfort altogether, the German airships were taking passengers in great style to the Argentine, Brazil and New York.

It was not a poor man's hobby, and one often wonders why the rich chose to go by air when boats were so much more comfortable. If one had the money to travel first class, a sea journey from Europe to America, Australia or South Africa in the 1930s was by no means an unpleasant experience, except on those comparatively rare occasions when the Atlantic or the Bay of Biscay were at their worst and when even first-class passengers could hardly be blamed for thinking longingly of the delights of dry land. At most other times, however, the voyage was likely to be seen as a welcome holiday, with a comfortable cabin, abundant food and drink, attentive servants, a chance to walk about the deck or rest, as one felt inclined, and, with luck, agreeable company. To succeed, the airlines had to offer if not identical, then at least equivalent, attractions.

A point often forgotten nowadays, when even the well-to-do are accustomed to looking after themselves, is that during the period between the wars when the airlines were growing up there were still plenty of cheap servants to be had. In general, the kind of people who went first class on the railways or the liners in the 1930s would almost certainly have had servants, some of them quite a lot of servants. Their expectations so far as being looked after were concerned were consequently high, a fact of life which the airlines looking for business in Western countries had to keep constantly in mind.

On the other hand, some at least of the servant-hiring class in all countries could be bribed by the promise of thrills and adventure and by the knowledge that they were getting something that was beyond the purse of lesser mortals. Recruiting the rich to the ranks of air travellers was a highly skilled business. There were, of course, a few people whose time was supposed to be almost beyond price – statesmen, corporation presidents, prominent journalists – and they could be sold speed and speed alone. But, for flights lasting more than two hours or so, the recipe had to be comfort, service, punctuality, freedom from death or maiming.

In all these matters there were pace-setters – airlines and aircraft which set a standard not previously achieved or even thought of as a serious possibility.

The 'Graf Zeppelin', showing the passenger cabin and engine nacelles.

The 'Graf Zeppelin' lands, with passengers able to greet their friends through the open windows.

Just occasionally, the pace-setters overdid things, providing more than the market required, and becoming commercially rather ridiculous as a result. Western Air Express and its Fokker F.10s were a case in point. As a public relations trick these sumptuously appointed aircraft were brilliant, but commercially they were more than slightly absurd. The comparatively short distance, Los Angeles to San Francisco, simply did not justify comfort on such a prodigious scale. To decide on alligator-skin upholstery and walnut panelling was to put too much bait on the hook. The fish would have come for less.

On the other hand, a number of the features of this pioneering aircraft were valuable innovations, which were to form part of the normal equipment of airliners in later years – sound-insulation in the passenger cabin, call-buttons, folding tables, individual reading lights, baggage racks, coat-cupboards and refrigerators.

It is, in any case, a nice point as to whether WAE's Fokkers or the German airships contributed more to the overall raising of the standard of passenger services. In the mid-1920s a new German company, the Luftschiffbau Zeppelin, built the LZ 127, the 'Graf Zeppelin', which made its first flight in 1928. It flew to the United States in October of that year and subsequently cruised extensively over Europe and the Middle East, before making a round-the-

world flight at the end of 1929, with a crew of forty-one and twenty pass-
engers. Between 1932 and 1937 there were regular flights over the South
Atlantic, the route being Friedrichshafen (later Frankfurt), Seville, Bathurst
(Gambia), Rio de Janeiro.

On the 'Graf Zeppelin' the upper deck had ten two-berth cabins, each with a
wash-basin and clothes cupboard, down the centre, with a restaurant on the
port side and a lounge and reading and writing room on the starboard side. A
promenade deck ran the full length of each outer side, with large windows
angled outwards to provide a good view downwards. The windows could
always be kept open because, due to the airflow round the hull, there were no
draughts either inside or out. The lower deck contained a smoking room, bar,
lavatories, shower bath, officers' mess, kitchen and crew mess. The decks
were linked by two staircases. The décor and furnishings were fully up to the
standard of the most modern liners in service. The lounge of the 'Graf
Zeppelin' had couches, curtained windows, flowers and a Japanese-style
wallpaper. Tables in the lounge had lace-edged cloths on them and all the
floors were carpeted.

The lavish meals would not have disgraced a major hotel on land. Menu
cards[1] from the 'Graf Zeppelin' indicate what was provided. One of 1929 is
headed on the first page: 'First World's Tour; the Graf Zeppelin', and has a
picture captioned 'Soaring over Los Angeles Biltmore'. Inside is:

On Board Airship
Graf Zeppelin
Los Angeles to Lakehurst

First Luncheon
Honey Dew Melon au Citron
Hungarian Goulash
Cold Asparagus Vinaigrette
Eclairs
Coffee

and the name of the creators of the meal, 'Los Angeles Biltmore, Caterers'.

The other great German airship of the years between the wars, LZ 129
('Hindenburg'), made its maiden flight in 1936. It was designed specifically for
trans-oceanic services and carried fifty passengers (increased to seventy-two
on its eighth flight) at a fare, for the single journey from Frankfurt to New
Jersey or vice versa, of $450 if a cabin was shared, or $750 for a double cabin
taken as a single. Its fastest flight took just under forty-three hours.

The arrangements on the 'Hindenburg' were even more magnificent than
those provided on the 'Graf Zeppelin'. One boarded the airship via the lower
deck, B deck. At the top of the noble staircase leading to A deck there was a
bust of Field-Marshal von Hindenburg and just ahead of this one came to the

---

[1] Preserved at the Musée de l'Air, Paris.

twenty-five cabins, each with two berths, one above the other. There were three bars, open all day and most of the night. Breakfast was served from 8 to 10, luncheon at 12, afternoon tea at 4 and dinner at 7.

Smoking was strictly forbidden, except in the specially designated smoking-room, which measured $12\frac{1}{2}$ by $15\frac{1}{2}$ feet. This was pressurised against the entrance of hydrogen and sealed off by means of a door opening into an airlock. The door was under the control of the steward, who had to make sure that nobody left the room carrying a lighted cigarette, pipe or cigar and he was the only person allowed to use matches. A fixed electric lighter was available on a self-service basis for cigarette smokers and for cigars and pipes the steward was prepared to light just one match.

Tips for the stewards were included in the fare. Telegrams could be sent via the airship's radio station. There was a small library for the use of passengers – books were issued against receipts – and a sick bay, with attendants. Consideration had to be shown to people on the ground below the flight path and passengers were cautioned about throwing objects out of the window. Military security was also a problem on some sections of the flight and, to avoid possible charges of espionage from the air, passengers had to hand their cameras to the stewards for safe keeping when they boarded the airship.

The dining-room on the 'Hindenburg' measured fifteen by fifty feet. It had ten tables made, like the chairs, of aluminium. There were colourful paintings of travel scenes on the walls. The tables were laid with white linen tablecloths and napkins, fresh flowers, silver cutlery and a china service specially designed for the 'Hindenburg'. Examples of the china are displayed at the National Air and Space Museum in Washington in a mock-up of the airship's dining-room. The lounge contained a Blüthner baby grand, with an aluminium case covered with yellow pigskin. The writing-room was equipped with pneumatic tubes, which allowed letters to be sent direct to the mail room above the control car.

As an American passenger recalled many years afterwards, the promenade decks were one of the greatest attractions of a Zeppelin voyage:

Outboard of the public rooms, and separated from them by a low railing, were fifty-foot promenades connected by a cross-passage between the two sides of A deck. This afforded a walking distance of nearly 200 feet for transatlantic passengers used to the daily constitutional around a steamer deck. Outboard of the promenades were six large Plexi-glass windows, slanting outwards at $45°$, often left open as there was no draught in or outwards even at an air speed of eighty knots. Here the passengers stood or sat for hours on low cushioned seats, enthralled by the sight of foaming waves, tossing ships, forests, towns, rivers and cities, going by only a few hundred feet below. Curtains drawn at night between the promenade and public rooms enabled the travellers to enjoy the sight of moonlight on the waves, the brilliance of the stars, without the glare and reflection of the artificial lighting.[2]

[2] Douglas H. Robinson, *LZ 129 'Hindenburg'*, New York, 1964.

Breakfast in the 'Hindenburg', 1936.

'Hindenburg' made ten round trips across the Atlantic during 1936, but in the following year, on 6 May, after the first of the 1937 crossings, the airship burst into flames and was completely destroyed while landing at Lakehurst, New Jersey. Thirty-six people lost their lives, the first passenger fatalities in the history of commercial airship operation. The cause of the disaster was never satisfactorily established, but the most likely explanation is that atmospheric electricity ignited hydrogen escaping from a leak in the airship.

The 'Hindenburg' and the 'Graf Zeppelin' had no competitors. What they achieved was never achieved again, although for some years the British tried to keep in the race. Vickers built airships from 1908 to 1929, the last being the R100. In the R100 the passenger and crew accommodation was arranged within the lower hull in three decks nearer to the bow. The dining saloon seated fifty-six; it was on the centre deck and had a viewing promenade forty feet long on either side. A staircase led up from the dining saloon to a gallery lounge. The cabins, for a total of a hundred passengers, were on the middle and upper decks. They had either two or four berths.[3] 'The walls dividing the cabins were of fabric, so that a man snoring in the next cabin could be a real nuisance at night; so quiet was the ship.'[4]

The R100 made an experimental flight to Canada in 1930, which carried

[3] C. F. Andrews, *Vickers Aircraft since 1908*, 1969, pp. 31–2.
[4] Nevil Shute, *Slide Rule*, 1968, p. 103. As N. S. Norway, the author was one of the design team working on the R100.

Diamonds in The Sky

only technical staff. She never flew again, being broken up for scrap after the disaster to her sister ship, the R101, which had been built by the Air Ministry. The R101 crashed and caught fire near Beauvais at the beginning of a flight to India. Nearly all the people on board, technicians and officials, were killed, and fare-paying passengers never had the opportunity to enjoy a voyage on a British airship.

It should be emphasised that with airships, as with aeroplanes, the main aim was always to speed up the mail, rather than to carry passengers. By using the plane-airship-plane combination, the Germans were able, in 1932, to cut the mail time between Germany and Brazil to four days and from Germany to Chile to eight days. At the same time, experiments were being carried out, by both the Germans and the French, to catapult mail planes from ships, at the limit of an aircraft's range from land.

In their successful attempts to develop air services across the North and South Atlantic, the Germans were tackling the routes which were technically the most difficult but which, for them, offered the greatest commercial potential, since they had great economic interests throughout the American continent. This was where Germans wanted to go, and this was their most profitable mail link. The other major aviation powers during the 1930s – the United States, Britain, France and the Netherlands – had a somewhat different order of priorities. The British, French and Dutch still controlled empires and needed good communications between the colonies and the mother country; the Americans were anxious to consolidate and extend their commercial and political influence in Central and South America and in the Pacific. The air routes established reflect these interests.

The KLM scheduled service from Amsterdam to Jakarta (then Batavia) operated from 1929 until 1931 on a mail-only basis. The airline began regular services on 1 October 1931 with Fokker F.XII aircraft, which could carry four passengers as well as the all-important mail, and which had reclining seats for long-haul flights. These were followed a year later by considerably faster Fokker F.XVIIIs, which were equipped for twelve passengers on the European services, but, once again, only four on the Jakarta run. Even with the bigger DC-2, introduced in 1934, there was a limit of five passengers to the Far East. The DC-3, however, which entered service with KLM in 1936, took eleven passengers and by this time the speed had risen to 175 mph.

In November 1935, Mr W. H. Pilkington, of the English glass firm, decided to return from Australia by air. His very detailed diary of the journey from Brisbane to Amsterdam gives an excellent picture of what really long-distance air travel was like at that time. The Brisbane–Singapore section of the route was by Qantas, and Singapore–Amsterdam by KLM. The whole journey took him ten days, at an average speed, when he was in the air, of 138.3 mph, as he meticulously noted. There were night stops at Cloncurry, Darwin, Surabaya, Singapore, Bangkok, Jodhpur, Baghdad, Athens and Marseilles, since, apart from the problems of night flying, those were the

Opposite: American aircraft illustrated on British cigarette cards during the Thirties.

64

PLAYER'S CIGARETTES

DELTA AIRLINES: LOCKHEED "ELECTRA"

PLAYER'S CIGARETTES

EASTERN AIRLINES: DOUGLAS D.C.2

PLAYER'S CIGARETTES

EASTERN AIRLINES: LOCKHEED "ELECTRA"

PLAYER'S CIGARETTES

PAN AMERICAN AIRWAYS: GLENN MARTIN 130 FLYING-BOAT "CHINA CLIPPER"

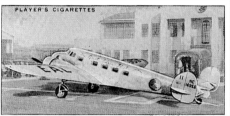

PLAYER'S CIGARETTES

AMERICAN AIRLINES: DOUGLAS D.S.T.

PLAYER'S CIGARETTES

NORTHWEST AIRLINES: LOCKHEED "ELECTRA"

PLAYER'S CIGARETTES

AEROPUT: SPARTAN CRUISER

PLAYER'S CIGARETTES

PAN AMERICAN AIRWAYS: MAIN AISLE. "CLIPPER" CLASS FLYING-BOAT

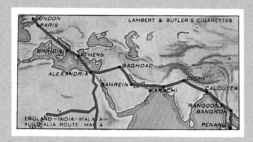

"HANNO" AT MUHARRAK, PERSIAN GULF

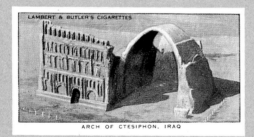

"HANNO" AT GWADAR, BALUCHISTAN

EL KADIMAIN MOSQUE, BAGHDAD

ARCH OF CTESIPHON, IRAQ

JERUSALEM—THE TEMPLE AREA

"HANNO" OVER THE DEAD SEA

REFUELLING "SCIPIO" IN ALEXANDRIA HARBOUR

sensible and humane days when it was still considered that human beings should spend the night in bed.

At Brisbane, he 'lay on the grass in the sun, waiting for the plane to be loaded'. He had taken trouble to cut his baggage down to only 55lbs and when the plane left he had only one fellow passenger, 'a fat motor salesman', who was going as far as Darwin. The thermometer he had bought at Brisbane allowed him to keep a check on the cabin temperature which during the journey went as high as 90°F and as low as 50°F.

After landing at Charleville, there was a long wait for the plane from Cootamundra with the Sydney and Melbourne mail, with lunch arranged at a hotel in the town, 'but too hot to eat much'. When the Cootamundra plane eventually arrived, two hours late, Pilkington heard the story of a new fellow passenger, an Australian called Dare, who was on his way to Amsterdam:

He told me that he had to go first to the railway authorities in Sydney to get special permission to leave the Melbourne express train at Cootamundra, though the train always stops there to drop the mail. This permit took two or three days to obtain. Having got it, he caught the 7.30 train last night, getting to Cootamundra well after midnight; he then got out and made his way to the local hotel and found an armchair to sit on until about four, when he was taken to the aerodrome. After waiting about there

The tri-motor Junkers Ju 52, one of the world's most successful passenger aircraft, was in service with Lufthansa between 1933 and 1945, in Europe, Asia and South America. It had seventeen seats and a range of nearly 600 miles.

Opposite: With Imperial Airways to the Middle East: another cigarette card series of the Thirties.

65

for some time, someone came in and made some coffee on a primus stove, the someone turning out to be the proprietor of the airline. After more delay they got into the plane – or tried to. It is a two-engined Dragon, similar to those used from Liverpool to the Isle of Man; but the cabin was so full of mail that the passengers had to fight their way through and finally got seats on and under the mail.

With its great load of mail, the plane was unable to fly at more than 1000 feet and the passengers had a very bumpy ride indeed. Conditions at the stopping places on the way to Surabaya were rough, with flies, great heat and dirt to make the passengers long to be airborne again. A sausage roll, at Daly Waters, eaten with the temperature in the 90s, made Pilkington ill. He was revived, however, by a bumper lunch put on board at Rambang – hot omelettes, macaroni, peas and salmon, tinned fruit, mineral water and tinned milk.

At Surabaya, there were better things to report. 'Stopped at a magnificent hotel, most comfortable, every room having not only its private bathroom, but a sort of balcony sitting-room as well.' The passengers borrowed a car to go sightseeing in the town. It was their last chance to take photographs, because the cameras were to be sealed at Singapore and kept sealed until the plane arrived at Amsterdam. A number of countries on the route disliked the possibility of their military and naval installations being photographed from the air. The airlines thought they were absurdly touchy on the point, but had no alternative but to take their passengers' eagle-eyed Kodaks away from them.

At Batavia, Dare had to be left behind, to follow later in another plane. The reason was a curious one. 'He has just been told that his suitcases are old ones and won't fit in the Douglas. He is being forced to unpack entirely and repack

The Fokker F.XVIII 'Pelikaan', which flew on the KLM Amsterdam–Jakarta service from 1932 to 1935.

in new ones here. Very much annoyed.' At Medan, after picking up an English stockbroker called Blake who lived in Malaya, they went on to Bangkok, dodging storms all the way. Once on the ground, the passengers' suitcases were examined 'by a cheerful and smiling Siamese soldier, who asked one of us whether he had any pistols or opium and picking up a light novel of mine suggested delightfully that it might be Communist literature.'

When the weather was good there were wonderful things to be seen from the air – jungles, where the brilliantly coloured tropical birds could be clearly made out, craters of extinct volcanoes and, over Rangoon, the Shwe Dagon pagoda, with a thousand small pagodas surrounding the great golden one in the middle. 'In the early morning sunshine and seen from above, it is one of the most beautiful sights imaginable.'

After Calcutta there was a full load of six passengers, five men and one woman. Dare had rejoined the plane by this time, and the others included a ship's doctor getting off at Allahabad, 'a Parsee and an Anglo-Indian lady'. From Singapore onwards they had seen the occasional Imperial Airways machine, either on the ground or flying below them. Pilkington never failed to note his pleasure at always passing the British plane, even when it had left the airport before them. His competitive streak may or may not have been typical of all long-distance passengers at this time, but it is clear that KLM had the power to inspire loyalty among the people it carried, even if, as in this particular case, they had to spend hours sitting with their feet on a mailbag. Pilkington certainly felt that to choose KLM was to choose the best. At Jask, for instance, he noticed an Air France plane. 'It had been delayed further out east and had reached Jodhpur some time early this morning when we were asleep. It had left almost immediately, and we caught it up and passed it an hour or so back. It is a three-engined Fokker, of the type formerly used by the Dutch – in fact, I believe that when they changed over to these Douglas machines they sold their old Fokkers to the French. It looks very uncomfortable by comparison and had only one weary-looking passenger.' KLM no doubt did little to discourage this kind of thinking.

Pilkington, of course, was in a superior position, a flying addict who had already flown out to Australia and knew the ropes. There is more than a touch of smugness in a diary comment he wrote as he was approaching Baghdad. 'There are five passengers in this plane, and every one of them is reading one of my books – no one else has come with sufficient literature to get them even as far as Baghdad.'

Once arrived in Baghdad, he spent an interesting evening touring the city with the Secretary of the YMCA. It was, he found, 'an interesting place, but, even in winter, smelly'. Palestine looked good from the air and at Gaza he was pleased to see ploughing done by camels.

Hannibal, the IA machine, arrived from Alexandria just after us. We look small beside it, but with so much more beautiful lines. Dare went up to the Captain to tell him that 'We were all travelling by Dutch Lines because IA was no use,' and seemed surprised when the captain did not like it. I suppose he can get away with that sort of thing in Australia. In any case the statement is an exaggeration, and they will be up-to-date soon.

And so back to Amsterdam, flying at 21,000 feet to avoid the bad weather, with no oxygen, and with the windows completely iced over.

I didn't even feel the usual slight pain in my little finger – the only physical indication I used to have on the way out whenever we were over about 15,000 feet. I suppose the difficulty the lungs have in forcing the blood to circulate affects the extremities first. Other people generally felt the height in some other individual way, but with me it was always and only the top joint of the little finger of my left hand.

In England, and on his way north by train from Euston, Pilkington indulged in reflection:

The first thing that strikes me is the noise of this train compared with the planes. Not only is it more noisy, but the noise is so variable that it is much more noticeable. The next thing is the unsteadiness – my cup of tea has spilt itself and I can't read my own writing – what I wrote while up in the air was occasionally legible even to others.

Then I can't see anything from here: the windows are steamed over, but when I wipe one I find the smoke from the engine obliterating the view, or else we are in a tunnel or a cutting. It certainly isn't as comfortable – I can put my feet up on a newspaper on the opposite seat, but I still have an almost upright back to the seat: the carriage is badly ventilated and no one has ever claimed for rail travel that it is clean.

Mr Pilkington's diaries – he kept one for the outward flight as well – are preserved in the archives of Pilkingtons at St Helens, and are rare and exceptionally valuable documents. They tell us exactly what it was like to make a long air journey during the years when one never knew quite what to expect next. They also help us to understand why people travelled in this way, when it would have usually been a good deal more comfortable to go by boat. There was not a great deal of difference in the cost – the air fare was about twenty-five per cent more than the first class on the boat – but the air trip was exciting, with plenty of interesting things to see and out-of-the-ordinary experiences guaranteed. The liner voyage, on the other hand, was, for most of the time, simply boring. Not everybody wanted excitement, of course, and there were those with a yearning for sociability and exhibitionism for whom a long sea voyage provided the perfect environment.

For some passengers on both the European and Empire routes there was excitement of a special and unwelcome kind. Crashes, especially those involving loss of life, were too frequent for the airline directors' peace of mind during the late 1920s and 1930s. They were of no help to those whose living depended on convincing the moneyed section of the public that flying was as safe as walking to church or to the grocer. Engines failed, planes came down in the Channel, drowning their passengers, and caught fire after crash-landings. Sea-planes hit obstacles in the water and turned over.

Why people chose to fly from Europe to Australia or South Africa is one

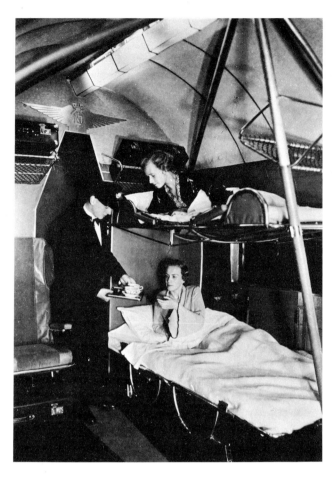

A KLM aircraft on the Far East route with bunks fitted for night travel. The two ladies are being served tea in bed, a pleasure not experienced by air travellers for very many years.

question; why the airlines went to so much trouble to persuade them to fly is equally interesting. Just before the outbreak of the 1939–45 war, a return air ticket from London or Amsterdam to Hong Kong or Brisbane cost £288. The planes carried a maximum of eleven passengers, which gives a possible revenue for the airline of £3168. With hotels and meals to be paid for out of this amount, and with all the expenses of running the plane, there was absolutely no profit to be made just by moving people from one continent to another. The basic answer can be expressed in one of two ways: either the passengers subsidised the mail or the mail subsidised the passengers. The two together made the service viable. There was, however, quite a different reason for wanting to carry people as well as letters and parcels. Passengers had an enormous public relations value. Carrying them thousands of miles in safety and to time was newsworthy and, although letters could not talk, Mr Pilkington could. The Pilkingtons were what are nowadays called opinion-formers and, if Mr Pilkington had enjoyed his trip, he would certainly tell his business friends about it and recommend them to follow suit. This, in turn, would be good for flying in general, because anyone who went by air to the Far East would certainly want to do the same within Europe. For KLM,

Diamonds in The Sky

Imperial Airways, Luft Hansa, Air France or any other airline operating both long-haul and short-haul flights, success over 4000 miles was a great help in getting business over 400. To be in the big league, it was essential for an airline to prove that it could organise services over long and difficult routes.

So they tried very hard to discover more Mr Pilkingtons and to make them happy. KLM presented its Amsterdam–Batavia passengers with a copy of a 100-page hard-cover book, *Wings Across Continenis*.[5] It was well illustrated and described the attractions of the route in considerable detail. There were maps of the towns chosen for overnight stops and the text was obviously intended to interest intelligent, educated people. An example illustrates this:

After England had become the mandatory power over Iraq, British, French, American and Iraqi interests founded the Iraq Petroleum Company. The spirit had to be brought from the oilfields near Mosul to a Mediterranean port of shipment, and some difficulty was experienced at the commencement in deciding which port was to be used. Great Britain wanted a pipe line from Mosul to Haifa in Palestine, also a British mandated territory. French interests demanded a pipe line to Tripoli, on account of their Syrian mandate. Agreement was reached by laying a double pipe line from Mosul to Haditha on the Euphrates, whence the English line goes via Rutbah to Haifa, the only port in Syria and Palestine capable of accommodating ships of big tonnage at its quays. From Haditha the French pipe line makes for the port of Tripoli in Syria.

The air route from Gaza to Baghdad owes much to these activities, for it runs for hundreds of miles parallel with the pipe lines and the motor road – a beautiful landmark – through the desert.

The passenger then looked out of the aeroplane window, saw the pipe line and the road and understood what it was all about. He was educating himself as he flew, with never a dull mile. Afterwards, he wrote to KLM in terms such as this:

We have made a perfect journey to Rangoon in PH-AIQ with absolute punctuality and at high speed. Nothing could have exceeded the consideration of Captain Smirnoff and his crew and the perfection of their arrangements to make our flight interesting and comfortable. I would especially commend the seating arrangements of the aeroplane, which have prevented any feeling of fatigue during the seven days we have spent on board.

That testimonial was from 'Lord Moyne and Lady Broughton, famous big game hunters'. This was from an even more distinguished address, 'The office of the Comptroller, HE the Commander-in-Chief's Household, New Delhi'.

I am writing at Lady Chetwode's request to inform you that she arrived safely at Jodhpur yesterday from Marseilles. Lady Chetwode wishes me to express her gratitude for all the arrangements made by your company, both for her homeward and outward flights. Everywhere she met the greatest courtesy and attention, and her whole journey was made most comfortable.

[5] Amsterdam, Andries Blitz, 1935.

Interior of an Imperial
Airways Argosy class
aircraft, early 1930s.

Whatever Mr Dare, Mr Pilkington's Australian fellow passenger, may have thought about the superiority of KLM to Imperial Airways in 1935, the difference had disappeared two years later. The British airline showed outstanding enterprise during the mid-1930s, on both its European and intercontinental routes. The most important services, to which Imperial Airways gave priority attention, were the so-called Empire routes, London–Karachi–Sydney and London–Johannesburg–Cape Town and, as in the 1920s, London–Paris. A great deal of research was carried out in order to discover exactly which amenities were most appreciated by passengers, especially on the Empire routes.

... space, good ventilation and heating, agreeable food, an attentive steward and, above all, his chair. By sea an outside room with bath is demanded, but by air the passenger's time is spent chiefly seated in a chair and, depending upon his mood, that chair must enable him to sit upright when taking his meals, or to loll back in luxurious comfort to read, and in it he must be able to recline or doze or sleep. All this must his chair fulfil, and that independently of his fellow passenger, who may require his chair to do quite the opposite and at the same time. Imperial Airways has recently com-

71

pleted a chair of its own invention which is fitted as standard to the new flying-boats and landplanes. Its comfort and adjustability show a marked improvement on anything of its kind yet in use; moreover, its weight is only 18lbs – a vital factor from the aircraft operator's point of view.[6]

Imperial Airways were extremely proud of this chair. They had researched it themselves, patented it and named it the Imperial Airways Adjustable Chair. It was manufactured under licence by Accles and Pollock and later, in 1938, by Junkers in Germany. Many thousands of travellers to Africa and the East had reason to be grateful to it.

KLM had been equally conscious of the importance of the chair in which passengers were required to spend so many hours. In their DC-2s they installed a special seat which could be transformed into a couch. In the upright position there was so much leg room that two suitcases could be placed on end, one behind the other, without interfering in any way with the comfort of the person occupying the chair in front.

Journeys on the Empire routes were leisurely. During the early 1930s, there continued to be difficulties with the Italian government, which refused to allow foreign airlines to fly over its territory, or to land or refuel at inland aerodromes. It was consequently necessary to fly passengers from London to Paris and then take them by train-sleeper to Brindisi, where the flight proper began. This somewhat tedious arrangement added another day to the total journey time, but by 1936 the problem had been solved and passengers were able to go all the way by air.

In 1933 the London–Karachi flight left on a Saturday and arrived on a Friday, with overnight stops at Athens, Gaza, Basra and Sharjah. London–Cape Town left on a Wednesday and arrived ten days later on a Sunday, the stops after Brindisi being Athens, Cairo, Wadi Halfa, Khartoum, Juba, Nairobi, Mbeya, Salisbury and Johannesburg.

The fares, to a modern eye, seem reasonable enough. In 1933, to travel by air from London to Karachi, a distance of just over 5000 miles, cost only £95, that is 4½d a mile in the currency of the time, or under 2p a mile in today's money.

With occasional lapses, the Far Eastern and African routes were remarkably safe and reliable during their early years, but there were occasions when it was an advantage to have strong nerves and an optimistic temperament. During a flight down the African continent in the early 1930s in a Handley Page Hannibal biplane, a plane which Imperial Airways proudly claimed 'had never killed a single passenger', a very seasoned traveller[7] was sitting alone in his seat in the after compartment, when the seat broke adrift during a violent bout of turbulence. A young officer assured him that the terrible vibrations were 'just turbulence', but on landing it was discovered that part of the wing had broken right off. Another passenger, an American,

---

[6] *Some Aspects of the Organisation of Empire Air Services.* The second Brancker Memorial Lecture to the Institute of Transport, 23 November 1936.

[7] Mr Walter Wren: conversation with Kenneth Hudson, 16 June 1970.

wanted to take a photograph of the damaged wing, but the pilot dissuaded him, on the grounds that it was 'not good advertising for flying'.

Although there was no night-flying on the route at that time, there were occasions when a plane was delayed and had to come in late. To guide it down, oil lamps would be placed on the airfield. On one memorable occasion[8] the pilot missed the beacon lights at Hyderabad, on the way to Karachi, and when he eventually reached Karachi he admitted he had been quite lucky, because he had only half-an-hour's fuel left. Regular passengers became very conscious of the time/fuel problem and considered it one of the inevitable hazards of flying. There was an alternative method of illuminating the air-field to make landing possible. The pilot lit wingtip flares on the plane, the noise being quite alarming for the passengers if they had no warning of what was about to happen.

Major Munday, who flew to London from Mpika, Northern Rhodesia, in 1932, wrote a little book which summarised what he had learnt from this and other flights and offered prospective passengers some practical advice.[9]

Passengers should be booked several weeks beforehand to avoid disappointment, as intermediate journeys by other passengers have to be fitted in with those of passengers undertaking longer flights. Cheques for the journey, if not sent with the order for booking, should be sent as soon as possible. The Station Superintendent at Mpika as a matter of fact took my cheque on the day prior to my departure, when I was issued with my ticket and weighed for the trip.

Some passengers, Major Munday had observed, were not at all suitably dressed for flying. He was reluctant to advise the ladies, except in the most general terms, but to his fellow males he had this to say:

An open neck shirt is almost necessary for the hotter days. Flannel trousers are the most comfortable. The average temperature is rather the same as in a railway train. During the early mornings it can be cold and at other times of the day very hot. Windows can be opened in some of the aeroplanes, but more than often this raises a complaint from some of the other passengers. On the whole journey clothes should be worn as on a car journey, with a jumper and good rain coat handy for varying temperatures of weather.

On the Empire routes, sweating or shivering passengers were a trouble to no one but themselves, but insects were quite another matter. An airline that operated over routes totalling thirty thousand miles had to face up very seriously to the risk of tropical diseases being carried in its aeroplanes from one country to another by insects. After much experiment, Imperial Airways eventually found the answer.

A portable vapourising machine has been designed which is similar to that used in many London hospitals for disinfecting the wards, and it can be used in flight without any discomfort to passengers or damage to the upholstery and fittings of the aircraft.

[8] Ibid.
[9] Major E. Munday, *A Report of a Flight made to London from Mpika 30 April 1932*, Livingstone: Northern Rhodesia, 1932.

The machine permeates the atmosphere with an insecticide distilled from a small wild flower, Pyrethrum, that is cultivated specially for this purpose and grows on the sunny slopes of Kenya and in the South of England.[10]

The biggest threat to health, however, was from food and drink consumed at the hotels and restaurants en route. Nowadays an airline can, if it chooses, take a load of passengers from Europe to Australia and feed them all the way with nothing but food prepared in its own kitchens at Heathrow, Schiphol, Frankfurt or wherever, establishing dumps of frozen food packs at airports along the route. In the 1930s, however, this was not possible. Neither food technology nor materials and equipment were sufficiently developed to allow it. The airlines had to rely on the local catering facilities in Basra, Khartoum or wherever the stop for lunch or dinner happened to be. Every attempt was made to select the most satisfactory places possible, but it would have been unreasonable to expect Cloncurry or Rambang to provide standards of hygiene equal to the world's best and cases of food poisoning among passengers were not at all uncommon. Mr Pilkington, one recalls, had a very nasty twenty-four hours after eating that sausage roll on his way back from Australia.

A point not to be forgotten in this connection is that crew and passengers stayed and ate together at the same hotels and rest houses. A serious attack of food poisoning or dysentery would lay everybody low, and consequently the pilot and his colleagues on the plane, who had a powerful incentive to keep themselves fit and well, were always on hand to keep as watchful an eye as they could on the food and drink served and to advise less experienced passengers on what to eat and what to avoid. But accidents did happen, even so, and more frequently than the airlines cared to admit.

While on the subject of food, one might usefully remember that, by comparison with people condemned to twenty-four hours on a plane today, pre-1939 passengers inevitably had a quite different attitude to meals. Physiologically, someone flying from London to New York, Bombay or Sydney today has very little need of food and none at all of alcohol. The less he eats and drinks, the better he is likely to feel at the end of his journey. The value of in-flight meals and apéritifs nowadays is psychological, not nutritional. They do something, but not much, to counter the boredom of sitting hour after hour dozing or looking out of the window at the sky and the clouds.

In the 1930s the situation was quite different. Lunch and dinner were proper, civilised occasions. One could stretch one's legs, enjoy the tonic of another environment, talk to new people, sit on a real chair at a real table and relax. And, greatest pleasure of all, after dinner one could in due course take one's clothes off, lie flat on a bed and go to sleep. There are so many references by passengers to the meals they had in exotic places that we are left in little doubt that, for the fortunate people who travelled this way in the golden days of flying, eating was an important part of the pleasure.

[10] *Imperial Airways Monthly Bulletin*, November 1938.

An Imperial Airways
pilot, *c.* 1930. These cards,
bearing the pilot's
signature, were given to
passengers as souvenirs
and talismen.

A KLM passenger from the Far East in 1935 reported:

At every intermediate landing something pleasant was prepared for us, a well-laid
table provided, and if any objection is to be made it is that we were offered in fact too
much to eat. This can only adversely affect the loading capacity of the aircraft, for it
was not only a question of the early snacks, breakfasts, luncheons and afternoon teas,
but on board we were continually offered tea, coffee or beef-tea with sandwiches and
biscuits. It is remarkable how one's appetite increases; presumably it is due to the
rapid change of climate, as a result not only of the horizontal but also of the vertical
changes in the position of the machine.[11]

It is an interesting theory, although there is, alas, no scientific basis for it.
But, however frequent they may have been, the in-flight snacks are unlikely

[11] 'Batavia to Amsterdam', by 'Passenger', *Shell Aviation News*, August 1935.

to have been memorable. A biscuit or a sandwich has to be very remarkable indeed if it is to stand out sharply against all the others one has eaten. On the ground, at the staging points, it was a different matter.

Here, for example, was a little refreshment at Waingapoe, on the Isle of Sumba, as it remained in the memory of a passenger who flew from Australia to England in 1936:

At the aerodrome we were escorted by a courtly old Dutchman to a spotlessly clean pavilion where a *light* breakfast had been prepared. Thick soup with bits of sausage floating about, into which we poured a delicious mixture of fried onions and coconut, eggs and ham, several sorts of pudding and very nice Dutch coffee.[12]

It was memorable and formed part of the rich pattern of the journey. What that pattern was – an agreeable mixture of scenery, native habits, and letting other people do the organising and the worrying – is clear from this extract from a letter written by a young British colonial officer in Bulawayo to his mother, after a pleasant flight back from leave.

We left Nairobi at 6.30 a.m. and arrived at Salisbury at 10.15 p.m., stopping at Moshi for breakfast, Mbeya for lunch and Broken Hill for dinner, with two other intermediate stops. It was a most interesting day. Shortly after leaving Nairobi, we flew low over the great game preserve and various herds of the buck – a gazelle type of animal – could be seen. A little later we ran into cloud and had to climb a little to get out of them. We then got some beautiful cloud effects, which I photographed. In a little time the snow-crested summit of Kilimanjaro (19,712 feet high) suddenly appeared out of the morning mists on our port bow, and to starboard a handsomer cone-shaped mountain, Meru (14,950 feet) rose straight from the plain.

At Moshi we had breakfast and at Dodoma we came down for fuel. All was cool, clean and civilised, and delightfully arranged refreshments on a snow-white tablecloth showed that some English woman (or at least British) was doing her bit to make the tropics better and brighter. Dinner at Broken Hill was a lively meal and the three-quarter moon just gave enough light to see things.[13]

6.30 in the morning until 10.15 in the evening was an unusually long day, but early starts were normal on flights to Africa and the Far East. Passengers travelling by both Imperial Airways and KLM had a card handed to them each day giving details of the overnight stop and of the programme for the next twenty-four hours. The Imperial Airways system worked like this:

When you are shown up to your room at any hotel where you stay the night, you find a card on the table which gives you instructions for the next day's flying. For instance, when I got back to my room at the hotel in Bangkok, I found a card informing me that I should be called at 4.30 a.m., so that my suitcase could be packed ready for taking away at 5 a.m. It gave me the ruling rate of exchange in case I wanted to buy local currency and stated that the car would be ready to take me from the hotel to the aerodrome at 5.30 and that the airliner would leave at 6.30 a.m. It further mentioned

[12] *Imperial Airways Gazette*, October 1936.
[13] *Imperial Airways Gazette*, September 1936.

that breakfast would be at Rangoon, lunch at Akyab and dinner at Calcutta, where we should be staying the night. [14]

One of the KLM cards, printed in Dutch on one side and English on the other, showed these timings for the morning:

Passengers and Crew will stay at the Grande Bretagne

	Time
Passengers will be called at	4.00
Luggage will be collected from rooms at	4.30
Breakfast will be served in the dining room at	4.00
Car leaves hotel at	4.45
Departure from airport at	5.30

This timetable may suggest that, immediately there was a knock on their door, passengers had to leap out of bed and rush straight down to breakfast in their pyjamas. The actual arrangements were more humane. Those who had roused themselves unaided and who were dressed and ready by four o'clock could breakfast at that hour if they wished. But by 4.30 all bags had to be packed and a quarter of an hour later the last piece of toast and marmalade should have been stowed safely away and the last passenger in his place in the car. A 5.30 take-off was exceptionally early. A passenger from Batavia to Amsterdam in 1935 noted approvingly that the earliest departure along the route was at 6 am, from both Jodhpur and Baghdad. 'From Athens we did not leave until eight o'clock and from Batavia even as late as ten o'clock.'

But early departures do not seem generally to have been considered an unreasonable hardship, and, in addition to the advantage of having some at least of the journey while it was still cool, it allowed the number of days en route to be shortened. This was especially important for people taking a short period of leave. In 1935 Mr S. C. Isaacs, [15] a lawyer working in India, flew from Calcutta to London in three days, with night-stops only at Karachi and Cairo. The return ticket cost £180, which compared favourably with the first-class fare by sea. Most Anglo-Indians, however, welcomed the long sea voyage as a holiday, and since the usual arrangement for people working in India was for long periods of service followed by long periods of leave, the time the sea voyage took did not bother them. It was those with short leaves who welcomed the opportunity to fly.

It is curious that for some years Imperial Airways paid no attention to Delhi, despite the fact that a steadily increasing number of people wanted to travel to and from the Indian capital. The company's advice to such people was either to use the train or to try to persuade a member of the Delhi Flying Club to give them a lift from Jodhpur in one of the Club's Gipsy Moths. [16]

[14] *Imperial Airways Gazette*, April 1936.
[15] Conversation with Kenneth Hudson, 9 June 1970.
[16] The Aviation Department of Tata Sons Ltd, the forerunner of Air-India, inaugurated the Bombay–Delhi service on 6 November 1937. The company began operations in 1932, with a mail service beteeen Karachi and Bombay, connecting with Imperial Airways' London to Karachi flights. In the first year the Tata planes carried a lot of mail, but only eight passengers.

KLM's first unac-
companied minor on
the Far East route.

Once the routes to Africa and the Far East were established, it became
possible for children at boarding school in England to rejoin their parents for
the holidays, a practice which is common enough nowadays, but was fairly
rare even as late as 1939. In 1938 a girl of ten, now Mrs Constance Halford-
Thompson,[17] flew from Amsterdam to visit her parents in India. She was the
first unaccompanied child passenger to be taken by KLM on this route and, as
a special favour, she was allowed to sit in the cockpit with the pilot. She

[17] Conversation with Kenneth Hudson, 1 July 1970.

78

remembers the steward telling the passengers that if anyone needed oxygen they should ask for it. When she asked, perfectly reasonably, how she would know if she needed it, the steward said a headache was the warning sign. At the first opportunity, therefore, she naturally claimed she had a headache, but when the mask was over her face and she breathed in oxygen she began to feel sick and decided her curiosity was satisfied.

On this trip all the other passengers, she recalls, were 'tough American oil-drillers'. They were very kind to her and took her on a sight-seeing trip around Athens. Some of her experiences were not so pleasant. The 5 a.m. starts often found her very sleepy and in Basra, when dinner was eaten late and outdoors, it was hot and rather dark, so that she was unable to see what she was eating.

Some of the schoolchildren returning home from school in England were very distinguished. As early as 1927, Imperial Airways was happy to be able to report that the heir to the throne of Iraq, who was returning from Harrow accompanied by his tutor, had travelled in the 'City of Baghdad' between Cairo and Baghdad, and throughout the 1930s a steady stream of boys – always boys – from aristocratic families flew back to India and to the Middle East for the summer vacation. But such exalted people, of whatever age, were always a small minority. Some passengers indeed, flying for the first time, were surprised to discover how ordinary their companions in the aircraft turned out to be. Before embarking on his flight to London in 1934, a South African businessman admitted that he had always looked on air travel 'as a sort of luxurious and mythical idea entertained only by the wealthy and demonstrative classes, so that they might be able to say to their friends, "I made the journey by air, dear."'[18]

During the 1930s, Ian Scott-Hill was one of Imperial Airways' managers in Egypt and his memories reveal certain things about the passengers and their habits which, had they been publicised at the time, might or might not have benefited the image of the airline. Thinking back to the thousands of passengers who passed through his hands at that time, Mr Scott-Hill distinguished certain clearly defined categories.

There were what would today be called the jet-set, the very rich who are constantly perambulating about the world. Africa was, of course, a mecca for the safari business. There was big business in transporting very rich people down to Africa, Kenya and Uganda particularly. That was perhaps two per cent of the passengers. The balance was made up almost exclusively of colonial civil servants going to and from leave and members of His Majesty's Services going to and from postings or leave, with or without wives, according to seniority.[19]

The Far Eastern and the African routes divided at Alexandria, and, for some at least of the male passengers, the attractions of Alexandria seem to

---

[18] *Imperial Airways Gazette*, July 1934.
[19] Interviewed for BBC TV, 7 July 1978.

have been memorable. As a good company servant, Mr Scott-Hill necessarily saw this from the Imperial Airways point of view.

It was desirable that the traffic staff would know the going rate for a lady of pleasure and what time the night clubs closed and what was the price for gin and tonic. If there were a sufficient number of passengers, as there frequently were, who found this the first fleshpot after perhaps two or three years' sojourn in the colonies or in extremely remote places, they would spend the night in a night club and we would offer to run the bus to the airport in the morning, say at 4.15 from the night club.

Imperial Airways had their own currency coupons in 2s.6d. and 5s. units. The idea was that passengers should take them to their Imperial Airways' representative at the hotel and cash them for local currency there, a practical and helpful system.

It does not seem, however, to have always operated quite as the company intended. The coupons were used as currency in passengers' dealings with the local residents. As another of Imperial Airways' managers, Pat Gillibrand, well remembers, the proprietress of at least one of the Egyptian brothels was in the habit of bringing batches of coupons to the Imperial Airways' office, in order to cash them for real money.[20]

Sir Malin Sorsbie, a pilot with Imperial Airways for many years, knew the passengers on the Empire routes as well as anyone did. He recalled:[21]

Our passengers on the India run were largely civil servants and their wives and I found them a pompous lot. There were very few British children in India in those days. We used to night stop at a desert fortress called Atsharjah on the Persian Gulf, where we had a Baluchi guard. One lady, who was a Governor's wife, reported me for not seating her on my right at dinner, and particularly the effrontery of seating the wife of a PWD official there instead, which the Governor's wife regarded as an insult to her dignity. A copy of this letter was sent to me by our Air Superintendent, who was an old fighter pilot from World War I and I think that he was probably highly amused by the complaint. Anyway, I replied, telling the truth, which was that the wife of the PWD official happened to be a very pretty girl and I heard no more about it.

The passengers on the Africa run were totally different. Personally, I found the South Africans rather an uncouth lot and the Rhodesians provincial, but the people from Kenya were gay and, in most cases, charming. They viewed the voyage as a great big lark and we had to put twice as much champagne on board as we had on the flight to India.

The passengers, as Sir Malin remembered them, were not often troublesome. They had few criticisms, provided the flight arrived on time.

In those days ships were not fitted with stabilisers and, therefore, anyone living in Africa was inured to the rolling of a ship, seasick or not, and the same thing happened to aeroplanes. The complaints were mostly about irregularity, but I can see from my Log Book that most of the flights were operated on schedule. Another thing, of course, was – a bugbear that still occurs in Africa – misdirected luggage, due to the porters being illiterate.

[20] Interviewed for BBC TV, 12 July 1978.
[21] Letter to Kenneth Hudson, 9 September 1975.

Only once in my entire flying career did I ever have any real complaints and that was when an engine caught fire and I managed to put it out by side-slipping. I think my passengers probably thought that I ought to have got out on to the wing with a fire extinguisher.

Passengers enjoyed the night stops which were at the very best hotels available and were all managed by Europeans.

Empire Flying-boat 'Corsair' on the slipway at Imperial Airways' base, Hythe, Hampshire. The Empire Flying-boats operated the trunk routes to Africa, the Far East and Australia from 1936 onwards.

Considerable ingenuity was displayed in making arrangements for the night and intermediate stops. While the flying-boat was refuelling off Crete, passengers were able to take tea on board the Imperial Airways yacht, 'Imperial', which was kept moored there for the purpose. On the Nile at Cairo the 'Mayflower' was used as a floating hotel, and at Mozambique another ship, the 'Richard King', was turned into a house-boat, with beds for thirty passengers. The 'Richard King', which was brought into service in 1939, provided accommodation of a very superior order. In addition to electric light and electric fans, there was hot and cold water in every cabin. The public rooms included a lounge, a dining-room and a bar. There was refrigeration for food and drinks and 'all the apparatus needed for the preparation of meals of the quality to which passengers are accustomed'.

Throughout the 1930s the Dutch services to the Far East were operated entirely by planes using airfields. Imperial Airways, however, made extensive use of flying-boats, to begin with between Brindisi and Alexandria, and later on complete routes, operating from Southampton Water. Two types were mainly used, the Short S17 Kent (Scipio class) and the Short Empire Flying-boat. The Kent was designed for operation on the trans-Mediterranean–East sections of the Far East and South Africa routes. The first of the class, 'Scipio', made its maiden flight in 1931. It had four engines and cruised at 105 mph. In the passenger cabin there was accommodation for sixteen people, in four rows of seats, with folding tables. The seats had air cushions, which could be used as life jackets in an emergency. The Empire Flying-boat was much bigger and faster. An all-metal four-engined mono-plane, it had a range of 800 miles and a cruising speed of 165 mph. It could carry twenty-four people on daytime flights and sixteen at night, together with a heavy load of mail and baggage. One of the Empire Flying-boats, 'Caledonia', made North Atlantic commercial survey flights in 1937, without a payload and fitted with extra fuel tanks.

Why, it is reasonable to ask, were flying-boats used at all? There were two main reasons. In the first place, no airfield was needed, and a heavily laden aircraft could have almost as long a run as it pleased before becoming airborne. Secondly, in the days before macadam or concrete runways became widely available, it was comforting to know that, whatever else happened to the plane, it was not going to sink into the mud while trying to take off or land. The all-up weight of the Empire Flying-boats was about eighteen tons, an impossibility for a wet grass or earth surface.

The Empire Flying-boats provided exceptionally comfortable and spacious conditions, bettered only by what was offered by the German airships. The company was justifiably proud of them.

. . . the midship cabin is located behind the mail compartments, kitchen and toilets and accommodates six passengers by day and four at night. Then, further astern, comes the big promenade cabin seating eight or resting four. On the port side is a rail for elbow resting by the windows and a surprising amount of space for promenading. Leg stretching space is always welcome on long trips. Above this cabin is a loft for bedding stowage, and behind it is a further cabin with six seats for daylight flying or sleeping accommodation for four. The rear wall of this cabin coincides with the farther step of the planing bottom and behind it, extending well into the stern portion of the hull, is another hold for mail, freight and baggage.

Every bunk has a little window above it with a cover flap and by each row of seats are universally mounted hot and cold air intakes and a light incorporating a switch and a bell-push for calling the steward. Little hold-alls are let into the walls at appropriate points. Light luggage racks of railway carriage design are installed to form back rests. The upholstery over the double sound-proofed walls and on the seats is mainly in a dark restful green.[22]

Twenty-eight of these aircraft were in operation by the end of 1937. Passengers paid tribute, not only to their speed and quietness and roominess, but

[22] *Imperial Airways Monthly Bulletin*, December 1936.

The promenade deck of an Empire Flying-boat.

also to the attentive service and to the efficiency of the catering arrangements. The stewards had well-equipped galleys, big enough to allow them to work properly and to carry good stocks of food and drink. Two specimen menus from 1937 show what was achieved.

Luncheon – the word 'lunch' is quite inappropriate for such a feast – in the 'Challenger' began with iced melon. This was followed by roast chicken, York ham and veal galantine, with tomatoes and asparagus tips. Then came fruit salad and cream, Cheshire, Cheddar and cream cheese, 'toast Imperial', assorted biscuits, crystallised fruit, coffee, and liqueur brandy.

On 'Corsair', dinner bore a strong resemblance to lunch on 'Challenger' – *pâté de foie gras* or grapefruit; roast chicken, ox tongue and York ham, with Russian salad or green salad; peaches and sauce melba; golden figs; Cheshire, Camembert and Kraft cheese; 'toast Imperial'; biscuits, dessert and coffee.

There was a respectable wine list, on which the intriguingly named 'Airway cocktail' received special mention.

Rex Holland, formerly of Cunard, Imperial Airways and BOAC, and now in charge of on-board catering for the American railway concern, Amtrak, has pleasant memories of British flying-boats in the 1930s. Even the train journey down from London was on the grand scale.

Diamonds in The Sky

A brief taxicab ride across the Thames to Waterloo Station, and a special Pullman parlor car right to dockside at Southampton – linen table-cloths, pink lampshades, attendants to stoke me with such morning snacks as toasted sardines on toast and a bottle of hock. Thence aboard a little motor ship out into the harbour and alongside a beautiful Imperial Airways flying-boat, which rode the boarding rain as easily and majestically as a sea gull.

There were no more than a dozen seats, up forward. We had orders that every passenger must be addressed by name. Any attendant who came aboard with a loose button, or who coughed or sneezed even once, was permanently on the proscribed list, and was demoted to tourist class, or else simply thrown away. At lunch or dinner, or at high tea, our attitude was always, 'A bit more of the lobster, Sir?'[23]

From 1938 until the outbreak of war in the autumn of 1939, part of the fleet of Empire Flying-boats was used on the Sydney–Singapore section of the flight from Australia to England. This section was operated by Qantas in co-operation with Imperial Airways. When normal civilian flying came to an enforced standstill, the Qantas flying-boats formed the nucleus of the Royal Australian Air Force flying-boat squadron which was to play an important part in the defence of Australia during World War II. Empire Flying-boats were also extensively used as troop carriers. When the Japanese advance in South-East Asia interrupted the Australia–England service, Qantas Catalinas solved the problem by flying non-stop from Perth to Colombo, across 3500 miles of the Indian Ocean.

British passengers seem to have attached great importance to being well fed and attentively served on a flight. The Americans, while by no means indifferent to these matters, gave a higher priority to speed, punctuality and safety. One reason for this may have been that Pan American, the principal US overseas carrier in the 1930s, flew routes where the transport previously available had been tedious, primitive and slow. Passengers on the British and Dutch Imperial routes compared airline service with what they received on large, comfortable ships, and complained loudly and often very nastily if the aeroplane fell below the standard of the boat. Pan Am's passengers, on the other hand, were more likely to make comparisons with slow, small and far from luxurious boats, with bad roads and with horses or mules. In these circumstances, gratitude was as probable a reaction as criticism. During the late 1920s and early 1930s, Pan American carried out a great deal of exploratory work in connection with possible mail and passenger services between North America and Europe, but negotiations over landing rights were infuriatingly protracted and it was eventually decided to concentrate for the time being on the Pacific, where there were fewer political problems. Hawaii, Wake Island, Midway Island and Guam were United States territories and, at that time, China was within the American sphere of influence. During the summer of 1935 complete flying-boat bases were built and equipped at Midway, Guam and Wake and those at Honolulu and Manila improved.

[23] *New Yorker*, 19 December 1977, p. 30

Cutaway diagram of a Boeing 314, with the passenger area divided to provide ship-type accommodation.

By then, suitable aircraft were available. In 1931, Pan American had produced a specification for a flying-boat with a range of at least 2500 miles, which would allow a service from California to Hawaii without refuelling. Acceptable designs were submitted by the Martin Company, for the M130, and by Sikorsky, for the S42, and these two aircraft went into production. A mail service to Manila was inaugurated in November 1935 and, after a year's operations during which safety standards were proved to be all they should be, the first trans-Pacific passengers were carried on 21 October 1936.

Pan American called their flying-boats Clippers, a name which became famous during the 1930s. The first Clippers were Sikorsky S40s. Then came the S41s and S42s and the M130s. Pan American, however, was looking beyond its third generation flying-boats even before they had begun to carry passengers and in 1936 the company placed an order with Boeing for six flying-boats, the 314s, which were planned to carry 40–72 passengers across the Atlantic in considerable comfort. In addition, in 1937, three Boeing 307s were ordered. These were four-engined, pressurised landplanes, not seaplanes, and Pan American wanted them specifically for the trans-Atlantic route.

In May 1939 the Boeing 314 'Yankee Clipper' flew the first Atlantic mail service on the southern route, New York–Azores–Lisbon–Marseilles, and a month later the same aircraft opened the northern mail route, from Shediac, New Brunswick, to Foynes, Ireland, via Botwood, Newfoundland. Passenger services on the same routes began a few weeks later.

The pre-1939 Clippers, like the Empire Flying-boats, offered passengers plenty of room and great comfort. The décor in the American planes was rather more chaste than in the British, however, and with its emphasis on

85

green and grey, probably better suited to hot areas of the world. Catering and general amenities were up to the Imperial Airways standard and there was a much-appreciated self-service area, equipped, in the best American tradition, with iced water on tap and throwaway paper cups. One could also help oneself to cottonwool, for ear plugs, and to bags to take and use if one felt air sickness approaching.

And that was a feature of life on all the flying-boats. Stanley Zedalis was a flight engineer on the pre-war Clippers. 'There were', he remembers, 'certain days when the storms were so bad and we had high winds, so we had to come down low. Sometimes, we were down so low that the spray from the waves actually came over the aircraft.'[24] Such storms made the passengers all too well aware of the excellent food served on board. As Mr Zedalis records, 'There were times when I had to go through the main cabin on inspections and I'd see these people with their heads in the bags all the time.'

And yet they flew. One is bound to ask why. Captain Haakon Gulbrandsen flew Clippers for years on the trans-Pacific route and he thought he knew the answer. Sickness or no sickness, flying represented a challenge. Looking back over those years, Captain Gulbrandsen saw the situation in this way:

We carried diplomats, royalty, business people and a certain number of rich people who just wanted to go because it was there to go. You know, like climbing the mountain, why did you climb it, because it was there.[25]

Boeing continued to develop its Clippers during the war years. The last of the series did both crew and passengers very well indeed. When necessary it could carry seventy-four passengers, but under normal operational conditions this was reduced to sixty-eight. It was, by the standards of the time, an enormous plane. It had ship-style staterooms, including a deluxe suite, and an elegant dining saloon. Apart from aircraft provided for the use of heads of state and the extremely wealthy, nothing with such a high degree of comfort and spaciousness has been seen since and very probably never will be.

It should be mentioned, perhaps, that throughout the 1930s the cabin staff on all long-distance flights, including those of Pan American, were always men, although stewardesses were employed for shorter journeys. This was partly a matter of conservatism – if the liners had only stewards, the airlines had to follow suit – but also in order to avoid possible complications during the overnight stops.

There could, however, be difficulties even with stewards. On one occasion a British passenger who had travelled by KLM from the Far East complained on arrival at Schiphol that both the co-pilot and the steward on his aircraft had been Indonesian and that, in consequence, he had been compelled to spend his evenings at the hotels and rest-houses en route in close company

[24] Conversation with Julian Pettifer, 12 November 1978.
[25] Conversation with Julian Pettifer, 13 November 1978.

with people who were not Europeans. The station manager at Schiphol who received his complaint was himself Indonesian.[26]

The stewards on the intercontinental services operated by Imperial Airways were always British and white. On similar services, Pan American used only white Americans.

On the whole, Americans, wherever they were travelling, usually tended to be more interested in an aeroplane's technicalities and speed than in the food and ambience. For the well-to-do British male – and Imperial Airways understood the type very well – the nearer conditions in an aeroplane approached those at a good London club, the more contented they were likely to be.

The world did, however, contain other kinds of people, people who wanted to fly long distances or had to, but who did not belong to the Euro-American business and social élite. Once off the prestigious routes, aeroplanes were likely to be inferior and conditions distinctly rough and ready, even in the late 1930s.

[26] Conversation with Mr F. Zandvliet, KLM.

Forward stateroom of Boeing 314 Clipper 'America', showing seats folded down to make a bed.

On the major routes at least, the need for rugs soon passed and by 1938 it was possible to tell ladies contemplating a journey by air:

There is no need to wrap yourself up. All aeroplanes are heated and air conditioned. If you do feel the need for a rug, rugs are provided – and on Empire routes foot muffs too.

These air liners are so spacious that there is plenty of room for passengers to walk about; the Imperial Flying-boats have a promenade deck. And there is no need to worry about noise, for the walls are insulated, allowing conversation to be carried on in a normal voice.

If the ears should get that 'full' feeling as they do sometimes when climbing high mountains, this can be stopped by swallowing hard or yawning several times or holding the nose and blowing with mouth closed.[27]

The achievements of the advanced nations – the Dutch, the Americans, the Germans, the British – in establishing the standards of comfort and service described in the previous pages deserve full credit, but they have to be put in a world context. By 1939, French airlines flying overseas had a higher total route mileage than either Britain or the Netherlands, although rather below that of Pan American, but for some reason they showed much less commercial enterprise, especially in the matter of making their passengers comfortable. The most probable explanation of this is that, at least in the 1920s and 1930s, the French middle classes – the market for air travel – did not live particularly comfortably. They ate and drank well, but in other respects they did not have or expect the same level of domestic and public ease as the same kind of people in Britain, the United States, Germany or the Netherlands did. The situation nowadays is quite different, of course, but in the 1930s France was not famous for the amenities of its homes, for its eagerness to buy and use the latest technical improvements or for the standard of its hotels and trains. It did not come naturally to a French airline, as it did to a British or an American one, to devote itself to the pursuit of comfort and convenience and, although the evidence is not as good as one would wish, one can reckon with some assurance that the passengers along the routes to the French colonies in Africa, the Caribbean and the Far East – the French imperial routes – were overwhelmingly French.

Yet, as early as 1931, Air Orient, one of the lines later merged to form Air France, was operating a Far East service fully comparable in distance and complexity with those of KLM or Imperial Airways. Paris–Saigon took ten days, with eighteen staging points. One went by flying-boat from Marseilles to Beirut, by way of Naples, Corfu and Athens, and at Beirut the landplanes took over, stopping at Damascus, Baghdad, Basra, Bushire, Jask, Karachi, Jodhpur, Allahabad, Calcutta, Akyab, Rangoon and Bangkok. Technically and administratively, it was a remarkable achievement, and yet KLM and Imperial Airways, not Air Orient, always seem to have got the publicity.

One should remember that what Air Orient was operating in the 1930s was

[27] *Imperial Airways Monthly Bulletin*, July 1939.

mainly a service for mail and for the kind of urgent freight required by a colonial government. In 1932, only 640 passengers went to Saigon by air and most of those were high-ranking officers and civil servants. The British and the Dutch certainly carried this kind of person as well, but they were also anxious to get the big-game hunters, the businessmen, the rich in search of a new experience, and, by aggressiveness and commercial astuteness, they did get them.

Within Europe, the French airlines went hard for business. However, a not untypical example of the publicity for their overseas routes is contained in a 1935 brochure issued by Air Afrique. 'The cost of board and lodging during the journey is not included in the price of the ticket. There is no reduction for a return ticket.'

Airport transport in Cambodia on an Air Orient Paris–Saigon flight, 1932.

FOUR

Salesmanship on the Domestic Routes

The Second World War, so far as civil aviation was concerned, was the Great Divide. During the decade which preceded it flying was becoming steadily safer, faster and more comfortable and, in the Western countries, about ten per cent more people each year were choosing to travel this way. But the numbers were relatively small and, socially, passengers were a fairly homogeneous group. By modern standards, they were cosseted to an extraordinary degree. They expected good service and, on the whole, they got it.

The war swept all this away. The pattern of flights so carefully built up over the previous twenty years was shattered. Flying was no longer a matter of simply buying a ticket and departing. The majority of services were cancelled and on those that remained a seat was a privilege granted only to people their governments considered important.

After the war, with a completely new generation of large aeroplanes at their disposal and an economic, social and political situation which bore little resemblance to that of the 1930s, the airlines virtually began again. Their business, as it now appeared, was to learn the new art of moving large numbers of people about the world fast and to contrive to make a profit. In the process, the old standards of comfort and service would need to be considerably whittled down and passengers would have to learn to accept it. Those who remembered the grand days before 1939 would be the casualties. They would, almost certainly, find the new conditions unpleasant, but for those who have known better things levelling down is always a painful process.

This chapter is concerned with the last pre-war phase of short-haul flying. If it sometimes appears nostalgic, one should perhaps console oneself with the thought that, as a result of the enormous broadening of the market, a thousand people make at least one return flight a year now for every one who was able to do so in 1939.

In looking back over its history, every old-established airline naturally takes pains to stress the importance of the innovations for which it was responsible, and it is not at all easy for an outside observer to act as a referee, partly because every airline has always had its good and bad points and partly because each airline operates within a different economic and social framework. An airline which, like Imperial Airways, Lufthansa and KLM, received a substantial subsidy from its national government, cannot be considered in quite the same way as one which, like Pan American or TWA, had to operate almost entirely on its own resources. In America, but not in Europe, the business had to pay its way. Not all private businesses, of course, are well managed, but in the conditions of the 1930s it is probably true to say that the American airlines had a greater incentive to be efficient and enterprising that the European. They had the possibility of bankruptcy always staring them in the face and that can be a considerable spur to effort and imagination. For this reason, it is not surprising that the Americans specialised in 'firsts'. They knew very well that the only way to survive and prosper in a highly competitive society was always to be one move ahead of one's rivals.

A look at TWA's achievements in the 1930s makes the point. The airline was the product of a series of mergers which culminated in the formation of the present company, Transcontinental and Western Air – TWA – in 1930. At that time, the need for a new aircraft was very apparent. The Ford Tri-Motor – the faithful 'Tin Goose' – the Fokkers, the Condors and the other pioneering aircraft of the late 1920s were obviously outdated. Nothing suitable as a replacement was available, so TWA commissioned the Douglas Aircraft Corporation to build a completely new aircraft to its specification, just as Pan American had done with its flying-boats.

Announcing the plane to its staff in a memo headed 'Private and Confidential to all TWA Personnel' – an effective way of making sure that the news got around and that other airlines began to shiver in their shoes – the company said the DC-1 would allow 'the fastest schedules ever offered to the travelling public', as well as being 'the most comfortable airplane in which to make long trips'. Normally, 'it will have a capacity of twelve to fourteen passengers, but it can easily be converted to carry eighteen to twenty-one passengers with maximum comfort. Equipped to carry twelve passengers, the seats will be mounted in rubber and arranged in two rows of six seats, allowing each passenger forty inches from seat back to seat back.' Today's passengers, knees aching and numb from the wretched thirty-four inches which is the maximum permitted to economy-class passengers by international agreement, are entitled to feel that progress in the air during the past half century has not extended to every detail of an airline's operations!

The DC-1 seats were made to TWA specifications and were not only adjustable but reversible as well so that, if they wished, passengers could face the rear of the plane. This was in answer to many requests that people should be able to face one another, in order to talk easily and to play cards while in flight.

The prototype of this all-metal twin-engined aircraft was delivered to TWA

One of TWA's DC–3 aircraft crossing the Grand Canyon.

in 1933. Known affectionately as Old 300, the DC-1 flew from coast to coast, Burbank to Washington, in just over thirteen hours, a time never previously approached. The production model, the DC-2, appeared in 1934 but it was the improved version, the DC-3, which revolutionised the aircraft industry and made other aircraft obsolete. It has a good claim to be the most successful passenger aeroplane ever designed. More than 10,000 were built by Douglas, both for civilian passenger flying and for military use during the Second World War. It cruised at about 180 mph and carried twenty-one passengers in reclining seats. Important safety innovations included wing flaps to slow the plane down on landing, the ability to fly on one engine, and an automatic pilot. The cabin was steam heated[1] and there was a lavatory and a galley for serving hot meals. Much attention was given to soundproofing the cabin, a feature greatly appreciated by passengers.

In 1939 passengers on some of TWA's DC-3s were provided with the ad-

[1] The steam was produced by a small plant on the port engine nacelle.

ditional pleasure of in-flight broadcasts. Twenty-two of the fleet had this facility. The master-receiver in each aircraft was controlled by the air hostess. Each passenger could have, on request, his own individual loudspeaker, which was plugged into a socket by the side of his seat and fastened to the back of the seat in front. 'Hostesses controlling the master receiving unit will tune in on stations near the plane's course and offer programmes appealing to the majority of passengers on each flight. Because of the speed of the planes, other stations will be tuned in whenever necessary to maintain proper volume for all receivers.'[2]

It was a task requiring nice judgement and a sound knowledge of the tastes and habits of one's fellow citizens. 'Programmes appealing to the majority of passengers' would nearly always mean programmes of a popular nature, and one or two people on each flight would probably not enjoy the fare provided, especially since it was being retailed by means of loudspeakers, not headphones.

The same circuit and the same loudspeakers were used to allow the pilot to make in-flight announcements about 'flight location, altitude, arrival time at airports, and other comments of general interest'. For better or for worse, intercom had established itself as a feature of passenger flights.

The DC-2s and DC-3s always carried a stewardess, who was a graduate of TWA's new Hostess Academy. TWA, however, could not claim air hostesses as one of their own firsts. That honour belonged to Boeing Air Transport, which later became part of United Airlines, after the US Government had brought in legislation forbidding aircraft manufacturers to operate airlines. Boeing was employing eight hostesses in May 1930, and no other company adopted the idea until 1933, when TWA took on its first batch for training.

The eight pioneers were all registered nurses. They wore white nurses' uniforms during a flight and green woollen twill suits, with capes and berets, on the ground. They earned $125 a month for a hundred hours' work. One of them, formerly Inez Keller and now Mrs Richard J. Fuite, has recalled her days as a stewardess.[3] She flew in Boeing 80As, taking a dozen passengers the 950 miles between Oakland and Cheyenne, Wyoming, with five stops. 'It was supposed to take eighteen hours, but it was usually more like twenty-four. If the weather got bad, we would land in a field for a while and wait for the storm to clear up.' The planes flew at a height of 2000 feet. They were not heated, pressurised or air-conditioned. Mrs Fuite found the absence of pressurisation the most difficult to tolerate. 'One day, after I had been flying four months, I lost the hearing in my left ear when the plane hit an air pocket near Reno and dropped 500 feet. I quit a few days later, because I didn't want to go deaf in my other ear.'

The work of these stewardesses was a good deal more varied than it is nowadays. 'We had to carry all the baggage on board,' Mrs Fuite remembers,

---

[2] *TWA Skyliner*, 15 December 1939.
[3] *New York Times*, 15 May 1970.

'and if the seats weren't fastened down tightly, we had to screw them down ourselves. Then we had to dust the whole plane. Some of us had to join bucket brigades to help fuel the airplanes. We also helped pilots push planes into hangars. And we had to make sure the passengers didn't open the exit door by mistake when they were going to the washroom.' If all the seats were full, the stewardess had to sit on a mailbag or a suitcase in the rear of the plane.

Another member of Boeing's first eight was Ellen Church, a registered nurse from Cressbill, Iowa. Her tasks, she recalled, included handing out box lunches, caring for passengers afflicted with air sickness – a common occurrence whenever the small, poorly ventilated planes encountered rough weather – and pointing out places of interest down below on the ground. If, as sometimes happened, bad weather forced the plane to land in a field at some remote place, the stewardess was expected to help with the five-gallon cans from which the tanks had to be refuelled and to find overnight shelter and bedding for the stranded passengers.

Mrs Cornelia Tyson, then Cornelia Peterman, was taken on as a stewardess by Boeing, after Ellen Church had interviewed her for the job. With the statutory nursing qualification, she received $125 a month, plus uniform and the cost of having it regularly cleaned, plus $6 a day for a meal.

The Boeing stewardesses, in Mrs Tyson's memory,[4] had to make sure that the cabin 'was clean and shipshape', before passengers got on board. They had briefcases 'in which we carried certain things that were taken off the aircraft every time, like ashtrays'. The airlines learnt fast.

If the weather was bad, 'the mail would go in a single-engined plane with the pilot and then the stewardess would keep the passengers, take them to a hotel and put them on a train, depending on what they wanted to do'.

The work was certainly varied and the responsibilities were never-ending and unpredictable. But relationships were on a very personal basis.

If we had more than four passengers we thought we were overworked. We did not serve box lunches.[5] They did, I think, at one time, when the pilots served food, but we had china and silver and food was prepared by the P-House in Chicago and it was good. We had chicken and rolls and what everybody liked were the fruit cocktails, which were laced with brandy. They were really pretty good, and this was during prohibition, you know.

The passengers took to the new stewardesses very quickly, but the pilots were less enthusiastic. Mrs Fuite remembers:

The pilots didn't want us at all. They were rugged temperamental characters, who wore guns to protect the mail. They wouldn't even speak to us during the first couple of trips. The wives of the pilots weren't very excited about the idea, either. They began

[4] Revealed in a conversation with Julian Pettifer, 15 November 1978. Boeing wanted, she understood, 'someone mature enough to handle any given situation and they didn't want people who were flighty'.

[5] The disagreement between Ellen Church and Cornelia Tyson on this point illustrates the need to be cautious in interpreting and evaluating word-of-mouth evidence.

Opposite: Ellen Church, one of the first airline stewardesses, standing in the doorway of a United Airlines DC–3.

a letter-writing campaign to Boeing, saying that the stewardesses were trying to steal their husbands and requesting their removal. One pilot's wife in Salt Lake City always met her husband at the plane. She was really jealous.

Gratitude, rather than jealousy, seems to have been the usual reaction of the passengers to this latest addition to the amenities provided by the airlines. One seasoned traveller[6] recalled that before the days of air hostesses he made a habit of saying this prayer before take-off: 'Please God, take me safely to where I'm going' (he would specify his destination), and on landing he always used to say, 'Thank you, sir.' After the introduction of hostesses, however, he no longer felt impelled to ask for divine protection. These uniformed young women filled him with confidence. If they were brave, then he should be, too.

'There is still a newness about air travel, and, though statistics demonstrate its safety, the psychological effect of having a girl on board is enormous.' A stewardess had to be under twenty-five, unmarried, maximum height 5 ft 4 in, maximum weight 8 stone 8 lbs, and a trained nurse. The reason for the last requirement 'was not that a nurse would be required in her professional capacity, but rather that her training has given her other essential attributes. She has been taught to obey orders. She has learned how to put people at their ease and how to be pleasant to them. She has acquired tact and consideration.'[7]

United Airlines, said their Western Traffic Manager in 1935,[8] used four criteria for running their services – 'safety, speed, comfort and economy'. Comfort was to a large extent in the hands of their stewardesses, 'chosen for personality and character'. Each of these stewardesses, said United, was considered a very important member of the crew.

It is her pleasant duty to look after the needs of the travellers, to make them comfortable, to point out various scenic points of interest and to serve specially prepared meals. No effort or expense has been spared to obtain the very best of food for these meals. United recently signed a contract with a famous San Francisco hostelry to supply outgoing aircraft with de luxe meals. An unusual feature of this service is that each lunch is kept cool and fresh by the use of dry ice, actually the first time that dry ice has been used aboard a commercial aircraft. The ice is so wrapped in cellophane that the food is never allowed to freeze, but simply ensures that the natural moisture and freshness of the food is retained. Usually these meals consist of such delicacies as chicken and fruit salads, cold meats, light sandwiches, cheeses, ice cream, pastries, etc. Hot coffee, cocoa, tea and soups are kept in large thermos bottles.

In Europe, Swissair engaged its first air hostess, Nelly Dienter, in 1934, KLM in 1935 and Lufthansa in 1938. The experiment on KLM was very short-lived. The girls received so many proposals of marriage while in the air that

[6] Mr Walter Wren: conversation with Kenneth Hudson, 16 June 1970.
[7] *Aviation: the National Air Magazine of Ireland*, November 1935.
[8] Quoted in S. A. Stimpson, 'The Progress of Air Transport', *Shell Aviation News*, October 1935.

they were apt to remain in the job only a few months. The KLM management came to the conclusion that it was all too much trouble and decided to do away with the stewardesses altogether.

At a press conference held in 1938, Lufthansa's Director of Operations, Hans Bongers, explained the kind of girl the company was looking for as a recruit to the select corps of stewardesses. 'We require', he said, 'ladies of education and breeding, with the ability to give the aircraft cabin a homely, domestic atmosphere.'[9]

Imperial Airways would have nothing to do with stewardesses, believing that the British style of flying demanded men, and that having this curious hybrid of a nurse and a waitress on board was neither the only nor the best way of putting passengers at their ease. In any case – and this was probably the main reason for not employing women – Imperial Airways believed they could get more work out of men. 'Our aerial stewards', they told the world, 'are men of a new calling.'[10] They had to be, since much was expected of them. 'In less than an hour,' said their proud employers, 'a couple of flying stewards can serve six courses, with wines, to between thirty and forty people,' and of how many waiters on land could that have been said?

By the mid-1930s, the American airlines had begun to leave this kind of publicity behind them. They had proved to the satisfaction both of themselves and of the public that they could transport passengers quickly and efficiently and serve them substantial meals in the air. Their task now was to get more passenger business and to persuade the US Government to pay a more realistic airmail subsidy. United Airlines had examined the financial structure of the American airlines with great care and in 1935 S. A. Stimpson, their Western Traffic Manager, published the conclusions:

It has been demonstrated that a reasonable rate for carrying the mail must be obtained by the air lines if their operations are to be profitable, or if they are to maintain the present standard of service. Although they receive less than one-ninth of the direct government aid per mile given to European companies, air lines in the United States are carrying passengers and air mail on an average at a speed of forty miles per hour faster. The average direct government aid per mile flown in France, the British Empire and Italy was $1.17 per mile, compared with 18.9 cents per mile in the United States at present. Although the actual rate paid for aircraft carrying mail in America is 26.8 cents per mile, this can never be fully realised, because of the many schedules flown, for which no fee is paid, on which air mail is carried free on strictly passenger aircraft.[11]

In this situation, the salesman came into his own. Passengers had to be got off the railways and the roads and into the aeroplanes. There was plenty of room for enterprising salesmanship. In 1935 the Federal Coordinator pro-

---

[9] 'Wir brauchen Damen von Format, die Flugzeugkabine eine häusliche Atmosphäre zu geben wissen.'

[10] *Imperial Airways Gazette*, October 1933.

[11] *Shell Aviation News*, October 1935.

duced his usual annual report of passenger traffic. It showed that during the previous twelve months railways in the United States handled seventy-four per cent of the traffic and received eighty-two per cent of the revenue; highways twenty-five per cent of the traffic and fifteen per cent of the revenue; and airways less than half of one per cent of the traffic and three per cent of the revenue.

The average railway coach earned twenty cents a mile, the bus twenty-two cents and the aeroplane fifty-five cents, of which 41.4 cents was for mail. This disparity of revenue between air transport and its competitors showed that the airlines had allowed their two main sources of income, mail and passengers, to get out of balance. Too small a proportion of the total was coming from conveying people and the principal task facing the salesmen was therefore to get more passengers. The way to do this, said Mr Stimpson, and the other American airlines would not have disagreed with him, was to aim at the top and to persuade the corporations that it paid them to send their senior people by air. It made nonsense to pay a man $30,000 a year and then throw away a large part of his salary by sending him long distances by rail, when, with night flights and time changes, 'it is possible to travel without the loss of a single business hour from New York and many eastern cities to any major point on the Pacific coast'.

The Douglas Sleeper Transport, brought into service in 1936, had the $30,000-a-year man and his wife, in whom the salesmen were equally interested, very much in mind. It was designed to carry twenty-eight passengers by day and fourteen at night. The specification, issued in 1935, makes very sad reading for anyone who has to undertake long night flights today.

The cabin will be 7 ft 8 in wide and 6 ft 6 in high, with eight roomy sections, four on each side of a broad aisle. Each section will have two seats, each 35 inches wide, facing each other. By night, the backs and bases of these seats will fold together to form a thick, soft foundation for the mattress of the lower berth. The upper berth and mattress will be dropped into position from the ceiling of the section. Each berth will measure 6 ft 5 in in length – several inches longer than the standard railway sleeper berth – which will enable even a tall man to lie in complete comfort. The lower berth will measure 35 in wide and the upper berth 29 in. The bottom of the lower berth will be 5 in above the floor, leaving a space for the storage of small hand luggage. The thick soft mattress and springs will add another 9 in to the height, holding the sleeping passenger 14 in above the floor of the cabin; the upper berth will be 46½ in above the floor, giving an ample clearance above the lower berth and steps will be provided to enable a passenger to enter this berth. The cabin windows will light the lower berth and a similar window, at the head, will provide light in the upper. Each berth will be complete with a reading light, a net for clothes, a baggage rack and a bell for calling the stewardess; separate dressing rooms will be provided for male and female passengers at the rear of the cabin and will be complete with running water, mirrors and towels. Toilet facilities will be provided at the rear of each dressing room.[12]

[12] *Shell Aviation News*, December 1935.

98

By 1937 the American airlines were competing with the railways on price. In that year TWA was charging $224.92 for its New York–San Francisco flight. It cost $229.20 to make the same journey by rail, including the sleeper supplement.

Many film stars earned much more than $30,000 a year and the airlines certainly wanted the pleasure and publicity of transporting them. Until 1935, however, all American film stars were barred from flying, under a special clause in their contracts. The withdrawal of this clause was an official acknowledgement by the film industry that flying could now be considered safe and that the studios' valuable properties were no longer at risk in an aeroplane. It was an important event for TWA, United and their competitors.

It would be quite wrong to suggest that the European airlines displayed neither enterprise nor business sense in the 1930s and that the Americans formed a league to themselves in these matters. The difference was simply that the Europeans had a softer cushion. The Americans had to make money quicker and sell themselves harder.

Everybody has his own concept of what is tedious, inconvenient and unnecessarily time-consuming and most of the sales techniques employed by airlines anywhere in the world consisted of identifying these unpleasantnesses and offering to remove them. In the United States, the main problem facing the traveller before the days of aeroplanes was likely to be the length of his journey; in Europe, it was such things as the rough seas often encountered when crossing the Channel or the Irish Sea[13] and the great nuisance of moving oneself and one's belongings from train to boat and then from boat to train again. On routes like this it was difficult to go wrong. In 1937 passengers bound for Paris could leave the London terminus at 8.45 in the morning and be in the centre of Paris at 12.30. By train and boat it would have taken them another four and a half hours and, apart from the possibility of a nasty crossing, they would have had to face up to smuts from two locomotives – an unpleasant hazard in the days before diesel and electric traction – and all the problems and labour of finding seats and stowing and re-stowing their belongings. London–Le Bourget, with eight services a day in each direction and, by 1939, a scheduled flying time of seventy minutes, solved the problem.

Looking through the files of advertising material put out by both the French and the British during the 1930s, one is struck by what appears to be the disproportionate amount of attention given to the London–Paris route. There were two main reasons for this. One was, of course, that this particular route had about 700 seats to sell every day, far more than on any other service, and it was obviously good business to make sure that as few of them as possible remained empty. The other reason was that London–Paris was the shop window. If people could be persuaded to travel by air between these two

---

[13] For many people, sufficiently frightening to make foreign travel unthinkable.

Victoria Air Terminal,
London, in the late 1930s.

cities – and the English Channel helped the salesmen a great deal – there was a good chance that they would develop the flying habit and, in time, try making other journeys the same way. The London–Paris service certainly responded to encouragement. Between October 1930 and March 1932 the average number of passengers carried each month doubled, and between then and March 1935 it doubled again. It was a route worth the loving care bestowed on it.

Shortly before the Second World War, travellers between London and Paris were able to enjoy the luxurious pleasures of Imperial Airways' latest achievement, the Frobisher aircraft. One observer wrote:

The cabins are furnished after the luxurious style of interior decoration which makes me feel that the Flight Steward should be called Head Waiter. There are three cabins. But cabin is a mean word to give to these three areas, carpeted richly and deeply, not shaped in front but nearly square, with sofa-like double seats on either side of the through walk down the middle. The three cabins have the same floor level, and the

100

ceiling is low, 6 ft 2 ins in the middle and rounded to the window lines' sides. Perhaps it is partly these lower ceilings of the Frobishers that make them still more comfortable than their big cousins, the Ensigns and the Imperial flying-boats. And the dark fawn colour scheme is entirely pleasant – carpet, sofas, curtains, cloth-covered ceiling and walls and all in tones of fawn.[14]

The Germans had brought luxury to the same pitch, in their new forty-seat Junkers, the Ju 90. It was a notably quiet aircraft, and it had a number of other agreeable amenities, admiringly described by someone who had experienced them in these terms:

A passenger sitting comfortably in his armchair has only to take hold of a tassel, and immediately receives fresh air from outside – without his neighbour in the next chair having any grounds for complaining of a draught. Again every seat has its own special reading lamp – an amenity which is not to be underestimated. There are five divisions to the passengers' cabin and passengers have the choice of a smoking or non-smoking compartment. At night the forty chairs are converted into beds.

Another advantage is that all the chairs can be made into single seats facing the direction of the flight. Above and below the seats there is ample room for hand luggage and the padded seats are each 1.25 metres wide. There is a far larger space than is allowed in the first and second class compartments of an express train.[15]

Aircraft like the Frobisher and the Ju 90 made the salesman's task relatively easy. They were used on routes where well-to-do travellers were reckoned to exist in promising plenty, routes serving such large and commercially important places as Berlin, London, Paris and Amsterdam. Other European cities were not so lucky. The case of Dublin is the greatest puzzle of the 1930s, a commercial opportunity of real size which the airlines failed to seize. The sea crossing between Ireland and either England or Wales was long and notoriously rough and, even when the London-bound traveller had reached Holyhead or Fishguard, he still had a tedious journey ahead of him. Dublin–London would have seemed to be one of Europe's most obvious airlinks, yet it took a surprisingly long time to develop.

By the mid-1930s there was considerable feeling about the matter, with reference to 'the absurdity and disgrace of being the only nation in Europe unconnected with the European air system'.[16] One body of opinion believed that, by not establishing a London–Dublin service, Imperial Airways was an instrument of the British Government's policy of punishing Ireland for its political secession after the First World War. Another, more in sorrow than in anger, regretted that a great commercial opportunity was being missed. A third castigated the Irish Government for failing to begin a service on its own account.

When the service to London did eventually get started in 1936, it was hardly the most distinguished in Europe and the salesmen had a hard time

[14] *Imperial Airways Monthly Bulletin*, December 1936.
[15] *Aviation: the National Air Magazine of Ireland*, December 1937.
[16] *Aviation: the National Air Magazine of Ireland*, January 1935.

The first Aer Lingus aircraft, EI–ABI de Havilland Dragon *Iolar*.

persuading people to use it. Criticisms abounded. They referred to many shortcomings or supposed shortcomings – the aircraft, the airport facilities, the general amenities, the pilots' alleged lack of skill. The safety measures came in for their share of criticism as well.

We were flying in a machine fitted with landing wheels only, and, having to cross the sea, the possibility of a forced descent should be taken into consideration. Under each passenger's seat was a most efficient flotation outfit, but no instructions of any sort were either given to us or placed in a prominent position, as to where this suit should be used.

It would seem obvious to me that on the back of each seat, so that it would face the passenger behind, there should be – as one finds on steamships – an illustration of how the suit is to be put on, blown up and worn. It may be that the reason for this omission is that the Air Company felt that ample time will be given to the pilot to instruct all passengers before a descent is made, and that prior warning might make a nervous passenger more so. I do not agree with this. Does lifebelt and boat drill frighten passengers on board ship? No, surely on the contrary it gives them confidence.[17]

Not even a cup of tea was to be had at Dublin's makeshift airport.

Eventually, in 1937, the Irish Government took a hand in the business. Aer

[17] Captain H. St. G. Harpur, 'London to Dublin by Air', *Aviation: the National Air Magazine of Ireland*, August 1935.

102

Rianta was founded in April of that year as the holding company, the capital being in the form of shares held by the Ministry of Finance, with the exception of a few qualifying shares owned by directors and subscribers. The operating company, Irish Sea Airways, later became Aer Lingus. Its sole aircraft, a 7-seater DH Dragon, bought second-hand, could hardly have been described as luxurious. Flights were from Baldonnell Airfield, Dublin, to Whitchurch, Bristol. The Dragon was later sold to an English buyer and came to a sad end. On 3 June 1941 it was shot down by the Germans while on a flight from Land's End to the Isles of Scilly.

By 1936 the Irish company was operating regular services to Croydon and in that year the single fare from Dublin to London was £3 6s. 8d., a much better bargain than that from London to Paris, although not sold anything like as hard as one might have expected. Better airport facilities were available at Collinstown, the site of the present airport, by the beginning of 1940 and from then until the end of the war the number of passengers was between 5000 and 7000 a year, or about a hundred a week, which would hardly have kept the airline in business if the government had not been nurturing it. Whether or not there would have been more passengers if more aircraft and more seats had been available is difficult to say.

During the 1930s most European airlines ran some sort of campaign to capture more business traffic, realising that businessmen have the great virtue of travelling all the year round and not merely at holiday times. One of the most interesting campaigns of this kind during the 1930s – in many ways ahead of its time – was carried out by a private British company, Crilly Airlines. A reporter noted:

For business houses and tourists special travel vouchers permitting 1000 miles of air travel for ten guineas are available on all Crilly inland air routes. These vouchers are transferable and exhausted by mileage only. Thus on one ticket owned by a firm representatives may travel singly or together on any number of trips within the 1000 mile limit; or two or more friends may share the same ticket on an air holiday tour. The voucher avoids all last-minute booking troubles, and in business circles is becoming steadily appreciated.

A further service calculated to be of substantial aid to the commercial man is to be introduced by Crilly Airways. This is the provision of private secretarial services in the company's offices at each airport the line touches.

In future there should be no need for a busy man to land at an airport and rush, possibly some miles, into a city to keep an appointment. He will simply telephone his friend in advance, meet him at the airport office and there transact his business with dispatch.

In existing circumstances, for instance, a traveller by Crilley (sic) Airways can leave Croydon at 12.20 p.m., arriving in Bristol 1.30 p.m., leave at 3 p.m., be in Leicester or Nottingham a little over an hour later, and back at Croydon in the early evening, with his business completed – a round trip of some 400 miles, costing on a travel voucher only four guineas.[18]

[18] *Aviation*, June 1936.

How, for this kind of fare, did the airlines, large or small, manage to stay alive? Wages and salaries, of course, were low, fuel was cheap, aircraft were cheap to buy and maintain, strikes and 'industrial action' were rare. The companies also managed to get a prodigious amount of work out of their pilots, who were not at all the exalted and privileged people that they are today. Sir Malin Sorsbie, who has been mentioned previously in connection with the Empire air services, worked for a number of years for Imperial Airways on the London–Budapest and London–Brindisi runs. 'We were paid,' he said, 'on a somewhat iniquitous system of a low basic salary and so much a flying hour. Greed, therefore, forced me to fly as many hours as I could. I used to try to average about a hundred hours a month, which is about double the number of hours operated by pilots today.'

Those were the days when pilots bicycled to the airport and sustained themselves on sandwiches and a flask of coffee brought from home. The salaries they were paid demanded simple tastes. On the other hand, a number of them became well-known public figures. Several airlines, among them KLM and Imperial Airways, issued passengers with signed, postcard-sized pictures of the pilot in charge of their flight. Regular travellers built up a collection of these cards.

The publicity and public relations work carried out by airlines has always been of two kinds – direct selling of particular services and activity designed to create a favourable attitude to both flying and the company. The second kind can never stop, the first depends entirely on whether the company feels that a service is reaching its full potential. It is a fact of life in the aviation field that the profit lies in selling the second fifty per cent of the seats, a truth which was gradually and sometimes painfully learnt in the 1930s. The methods chosen to sell this fifty per cent varied enormously and some airlines were noticeably better at it than others.

One could, for example, decide, as Swissair and Imperial Airways did, to market the Switzerland–London services as a whole, and to emphasise simply the time taken and the price. Prospective passengers could then assess the bargain for themselves, on a purely factual basis. The details were certainly impressive. Those given below relate to the summer of 1939:

London–Zürich	3 hours 35 minutes	£13 16s. 0d. return
London–Basel	2 hours 45 minutes	£12 15s. 0d. return
London–Lausanne	4 hours 25 minutes	£15 1s. 0d. return
London–Berne	3 hours 40 minutes	£14 4s. 0d. return

By train and boat all these journeys took not far short of twenty-four hours. These, of course, were the sort of times that were normal in Western Europe. In the Soviet Union everything was on a far larger scale. In 1935 Aeroflot was offering Moscow to Vladivostok, ninety-six hours for the 8190 kilometres, Moscow–Tbilisi, thirty-eight hours, and Moscow–Tashkent, thirty-two hours. With their numerous stops, these long flights averaged no more than

Airport restaurant, Nazi style, at Tempelhof, Berlin, in 1936.

87 kilometres an hour, but this was at least twice as fast as anything even the best trains could accomplish. On shorter routes, however, much better times were achieved. The average traffic speed of the local air services in 1935 was 140 kilometres an hour and, since 'local' in Soviet terms meant anywhere within eight hours' flying distance, the saving of time was clearly important.

The Aeroflot services were not, however, promoted in the Western sense of the term. They existed and it was not easy for ordinary citizens to use them. Soviet airlines were seen as forming an essential part of the economy and government of the country. They were not intended for holidays, shopping trips or visiting one's friends and relations, and in certain instances they were not only useful, but indispensable. The service between Irkutsk and Yakutsk, for example, with its link with the important gold-mining region, covered a district in which the only other means of transport was by boat on the Lena, which is closed by ice for four to six months of the year.

In any case, the airlines in the Soviet Union, unlike those of the United States and Western Europe, could not go bankrupt, any more than the postal services or the railways could. They were a State service and, having decided on the correct level of provision, the State made available whatever funds were required. The Western airlines, however, had to go for business all the time – Paris shopping trips, tea-flights over London, half-price tickets for children, honeymooners' discounts, inclusive tickets to the Grand National, charter flights to business conferences and many other enterprising offers.

105

One of the most ingenious – totally outside Aeroflot's mandate – was Imperial Airways' Sunday Special to Le Touquet. The fare of £3 15s. 0d. included tea at the casino and dinner in the air on the return flight. With each ticket there were instructions as to how to play roulette, with a diagram of the table.

Packaged tours by air were coming in just before the outbreak of war in 1939. In Britain, where the travel agents were exceptionally enterprising in this respect, travel bargains by air, with hotels and meals included, were being offered during 1938 and 1939 by all the main concerns – Thomas Cook, Pickfords, Frames, Swans, Hickie Borman – and in the United States American Express was taking an active interest.

Specialised packages were also available and were vigorously promoted.

Fly to PISTANY SPA,[19] famous for the successful treatment of RHEUMATISM, Arthritis, Neuritis, Sciatica, Lumbago, Gout, by Imperial Airways. Quickly and Comfortably. All services operated by 4-engined aircraft. Special facilities for invalids. 70% reduction on Return Fare for a stay of 3 weeks or more.

The Ala Certificate (price 7/6) entitles the holder to 70% reduction on the cost of the homeward journey.

Leave Croydon 09.45   Arrive Pistany 18.35

Outward Journey   £12 10s. 0d.

Homeward Journey   £3 15s. 0d.

(to holders of an Ala Certificate) Available until 2nd October.

3 weeks stay, including cure costs at the two famous cure Hotels:

Grand Hotel Royal   £22

Thermia Palace Hotel £31

Full information and Special Kronen Travellers' Cheques.[20]

There were some advantages in being ill.

Systematic market research began fairly early. It was important for the airlines to discover what their passengers felt about the services which were being offered to them. One of the pioneers in this field was Swissair. In 1933 it carried out an investigation into the reactions of passengers to its Zürich–Vienna express service, for which a supplementary charge was made. Since the findings were generally favourable, they were published. There were four main conclusions:

1. All passengers praised the punctuality of the service which aroused confidence and was adhered to with few exceptions.
2. No physical discomfort of any kind was felt by passengers as a result of the high flying speeds.
3. No cases of air sickness were reported, in spite of squally weather, as the machines do not roll and the length of flights was comparatively short, owing to the high speed.
4. Corpulent passengers wanted a somewhat larger cabin, like those they had been

---

[19] Pistany or Piestany, Czechoslovakia, is 80 kilometres north-east of Bratislava. It is the most important of the Slovak spas.

[20] Imperial Airways brochure, 1937.

accustomed to in the case of the large triple-engined aeroplanes. The heaviest passenger, a gentleman from Zürich, was 120 kilos (18½ stone) in weight, but he had sufficient room next to 3 fellow passengers.[21]

Union Terminal, Cincinnati, Ohio, 1933. Railway architecture prepares the way for a new generation of airports.

The story of air travel could almost be written in terms of airports. As with railways, commercially and politically important places had airports which were, by the standard of the time, impressive, and passengers tended, quite naturally, to judge the efficiency of air transport very largely by the way they were dealt with at the airport. This was not altogether fair to the airlines, who did not themselves own the airports from which they operated – these belonged sometimes to municipalities, sometimes to companies created for the purpose – but the travelling public has never made this distinction, largely because airports grew out of railway stations and there has never been any doubt that railway companies do own and operate railway stations. The link between railway stations and airport terminal buildings is in any case fascinating and worthy of much closer attention than it has so far

[21] *Shell Aviation News*, January 1933.

received. A laboratory example is the former Union Station at Cincinnati, in the United States. This huge and remarkable station was completed in 1935 to serve the various railways operating in and out of the city. Ironically, it was opened at a time when the American railways had already begun their decline, a last grand gesture of defiance and confidence. Standing inside its now disused but fortunately still standing concourse, one finds it difficult to make up one's mind as to whether one is in fact at an airport or a railway station. The bookstalls, bars, hairdressing saloons, restaurants, waiting rooms, post office, everything is in what one thinks of as the airport tradition, and the question naturally arises in one's mind: 'Was Cincinnati trying to compete with the new, upstart airports or were the airports trying to compete with Cincinnati?' The answer is, 'Both'. What we are looking at is passenger terminal architecture, 1935 vintage, and at the time it was designed and built, the purpose of any major terminal, for whatever form of transport, was partly to do the job efficiently, but also to put the passenger in the right frame of mind for his journey. It is, in fact, a transport industry's greatest and most telling public relations exercise, whether the form of transport happens to be aeroplanes, railways, passenger liners or buses. This is the point at which all the activities of the industry come together under the public spotlight, the point at which they are judged. The 1930s are a key decade in aviation history for this reason. The novelty of flying was beginning to wear off and preparing to fly had become as important as the actual flying.

Consequently, the airlines could not dissociate themselves from the airports. The reputation of the airlines, and of flying in general, was closely and inextricably connected with what went on at airports, and the airports had to be kept up-to-date, since the expectations of the public were rising all the time. Sometimes the only answer was to pull the old buildings down and start all over again. This was done at almost every airport in the world during the 1950s, 1960s and 1970s, but it was already starting in the 1930s. At Le Bourget the original buildings were demolished and new ones put up in 1935-7. Schiphol and Croydon, on the other hand, decided, since their buildings were of more recent date, to improve and modernise terminal buildings to provide better passenger handling facilities. At Schiphol, in order to cater for the heavier and bigger planes which were being introduced – a take-off weight of sixteen tons, compared with the two tons and less of the early 1920s – new runways were laid in place of grass.

Much attention was devoted to night flying aids during the 1930s. Croydon had an elaborate system – flashing red boundary lights, red lights on church towers, factory chimneys and other tall structures in the vicinity of the airfield, a red flashing neon direction beacon visible for eight miles and landing floodlights. At both Croydon and Le Bourget there was an illuminated wind-direction indicator.

In most parts of Western Europe, it was not too difficult to find suitable sites for airports, but in Scandinavia, apart from Denmark, the problems were

immense. Lakes, mountains and rocks abounded and adequate areas of
reasonably level ground rarely existed close to the main towns. Consequently
Norway, Sweden and Finland were accustomed to operate many of their
services with sea-planes, fitted with floats in the summer and with skis in the
winter. When, with the development of international services, it became
essential to have airports which could take landplanes, the only answer in
many cases was simply to blast runways out of the rock. This is what was done
at Bromma. Opened to traffic in 1936, as Stockholm's first land airport, it was
also the first airport in Europe to have paved runways, an unavoidable
decision to take, since the runways were built on solid rock.

The process of replacing and improving old airports was going on all over
the world in the 1930s, but it is easy to forget how relatively simple the
problems facing airports were before 1939. Compared with today, the number
of passengers passing through the busiest of airports every day even in the
late 1930s was very small. Croydon and Le Bourget would have to deal with a
maximum of 2000 passengers and forty to fifty aircraft movements a day. For
all the progress that had been made, operations were still on a very small
scale. Imperial Airways' sales and publicity campaign produced just 22,000
passengers in 1938.

Night flying aids at Newark, New York's airmail terminal which came into operation in 1929.

In the 1930s Brian Haimes lived on the outskirts of Croydon Aerodrome and spent much of his boyhood watching what went on there. He recalled:

There can only have been a dozen or so arrivals and departures per day, and each of them was an Occasion. When the H.P.42, or whatever, had been loaded and was ready to go, an imposing fellow in uniform with a peaked cap would stand to attention and solemnly salute the captain. Or perhaps he was saluting the Union Jack which flew from a flagpole above the cabin. The flagpole would slowly retract, and the great silver beast would roll breathily away off the tarmac and on to the grass for take-off. As an observer one felt vaguely that one was assisting at a significant ceremony. If all the rites were properly observed the sun couldn't possibly set on the British Empire, but if they weren't, the Foreign Peril might be at our gates in a flash. [22]

With a dozen departures a day, ritual of this order was possible, and to have been able to witness it was indeed a privilege. But there was little of it left after the war and when passenger flying began to creak its way back to normal six years later, it was on a completely different scale and with a very different philosophy. The poetry and dignity of aviation had gone for ever and mere transport had taken over.

[22] 'When Summers Were Hot', *Shell Aviation News*, September 1970.

FIVE

In and Out of the War

It is interesting to wonder how civil aviation would have developed if the Second World War had never taken place. The superficial effects of the war on aviation are easy to see and easy to state – the disruption and, in many instances, total closure of international services; the great technical advances due to the development of more advanced types of military aircraft; the production, as during the First World War, of large numbers of men trained to fly aeroplanes and to administer their operation; the creation of a worldwide aircraft industry hungry for civilian business. But there were other results of six years of war which were more widespread, less immediately obvious and more profound. The more important were the ending of years of unemployment and economic misery for working-class families; a remarkable rise in general living standards and spending power; a considerable weakening, if not destruction, of the old, hierarchical social order; and the growth of a very large number of men of many nationalities who had compulsorily spent several years of their twenties or thirties living abroad, often on another continent. Post-war flying grew out of both kinds of change, the technical and professional and the social and economic.

Before the war very few people inside or outside the airlines had the slightest notion of what passenger flying was going to be like once life returned to 'normal' again, whatever 'normal' might mean. The general view, naturally enough, was that everything would be the same as before, but, with reasonable luck, better. Going by air would become increasingly common and more gracious. How unreal this forecast eventually became can be seen by studying an article[1] written towards the end of 1939 by Mr Howard Ketcham, the President of Howard Ketcham, Inc., a well-known American company specialising in interior design. Mr Ketcham had been responsible for the interiors of a number of large airliners, including the Fords Tri-motor and, at the time the article was published, he was working on designs for United Airlines' new DC-4s. These aimed at 'commodious luxury', and his

[1] Published in *Aero Digest*, October 1939.

111

'How the rich fly', as seen by *Punch* in 1939.

sketches make a modern reader gasp. The lounges he envisaged – the war put a stop to their realisation – were as spacious as those of a West End club, with no sign of seating in rows or crowding of any kind. They were based on the belief that the passenger should be made at least as comfortable as in a large car or in a Pullman train. 'Pullman travel', Mr Ketcham pointed out' 'currently attracts about twenty times that of air traffic,' and he went on to say that passengers would only be won over from the railways by being provided with conditions better than those to be found in a Pullman car. The objective was 'gracious cabins', with armchairs facing port-holes, exactly as on a ship. 'Chairs by the window are located so that the passenger is constantly presented with the spectacle of a fleeting terrain below without having to crane his neck.'

In pre-war days stewards gave the kind of service one expected and received on first-class liners, deferential porters were always available to carry one's luggage, everything was orderly and unhurried and flying, usually, was a pleasure. Talking to people who remember the days before the old order collapsed is like meeting beings from another century or even another planet. Consider, for example, Mrs Leonie Smith:[2] her first scheduled flight was in 1936, from Croydon to Budapest, on her honeymoon. She had flown a good

[2] Her flying reminiscences emerged during a conversation with Kenneth Hudson on 9 June 1970.

deal previously on joy-flights from Lympne and enjoyed the experience. Between 1936 and 1939 she travelled a great deal by air between London, Paris and Le Touquet. Among the features of flying in pre-war days which remained firmly implanted in her memory were the fact that the plane was never full; that there was little conversation between passengers, because of the engine noise – 'If you wanted to talk, you had to make an all-out effort'; that the passengers were 'upper class'; that the staff were extremely attentive and helpful – 'They held your hand as you walked down the steps from the aeroplane.'

She never went in an aeroplane again after the war, although she could well afford to do so. 'Having flown in comfort, with VIP treatment for every passenger, I couldn't bear to be herded like cattle.' She was frightened, too, of claustrophobia under post-war conditions, with large numbers of passengers crowded into the aircraft.

Mrs Smith had known better things, which is always an uncomfortable situation in which to be, and, in a sense, she was the kind of passenger the post-war airlines preferred to forget, the spectre at the feast. But, fortunately for Imperial Airways, KLM, Air France and the rest, the new age did not follow immediately on the old. There was a convenient buffer period of a major and long-drawn-out war between the two. During this period, the Americans consolidated their advantages.

The outbreak of the Second World War severely cut into Pan American's activities over the North Atlantic, which had begun so promisingly a few months earlier, but further expansion was possible elsewhere. In 1940, a Boeing 314 opened the South Pacific service to New Zealand and in 1941 the Central Pacific route was extended to Singapore. An African service to Leopoldville, via Bathurst and Lagos, was opened on 6 December 1941, the day before the Japanese attacked Pearl Harbor. This service, which started at Miami, was set up very rapidly, and formed the basis of an elaborate system of ferry services providing men, materials and aircraft for the Allied forces in North Africa.

There were also developments in South America, where Pan American had been establishing itself steadily since the late 1920s. A new airport was built at Barreiras in Brazil, and in September 1940 Pan American opened a Boeing 307 service to Belem, connecting with a DC-3 for Rio de Janeiro which arrived on the coastal route via Belize. The Boeing 307 Stratoliner was the world's first pressurised airliner. Although only a few of them were built – Boeing had to transfer its attentions to the production of bomber aircraft during the war – the 307s had remarkable stamina and a number of them were still flying thirty years later in various parts of the world.

Pan American and its associate company, PANAGRA, exercised considerable and successful pressure to eliminate German influence in Latin America. In 1941 PANAGRA services replaced those run by the German-supported airlines in Ecuador, Peru and Bolivia. German crews and maintenance staff

The Boeing 314A. Three of these very reliable flying-boats were bought by the British Government in 1941 and operated on a Foynes–Lagos–Baltimore route until 1945. After the war they were transferred to the Baltimore–Bermuda run. In their six and a half years of service, they crossed the Atlantic 596 times and carried 42,000 passengers without accident or injury.

were removed from the Colombian airline, SCADTA, and the Condor airline in Brazil, centre of all German operations in South America, lost both its staff and its identity. Later, between 1943 and 1945, Pan American bought substantial holdings in the national airlines of nearly every country around the Caribbean.

During the war years a large part of the Pan American fleet, including all its B.314s, worked for the United States government. They were on regular runs to Egypt and China, to Africa and Brazil, from where they brought back rubber and scarce materials. Many of TWA's larger aircraft were similarly engaged. Its Stratoliners made nearly 10,000 Atlantic crossings, carrying war material, diplomats, troops and sick and wounded soldiers.

One could, perhaps, summarise the wartime experiences of the American airlines by saying that those flying overseas, TWA and Pan American, spent a fairly prosperous five years, under difficult and often dangerous conditions, while the airlines responsible for its internal services carried on much as usual, despite recurring problems over fuel, aircraft and spares. For the United States, it should be remembered, the war did not really begin until December 1941. A reminder of the normality of life in America up to that time is provided by the opening of the world's first purpose-built town terminal in January 1941. Stone-faced and opposite Grand Central Station, New York City, it is still there, a significant item of airline archaeology, although no longer used for its original purpose. It provided five major American airlines with elegant and spacious quarters for downtown passenger reservations and ticket sales.

The European airlines were not so fortunate. What happened to KLM was typical. In the autumn of 1939, on the outbreak of war, all the European

114

services, except those to Belgium, England and Scandinavia, were suspended and the starting point of the Amsterdam–Batavia service was transferred to Naples. In April 1940 the Belgian and Scandinavian links went, and in May all services from the Netherlands came to an end. Eighteen aircraft were destroyed by bombing at Schiphol, where the terminal buildings were wrecked, and eleven aircraft were taken over by the Germans. Fourteen other planes of the KLM fleet remained under KLM control, however, being either in Britain or on the Naples–Batavia route at the time of the German attack and occupation.

The KLM management, despite the appalling difficulties with which it was faced, never gave up. In June 1940 the Batavia service had to leave from Tel Aviv instead of Naples and in February 1942 it was closed altogether. The Amsterdam–Lisbon service became Bristol–Lisbon, KLM undertaking the route on charter for the recently formed BOAC. In October 1942 this service was extended to Gibraltar, and in 1944 it got new DC-3C (Dakota) aircraft, which could carry up to twenty-eight passengers. The KLM management was transferred, first, in May 1940, to Batavia and then in September 1942, after the Japanese advance, to London, where it remained until the end of the war.

KLM was able during the war years to develop services in the West Indies, based on its colonial territories there. The Curaçao–Kingston route was inaugurated in August 1941, and Curaçao–Miami in August 1943. There were other services to Havana, Santo Domingo, St Martin and Port-au-Prince. In 1945 KLM's network in Central and South America covered fourteen cities in nine countries, with a total route-distance of 5761 miles.

Air France was annihilated as a civil airline during the war. In 1939 it operated the third largest network of routes in the world, being surpassed only by the United States and the Soviet Union. Parts of its overseas organisation had survived, however, at Algiers, Tunis, Dakar, Beirut and London, and these were integrated to form the Network of Military Airlines (Réseau des Lignes Aériennes Militaires), which carried out for the Free French territories and organisations much the same duties as the Air Transport Commands did for the Allies.

Imperial Airways was a war casualty. Its demise and replacement in 1940 by the British Overseas Airways Corporation – a merger of Imperial Airways and British Airways – formed part of the package-transformation of British-run airlines. Extensive flying operations were carried out throughout the war by BOAC planes, but they bore little resemblance to the Imperial Airways pattern which had existed in 1939. The former trunk routes from Britain to the Far East, Australia and South Africa were cut, and in their place came an important Britain–Cairo link, flights to the Soviet Union, and a complex system of North Atlantic and African services.

After Italy's entry into the war had closed the Mediterranean, the newly formed BOAC moved its Western base to Durban. From there, what became known as the Horseshoe Route was operated through East Africa, India and

A wartime boat crew mans the launch servicing a BOAC Boeing 314 flying-boat in Poole Harbour.

Malaya to Australia. Seventeen S.23 Empire Flying-boats were used on the route, with their luxurious peace-time fittings and furnishings removed and the very utilitarian seating increased to twenty-nine. The Japanese occupation of Malaya ended the Horseshoe Route and the eleven BOAC planes marooned at its eastern end joined the by now much depleted Qantas fleet. Ten of the eleven aircraft were subsequently lost in crashes or by enemy action and the sole survivor, 'Coriolanus', was the first transport plane to fly into Singapore after its liberation.

Thirteen of the S.23, S.30 and S.33 Empire Flying-boats survived the war, but they were all broken up soon afterwards, not one being preserved as a museum exhibit – a singularly disgraceful state of affairs.

In 1942 a number of Sunderland flying-boats were allocated to BOAC for the carriage of mail and priority passengers. To begin with they had a very austere type of bench seating, but this was later improved. After the war, the Sunderlands were refurbished and put on the newly opened Empire routes, as the Hythe class. When BOAC replaced them the Hythes did not follow the Empire Flying-boats to the breaker's yard. They were bought by Aquila Airways, which used them on regular services to Madeira and in the Mediterranean. These services lasted until 1958, after which no flying-boats were operated out of Britain.

116

The indefatigable W. H. Pilkington made three wartime business trips to Canada and the United States in 1940–2 by air, or partly by air, and just as he had done several years earlier on his way to and from Australia, he kept a diary of his experiences. On one trip, even with a fair amount of influence in high places, it took him a month to get a passage to Lisbon. Twelve hours before he was due to leave England, the service was suddenly suspended for an indefinite period and Mr Pilkington was asked to be ready to leave at twenty-four hours' notice whenever it happened to be resumed. Three weeks later, he was given an hour's notice to go home and pack and catch the train to Bristol, from where he was to take the KLM flight to Lisbon.

It was then the end of October and the weather in Bristol was clear and frosty. They left their Bristol hotel at 6 am, after an early breakfast, and proceeded to the airport at Whitchurch, on the outskirts of Bristol.

There were five passengers and three of the crew, and it took two hours for the eight of us to be taken carefully through all the important formalities of Customs, immigration, censorship, currency permits, and so on. The Immigration Authorities nowadays require to be satisfied of your bona-fides and of your reasons for travelling before they will let you out of the country – particularly in the direction of Lisbon, the last link with Europe. The Censorship Authorities are even more particular; travellers are expected to get their papers and printed matter examined and sealed up several days before leaving, but the examination of the few that had accumulated since my first disappointment took quite a long time to scrutinise, and questions were asked about several of them. As for money, a permit is required to take out more than £10, and I had been able to obtain a permit for £25, which was all liable to be needed if I were held up anywhere on the way. During all this two hours we were kept in a cold little room about ten feet square, with a military guard, but eventually everything was ready, and we went aboard. [3]

They took off in due course, but after forty minutes they were back again at Bristol. The weather off Portugal was so bad that there would have been no chance at all of landing at Lisbon. So, for seven successive days Mr Pilkington and his companions left their hotel at 6 am and went through exactly the same lengthy formalities at Whitchurch. At the eighth attempt, the pilot made the journey to Lisbon.

The original passengers included, in addition to Mr Pilkington, the Swiss diplomatic courier, who made or tried to make the trip once a week in order to take letters destined for prisoners of war in Germany; another Swiss, the London manager of a Greek bank, who was going home for a long holiday; the Press Attaché at the British Embassy in Lisbon; two Poles, one of them a diplomatic courier; the Greek Naval Attaché in Lisbon; and a young man with good connections from a Middle Eastern country who had been engaged on some kind of naval work in Britain. When the plane ultimately got away, three more passengers had been added, two members of the staff of the

---

[3] 'A Wartime Journey', *Cullet* (the house journal of Pilkington Ltd), autumn 1942.

Winston Churchill at the controls during a wartime crossing.

American Embassy in London and Mr de Geer, the Dutch Prime Minister at the time of the invasion of Holland. It was a not untypical wartime passenger list.

In Lisbon, there was great difficulty in finding a hotel room – 'there are tens of thousands of refugees from all parts of Europe, mostly waiting to get to America' – and trying to get a seat on one of the American Clippers to New York was even worse. After days of waiting, Mr Pilkington gave up the attempt and went to America, very uncomfortably, by boat.

On the way back, he got as far as Bermuda in a Pan American flying-boat, one of his fellow passengers being H. G. Wells. From there to Lisbon it was, once again, a boat or nothing.

On one of his other transatlantic trips, Mr Pilkington travelled from New York to Scotland via Newfoundland in a Liberator bomber. The passengers sat on bags of folded parachutes while the plane took off and after that they were free to walk about. The oxygen masks had been put out.

These masks were really rubber nosebags, with head straps similar to those of a civilian respirator; they are also fitted with a long rubber supply tube. There were

118

several oxygen cylinders strapped together in one corner of the well and from these lengths of metal tubing led to a number of wall points, probably three dozen in all, in different parts of the plane. Each point consisted of a gauge, a valve and a nozzle. The gauge was graduated in thousands of feet of altitude; the valve could be turned to increase the flow of oxygen through the gauge to agree with the altitude value given out by the captain. The maximum altitude shown on the gauge was 30,000 feet. In the United States Air Force it is customary for oxygen to be taken when the altitude exceeds 15,000 feet. The long rubber lead would permit considerable freedom of movement and presumably one could detach the lead from one point, attach it to the next vacant one and so move about the plane.[4]

They had supper.

Packets of sandwiches and seven large thermos flasks had been put on board at the flying field in Newfoundland. The mechanic came for three of the flasks and some of the sandwiches and carried them forward. The wireless operator had his supper upstairs in his cabin. The three passengers sat on the ledges. The two Dutchmen had brought emergency rations with them; M. carried their sandwiches. We had plenty of food. I poured out the coffee for the three of us, standing the cups on one of the wide ledges. I am quite sure that I did not spill a drop and I know that I filled the cups more than I would in a railway dining car. That is a testimony to the smoothness of the flight.

The passengers slept wherever they could find a vacant space, some in the bomb compartment, some in the tail. Pilkington was lucky enough to discover 'an upholstered ledge'. This was not flying as Imperial Airways and its pre-war passengers had understood it, but it allowed the distance to be covered quickly and probably with less danger than by sea.

Immigration procedure during the war years was difficult and tedious. Everyone entering Britain or any other country was automatically a suspicious character. What it involved has been well described by one of the British Immigration Officers[5] who dealt with sea-plane passengers after their arrival on the south coast. The control point was at Poole.

This was at first in the billiard room of the Antelope Hotel in the High Street, after being moved from Sandbanks, and the wooden staircase creaked to an incredible assortment of VIPs, escapers, suspects and 'government officials'. In mid-1942 the staff moved into better quarters in the Poole Pottery, where there were four cubicles suited to Immigration examination and a main showroom which served as the Customs Hall.

As may be imagined, the examination of these flying-boat loads was an extremely protracted business. Not for them the 45-second interview which the modern foreign businessman arriving at London Airport has come to expect. The Immigration Officers might take six hours to clear a flight.

In the autumn of 1942 the flying-boat services were temporarily transferred to Hythe, on Southampton Water. This was to give the Navy free use of Poole Harbour to launch a diversionary attack on the Normandy coast, should

[4] *Cullet*, October 1941.
[5] T. W. E. Roche, *The Key in the Lock*, 1969.

A Liberator bomber loads up during a snow blizzard at Dorval, Quebec, for the long crossing back to Britain.

anything have gone wrong with the landings in North Africa. At the Hythe base there was no building suitable for immigration control, so the Immigration and Customs staff installed themselves in a hotel half a mile away. There, the immigration part of the business was conducted in the greenhouse.

On the other side of the military and political fence, the German airline, Lufthansa, had a curiously mixed war, disastrous in some ways and remarkably normal in others. The years immediately preceding the war had contained some enterprising developments. Throughout the 1930s, Lufthansa had taken an active part in the development of aviation in China, by means of a joint Chinese–German concern, the Eurasia Aviation Corporation. Eurasia used Junkers planes and there were flights between Berlin and China via Siberia, Afghanistan, where Lufthansa installed a meteorological station in 1936 and, on the southern route, Bangkok, Hanoi and Canton. In August 1939, the last trial flight for a passenger service between Berlin and Tokyo was successfully completed, but the outbreak of war in the following month prevented the service from coming into operation. With the ending of the Eurasia arrangement in 1940, all German flights to the Near and Far East came to a halt, and Lufthansa had to wait twenty years before it was able to start them again. All the pioneering work, so carefully carried out for many years, was thrown away.

In Europe, the situation was quite different. The Lufthansa timetable for 1 November 1939, 'and until further notice', contained details of services to Denmark, Sweden, Italy, Austria, Greece, Turkey, Yugoslavia, Romania, Hungary and Bulgaria, with Berlin as the central point. By the following year, the routes to Portugal, Spain, Czechoslovakia, Norway and Finland were in operation again, with German control over most of Western Europe fully established, and matters stayed that way until the end of 1944.

Even in March 1945, with most German cities in ruins and military collapse only a very short way off, Lufthansa continued to run regular international services. They were, it is true, only a shadow of what they had been even six months earlier, but they existed. At this eleventh hour it was still possible to fly on scheduled services from Berlin to Norway, Sweden, Denmark, Italy, Austria, Czechoslovakia, Spain and Portugal.

With the end of hostilities against Germany and Japan, the reinstatement of air services was remarkably rapid. The story of the late 1940s is largely that of the introduction of new types of aircraft, badly needed to replace the ageing planes which had somehow kept services going during the war years and which no longer corresponded to modern requirements. It is natural to begin with the Atlantic crossings, since the biggest commercial prizes were on this route and the greatest efforts of both the airlines and the manufacturers had for some years been devoted to finding aircraft suitable for it.

American Export Airlines, an offshoot of the shipping company, American Export Lines, inaugurated the first non-stop service between New York and Foynes, Ireland, in 1942, using Vought-Sikorsky VS-44 flying-boats. American Airlines bought American Export Airlines in 1945, changing the name to American Overseas Airlines. The VS-44s were taken off this service in October 1945 and were replaced by a civil conversion of the Douglas C-54 Skymaster, later known as the DC-4. Unpressurised, this aeroplane marked the end of the flying-boat as a major item of airline equipment, although some companies, notably BOAC, continued with them for a number of years longer, mainly, one suspects, out of sentiment.

The pioneering four-engined pressurised commercial aircraft, the first plane capable of flying in calm air above the weather, was the Boeing 307 Stratoliner, introduced in 1940, but the first pressurised transatlantic airliner was the Lockheed L.049 Constellation, first operated by Pan American in January 1946. It carried forty-five passengers, at new standards of speed and comfort, and was the supreme long-distance aircraft for many years. In its developed form, the 1649A Jetstream, it had a range of nearly 5000 miles, and carried sixty-four passengers very pleasantly. Its main competitor, the Boeing 377 Stratocruiser, a development of the military C-29 Superfortress, entered service in 1948. It was faster, cruising at 340 mph, and had a bigger range than the Constellation, but it was considerably more expensive to run, a disadvantage which soon led to it being restricted to routes where revenue could be kept up by having a high proportion of first-class seats. It was very popular with passengers, however, probably because it had, alone among contemporary aircraft, a downstairs lounge bar, holding fourteen passengers. The main passenger cabin could take between fifty-five and a hundred passengers, depending on the seating density and arrangement. When it was

A United Airlines Boeing
Stratocruiser over the
Golden Gate Bridge.

fitted as a sleeper aircraft the 377 contained twenty-eight berths, in two tiers, and five seats. There were complete dressing-rooms for both men and women.

Fifty-five Stratocruisers were built and Pan American bought twenty of them. The other major operators were BOAC and American Overseas Airlines. The price of each aeroplane was a million and a half dollars, making the Stratocruiser much the most expensive commercial aircraft built up to that time. As a comparison, one might mention that the Short Empire Flying-boats cost only £61,000 apiece, or about $240,000 at the pre-war rate of exchange. The previous generation of airliners had been considerably cheaper even than this. The selling price of the de Havilland Hercules, which entered service in 1925, was £25,000. The later but smaller Boeing 247, available in 1933, cost only £10,000, considerably less than half the price of a Rolls-Royce motor car today. One could put this another way, by saying that to provide each of the twenty-four seats in the Empire Flying-boats cost about $10,000, while in the Stratocruiser, at a medium density of seventy seats, the figure was a little over twice that, but for a much faster aircraft with double the range. Equally important, the direct operating cost per seat-mile of the Empire Flying-boat carrying twenty-four passengers was nearly twice that of the twenty-one passenger DC-3. Flying-boats, too, have much higher overheads. Once adequate aerodromes were available, the flying-boat was doomed.

In the immediate post-war years, however, airlines had to make do with whatever aircraft they could get, and in some cases the only solution, as in the period after the First World War, was to buy and adapt ex-military planes. The Liberator bomber was used in this way. Even during the war, converted Liberators were operated by BOAC on its service from Hurn to Montreal, ferrying returning aircrew, together with mail and government officials, back to Canada. They were also used for direct flights from England to Egypt, Lisbon and West Africa. After the war and the end of the Atlantic Ferry, some of the Liberators went to Qantas for the Perth–Ceylon route and later for the Sydney–Karachi section of the Australia–England route. Others went to Scottish Aviation, Hellenic Airlines and to the Icelandic company, Flugfelag Islands.

The Avro Lancastrian, a conversion of the Lancaster bomber, was also used as a post-war stop-gap. The structural conversion involved little more than fitting nose and tail cones instead of the gun turrets. They cruised at 230 mph and had a range of 4150 miles. Operated by BOAC and Qantas, they came into service in 1945 and achieved a three-day schedule between London and Sydney, and in 1946 they opened British South American Airways' service to Buenos Aires and then on to Santiago and Lima. The Lancastrian was expensive to run. Only nine passengers were carried on the Australian

The lower deck cocktail lounge on a BOAC Stratocruiser.

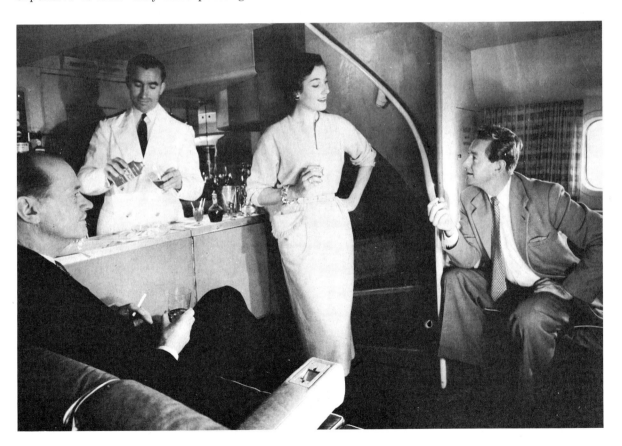

service and thirteen to South America, but at that time the prestige value of the remarkable timetable was felt to make the huge losses – £1,400,000 a year to Sydney – worthwhile.

The Avro York, which entered service as a military transport in 1942, went into quantity production in 1945. In this version twelve passengers were carried in a rear cabin, with freight in a forward compartment. Twelve Yorks were bought by British South American Airways and thirteen were fitted as twelve-berth sleepers for the England–Johannesburg service. The remaining Yorks, used by BOAC, were eighteen-seaters.

The post-war aircraft, even when they were converted bombers, completely changed passenger flying. They were much faster than anything in commercial service before 1939, they could travel twice as far without needing to refuel, and the new American types could carry a great many more passengers. They were also several times heavier than the landplanes of the 1930s, which meant that they needed longer distances to land and take off and that a hard runway was essential. The days of grass runways at major airports were finally over.

This was the second major effect on aviation of the war, the first being a general increase in airmindedness. Between 1939 and 1945 airfields had been built all over the world to entirely new standards. Grass runways were impossible for the heavy military aircraft used by both sides in the conflict. Concrete or asphalt became the normal surface for the runways of military airfields and post-war civilian airports adopted this method of construction as a matter of course.

The process of finding and developing airport sites which were suitable for the new generation of aircraft cost a great deal of money and in many cases an adequate area of reasonably level ground was to be found only by going a long way from the centre of a city. The bigger the aircraft, the further one usually had to go. Airports as much as fifteen and twenty miles from the town terminal were almost unknown to passengers of the 1920s and 1930s; they are increasingly normal today, when huge areas of land – 2000 acres and more – are required.[6]

The fact that progress in the air is rarely an unqualified blessing was realised very soon after the Second World War. An article in 1947 declared:

The increase in passenger comfort in the modern airliner has not kept pace with the increase in cruising speed, as anyone with memories of pre-war travel on, for example, the London–Paris run, will testify.

Passengers' convenience in terms of time spent between the airports and the terminals and in completing the various formalities has deteriorated. From the passengers' point of view, there is not much gain in reducing time spent in the air by an increase in cruising speed if the overall time for a journey is not also reduced.[7]

[6] Heathrow covers 2819 acres. Its perimeter road is 9.3 miles long. This is small by modern standards. Schiphol has 4200 acres.
[7] *Shell Aviation News*, July 1947.

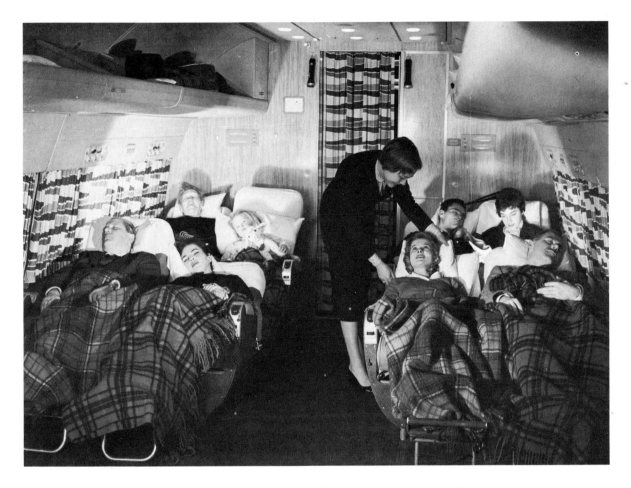

This has been the air passenger's complaint for the past thirty years and it is getting louder all the time. The people with the biggest grievance are those making short-haul flights, where the city-to-city time is what matters. What, they reasonably ask, is the point of shortening the actual flying part of the journey from, say, Paris to London, to forty or forty-five minutes, if it then takes an hour or more to get to the airport at either end, half an hour at the gate or waiting for the aircraft to take off, and a further three-quarters of an hour until one's baggage arrives? These irritations will be looked at more closely in later chapters. They are mentioned here only to show that they have their beginnings a long way back.

The history of the present London Airport illustrates the post-war problem of space very well. The pre-war terminal at Croydon, ten miles from central London, was surrounded by houses and too small for post-war aircraft to use. With its undulating grass field, it was inadequate as a major airport even before the war and by 1939 it had been long outclassed by other European airports. Gatwick, opened in 1936, was altogether more interesting. With its circular terminal building and telescopic covered ways leading to the aircraft, it was full of ideas for the future in a way that Croydon never was.

Interior of a Lockheed 1049G Super Constellation, 'Queen of the Air'. At this time the Atlantic flight lasted 17–20 hours, depending on intermediate stops, and to make passengers more comfortable during the night hours, the seats were designed for easy conversion to couches.

125

The infant Heathrow. Passenger reception tents and communications facilities in 1946.

At the end of the war, the main passenger terminal for overseas flights was at Hurn, near Bournemouth. It had very good runways, left behind by the RAF, but it was far from easy to get to. The American airlines in particular were tired of having to put their passengers down a hundred miles from London and then, after immigration formalities had been completed, a mile away from the airfield, being compelled to take a consignment of tired people to Bournemouth.

So the Government agreed that, from 31 May 1946, the terminal should be moved to Heathrow, a former RAF airfield, fourteen miles from Charing Cross. In the early days there were runways there, built for the RAF, but no terminal buildings. Everything, offices, passenger lounges, Customs inspection, immigration, had to take place in marquees and caravans. To begin with Heathrow was strictly for the long-haul flights of BOAC, British South American Airways and the American airlines. The recently created British short-haul company, British European Airways, was based first at Croydon and then at Northolt, eight miles from Heathrow, which also dealt with other countries' international flights. Soon after the opening of Heathrow, however, Air France transferred there from Northolt, followed almost immediately by KLM. In 1954 Northolt was closed to civil airlines and all the services of BEA and of the foreign airlines using Northolt were switched to Heathrow. The confusion from 1946 onwards has been remarkable. In 1946, June to December, there were 2046 aircraft movements and 63,151 passengers; in 1950, for a whole year, the totals were 37,746 and 523,357 respectively, and throughout this period there were no permanent airport

126

buildings. 23,000,000 passengers passed through Heathrow in 1976, and throughout the thirty-two years of the airport's life building work for extensions and modifications has never stopped. Things have always been in a muddle, and always changing, never finished, the principal cause of such a state of affairs being that, at Heathrow as at many other places, traffic has grown faster than the facilities to deal with it. It is and always has been an exhausting place and the fact that it is fourteen miles on busy roads from London does not make the traffic any less.

There are very few major airports in the world which still occupy the same site as they did in the 1930s. The most notable exception is the Amsterdam airport at Schiphol. A former military airfield, it was transferred to the municipality of Amsterdam in 1926 and converted into a civilian airport. During the following ten years it was continuously enlarged and improved. There was plenty of land for expansion, and the Annual Report of 1938 said:

As far as the dimensions are concerned, Schiphol has now joined the front rank of the airports, not only in Europe, but also on other continents, as a result of the extensions to the airfield, and with the runway system and apron now completed, the airport now has a gravel area of a perfection that cannot be found at any other European airport at this time.

Check-in and bar at Heathrow, 1946.

127

Diamonds in The Sky

Schiphol was totally wrecked by the Germans at the end of the war, after the Allied landings at Arnhem. Every building was systematically destroyed and the runways made unserviceable, but within three months after the liberation, temporary buildings had been erected and services started again.

The late 1940s, however, were not merely a period during which the pre-war airlines picked up the threads and began again. Countries which had never previously had an airline established one now, and others which had formerly operated only a domestic service decided that the time had come to think internationally.

The most spectacular new development was that of El Al. Founded in 1948, immediately after the end of the British mandate over Palestine and the establishment of the independent state of Israel, its main task for some time was not to function as a commercial enterprise but to bring in immigrants during the years when Israel was blockaded from all sides. To begin with it used army surplus planes, converted in a rough and ready fashion to take passengers. The majority of these were DC-4s and C-46s. To avoid Arab attacks, they were frequently and repeatedly overpainted with the livery and names of other airlines. In the early years, El Al veterans recall, the airline spent more on paint than on any other item. The planes bringing immigrants to Israel, especially from the Yemen, were usually seriously overloaded.

He faced a problem. The plane would normally carry about fifty passengers. 'Shove them in,' he decided. Thin as they were, five people could sit in seats meant for four. The unorthodox arrangement was euphemistically nicknamed 'special immigrant high-density seating'. The plane left the field with about 150 people packed in the aircraft. The flight was murderous. The Yemenites were strapped in to prevent them from falling off their benches with every movement of the plane.

The Yemenites were grand passengers, the best ever, according to Lewis. They were quiet and did not complain. But they were afraid. Most did not know what an automobile was, let alone a plane. If many had not been convinced that this was the answer to the biblical prophecy, they would never have entered the cavernous monster. During the flight, people prayed, were sick, sometimes relieved themselves where they sat. Hardier souls ate meals of dates and sunflower seeds, strewing these in mounds in the crowded cabin.[8]

By 1950 El Al had negotiated landing rights in London, Paris, Rome and Zürich and it was in the international airline business. It had also, in 1950, formed a separate company, Arkia – Israel Inland Airlines – to look after domestic flights. The main purpose of Arkia was to build up Eilat, Israel's southern port. The airline provided an essential link to this otherwise inaccessible place. It flew expectant mothers and other hospital patients north and immigrants, businessmen, and sometimes water, south. In the course of time, Eilat became mainly a holiday and tourist resort, but this was a development of the 1960s.

---

[8] Arnold Sherman, *To the Skies: the El Al Story*, 1972, p. 34.

Interior of a DC–3,
showing early post-war
austerity conversion.

When it set up El Al, Israel was a country with extremely slender resources. In the financial sense, it could not afford an airline at all, but it could
equally not afford not to have one. The money somehow had to be found, and
the flying crews and maintenance staff recruited and trained. The problems
were entirely different from those facing rich industrialised countries, such
as the Netherlands, France or Britain, which had merely to extricate themselves from the mess left behind by the war, or other fortunate countries – the
United States, South Africa and Sweden[9] are good examples – on which the
war had made little or no material impact. El Al, like all other Israeli
expenditure, had to be paid for out of the pockets of poor people and by what
amounted to foreign charity. But its prestige and propaganda value, for a new
state, was very high. El Al was Israel abroad, and it was the first of many
other airlines established during the 1950s and 1960s by the developing
countries, who saw an airline as a great opportunity to wave the flag at
foreigners. The expense was a secondary consideration.

In a sense, these former colonial territories were doing only what their
former masters, the French, the British or the Dutch, had already done. A
proof of independence, of a country's right to be considered grown up and out
of tutelage, was the ability to run one's own airline. The landing of Air-India
International's Constellation at Heathrow on 9 June 1948, to inaugurate its
Bombay–London service, was much more than a mere commercial flight. It
was a symbol of the fact that the new Indian state had, in more senses than
one, arrived.

The most significant aviation event of the 1940s, however, was almost
certainly the flight, in 1946, of the first jet-propelled aircraft in the world. The
aircraft, a flying test-bed, was one of the invaluable Lancastrians. It flew
perfectly satisfactorily and nothing in the airline world was ever quite the
same again.

[9] During the years immediately following the war, Sweden, Norway and Denmark
continued to run their own separate national airlines. They were amalgamated to form the
present SAS in 1948.

SIX

Low Fares or Luxury

In January 1950, IATA held its Annual General Meeting in Brussels. It was an important meeting, with the financial problems of the member airlines well to the front of the discussions. In some ways it was curious that this should have been so because, from the available statistics, it would have appeared to an outside observer that the airlines were doing rather well. During 1949 American Airlines became the first company in the world to carry more than three million passengers in one year. Its total of 3,263,760 passengers represented an increase of 15.9 per cent over 1948. BOAC's passengers went up from 119,000 to 150,000, a jump of twenty per cent, and BEA's from 565,000 to 708,000. All in all, IATA's Director-General Sir William Hildred told the meeting, the world's scheduled airlines had carried more than twenty-five million people. Yet they were losing money, in some cases because of bad management but more often because the public – a very different public from that of 1939 – considered fares too high. 'As soon as the world's air lines begin to tap the mass-travel market,' said Sir William, 'their economic problem will disappear.' What this really meant was that the airlines were geared only to providing first-class travel, on the basis of which their business had been built up in the 1920s and 1930s, and had never come to grips with the problems of giving ordinary people in aeroplanes what ordinary people have always had in trains and boats, second- and third-class travel.

In 1950 passengers travelling by air in Europe had to pay a little over 3.5p a mile on international routes and slightly more than this on domestic routes. This was rather above what the railways charged its first-class passengers. The argument used by the airlines was that the small difference in fare involved in going by train or going by air was more than outweighed by the saving on meals, tips and other incidental expenses which surface transport involved. This, however, was to miss the point, which was that, in order to fill their seats and prosper, the airlines had to make a successful appeal to second-class railway passengers, not merely to the relatively small number of first-class. And that would mean bringing air fares down by twenty or thirty per cent, to about 2.75p a mile, which the companies concerned said would lead to bankruptcy.

The truth was that the international air transport industry was being run on a quite unnecessarily lavish scale. With State funds always available to meet the annual deficit there was no incentive to be economical, no reason to adopt measures which would make the business pay. E. P. Johnson wrote in 1950:

No other transport medium has required the best possible West End sites for its booking offices, or the latest ideas in shop fittings to attract custom, yet the string of luxurious premises rented by the air lines in London is duplicated all over the world from Rio de Janeiro to New York, from Rome to Rangoon. The cost of all this is incorporated into the fares that passengers pay, although there must be few who would not rather be charged a few pounds less for their passages even although it meant buying their tickets in less accessible and impressive surroundings.[1]

Another contribution to the same journal put the matter more colourfully. 'The sooner air transport grows out of the salmon and champagne era and gets down to kipper and tea traffic,' the author believed, 'the sooner it will be able to justify its existence.'[2] He went on to explain what he meant by 'kipper and tea traffic'. The essence of such a policy was 'packing as many paying customers as decently possible into one's aeroplane', bearing in mind that 'it is perfectly possible to be decent without providing powder-rooms, cocktail bars, promenade decks and all the rest for the benefit of those relatively few passengers, usually travelling on expense accounts anyway, who can afford to pay the extra fare that these luxuries inevitably cost.'

There was reliable evidence, based on the cut-price group travel that had already been possible within the IATA regulations, that people were prepared to do without 'luxury', if they got a cheaper fare as a result. In any case, no airliner could provide comfort equal to that of a transatlantic liner and any attempt to do so was economically futile. The aim of air transport consequently had to be to get the passenger to his destination quickly and safely. 'The quicker the journey, the less luxury he requires to keep him quiet' should be the industry's motto, in E. P. Johnson's opinion. Johnson made a number of other far-seeing observations which, had the European airlines followed his advice, would have enabled them to make a profit, instead of worrying that each year's operations were going to show a bigger loss.

First, he said, saving time was nothing like as important for most people as the salesmen seemed to believe. 'Pounds, shillings and pence are a weightier consideration than hours, minutes or seconds, and to many people time is *not* money, or at least not enough money to enough people to keep all the world's airline aeroplanes steadily flying at a really economic utilisation level.'

Second, it had to be realised that a large number of people were frightened of flying, 'and until air travel ceases to be considered even mildly

[1] *The Aeroplane*, 6 January 1950.
[2] *The Aeroplane*, 9 December 1949.

The 'first-class mentality' that caused financial problems to the airlines in the early 1950s.

hazardous by most people, only the economic consideration of money-saving through cheaper fares will serve at least to some extent to neutralise this fear factor which deprives the air companies of so many potential customers at present.'

Third, airline managements had to rid themselves and their staff of the 'first-class mentality' which prevented them from running an efficient, profitable transport system. 'Two-class air travel is obviously long overdue for general introduction. The minority who are prepared to pay extra for such additional comfort as can be built into an aeroplane must be catered for; the majority who just want to travel cheaply are the natural market for the airlines, who will not begin to justify their existence until this majority is offered what it requires.' There were problems about two-class travel on aeroplanes, the chief of which was to find a way of stopping the two classes from mixing. This, however, was largely a matter of the size of the aircraft and would disappear as a problem when aircraft became bigger.

Johnson urged the European operators to take a close look at what was happening elsewhere. One South American company, using Catalina flying-boats, charged only seventy per cent of its competitors' fares, but nevertheless made a respectable profit. The Catalinas were old and slow, which is why

132

they were permitted to offer lower fares, but, because they were cheap, they were always full. The directors and principal shareholders occupied active positions on the staff, both on the flying and the commercial sides, the pilots helped to load and unload cargo and baggage, the offices were not in the most fashionable parts of town and many of the maintenance staff also travelled the routes as flight engineers. As a result of this very practical type of organisation, thousands of people were able to fly who would otherwise never have been able to fly at all.

The European airlines were sensitive to this kind of criticism, and especially to comparisons between Europe and America. Proposals like those made by Johnson could be dismissed as mere theory, but what could not be denied was that American aircraft were much more fully used than European, fifty per cent more, and that their fares were considerably lower. America had made it possible for the masses to take advantage of air transport; Europe was trying to reconcile high fares and low income levels, an impossible task.

Some of Johnson's suggestions – and they were by no means peculiar to him – have since become a reality. Two-class air travel is now more or less normal, at least on the long-distance routes; on some transatlantic services, especially those run by Laker Airways, people now pay only for the services they actually want; and airlines have, very belatedly, accepted the idea that cheap fares fill seats. But in one respect there has been no advance at all. In every major city, the offices and sales centres of the international airlines are still to be found in the most fashionable and expensive areas and they are still very lavishly designed and furnished. No airline dares to be the first to house itself less elaborately and to present a simpler face to the world. To do so, it is feared, would inevitably lead to a drop in the airline's prestige, and therefore sales. So the snobbish charade continues. The 'first-class mentality' is still very much in evidence.

Not all critics of the aviation industry and the airlines agreed with E. P. Johnson, however, that, provided the emphasis was on speed, safety and low fares, all would be well. In 1950 Robert L. Turner, General Traffic Manager of Eastern Air Lines, read a paper[3] at a meeting of the Society of Automotive Engineers in New York. In this paper he put his finger on what he felt were some of the more serious shortcomings of the aircraft then in service. He told his audience:

Some of us in the sales end of the airline business have often felt that transport airplanes were designed for, first, making the pilot comfortable; secondly, making it easy to maintain; thirdly, providing enough gas capacity for the range desired, and last, taking what is left over and saying this is where and how we will move the traffic.

Mr Turner went on to list a number of the items which customers said they would like to see in an aircraft. The first was better visibility:

[3] Summarised in *Shell Aviation News*, January 1951.

Diamonds in The Sky

They want to be able to see out. With the advent of aircraft operating at high altitudes with pressurised cabins, you may think this becomes less important. However, immediately after take-off and while approaching for a landing, the customers want to see the country. In addition, one of the features of air travel which the customers like to see is cloud effects at high altitudes, particularly at sunrise and sunset – so let's fix it so the customer, even on the aisle seats, can see outside the aircraft. Some improvement can be made over certain modern airplanes, even without enlarging the windows, by relating the position of the windows to the position of the seats. Another thing: what can you do for the majority of customers who sit directly over the wing of all modern transports? The only thing they can see is some beautiful shiny aluminium.

Second was less noise:

We need to provide a quieter ride for passengers. Unquestionably there has been a lot of improvement in recent years but we have a long way to go. In my opinion, only a small part of the present-day problem is engine and propeller noise. In some modern aircraft, the noise from the ventilating system is a source of annoyance to passengers. I have been in certain aircraft where the noise of air flowing through the outlets has made ordinary conversation completely impractical.

Meals should be served more quickly:

We must have the ability to serve meals quickly but in a way that will create the impression of gracious, unhurried service. We are already at the point where it takes three hundred miles to serve a meal in the modern transport. Some provision must be made to serve a palatable meal rapidly. This is another reason why it is important that the aircraft for local operations have the ability to get to smooth air quickly – no one likes to wear their meal.

Baggage handling must be faster and more convenient:

Today we fly between Washington and New York in one hour block to block. Does it make any sense for the customer to wait up to twenty-five minutes in order to get his baggage at the other end? This is what is sometimes happening today. Even in recent years, new aircraft have come out with completely inadequate cargo space. Please give us room to stow the stuff and make it easy for us to get to it.

Also, we need to provide more facilities for carrying baggage in the cabin. Every day we get more and more commuters – the kind of business that really pays off because we get the revenue with a minimum of sales expense. These people want to carry their baggage with them and to get going as soon as they hit the ground. Why do we put overhead racks in an airplane and then turn round and tell the customers they can't use them for anything heavier than a hat or overcoat?

'Serving a palatable meal rapidly' is no easy matter. The question always has to be asked, 'palatable to whom?' Before the Second World War, the passengers on most international flights were a fairly homogeneous body of people. They were middle- or upper-class and they appreciated good cooking when they saw and tasted it. Once mass transport got under way, however, the problems facing the airline caterers were much more complicated. The social range of the passengers they had to feed was widening every year and

The galley in a Pan
American Stratocruiser.

so, too, was the range of tastes in food. The change affected both first class and economy alike. The task has been, broadly speaking, to provide in the first-class cabin meals which would please, or at least not antagonise, duchesses, bookmakers and vulgar vice-presidents, and in economy class to make an extraordinary variety of passengers of all conceivable tastes, ages, incomes, backgrounds, nationalities and religions reasonably contented with what they were given to eat and drink.

Until the early 1950s, some airlines were still attempting to feed as many of their passengers as possible on the ground, but others, such as Air France, preferred to serve meals in the aircraft, in order to make flights less tedious for passengers. In 1951 it was calculated that on an average of all long-distance services, about sixty per cent of all meals were served on the aircraft. The cramped conditions in aircraft galleys made it essential that, as far as possible, meals should be prepared before the food was put on board so that they merely had to be kept hot or heated-up in the galley. With the equipment and processes available at that time, this presented considerable problems if the meals were still to taste reasonably fresh by the time they were eaten and if the endless repetition of cold dishes was to be avoided. The introduction of deep-frozen food in about 1950 seemed to have provided the answer to most of the caterers' difficulties. By this means a complete meal was first cooked and then put in a temperature of thirty degrees below zero Fahrenheit for three or four hours. Afterwards it could be kept in cold storage for very long periods, at a temperature of minus five degrees Fahrenheit, and taken to the aircraft as required. On board it was put into electric ovens and defrosted, then heated to the required temperature.

The results were not to everyone's liking, but, like all forms of standardisation, they offered a reliable, if unexciting, product anywhere in the world at any time of the year. If hot meals were to be provided at all hours and in all climates, this was one way to do the job. The phrase 'airline meal' has subsequently become almost synonymous with predictable food that can be eaten reasonably easily with the elbows kept tightly against the body. However, given the circumstances, the only real alternative was sandwiches, and in hot climates sandwiches have a way of not remaining agreeable for very long after they are cut – and, in 1950, polythene wrappings were still experimental.

The advantage of deep-frozen food was quickly realised – the elimination of waste and unnecessary weight, the small space in which the frozen meals can be packed, and the ease of preparing them aboard the aircraft. But, in fact, the idea did not catch on as quickly as might have been expected. Little came at that time of plans to establish refrigerated stores of deep-frozen food at stops along the route where local catering facilities had proved unsatisfactory and in 1952 BOAC, for example, was using deep-frozen food only on services starting from London, and even then for no more than a quarter of all meals. The main drawback was the weight of the equipment required to prepare the food from the frozen state, but personal and national prejudices also played a part. American passengers appeared to have no objections to it, but for many years Air France refused to use frozen food at all. Their catering adviser agreed that it tasted perfectly good, but added the crushing comment, *'Mon Dieu!* Who wants to eat food cooked two years ago?' and continued with his *Terrine de Caneton Nantaise* and *Coeur de Charollais sauté aux champignons*, prepared in the airport kitchens and put on board the airliner in portable refrigerated containers.

It was reckoned in the early 1950s that galley equipment and food amounted to a total weight of about twelve lbs for each passenger carried. The weight of actual food carried aboard the transatlantic Constellations was 400 lbs, which was sufficient for two main meals and light refreshments for the forty-three passengers and the crew. The bar stocks amounted to a further 104 lbs, making 504 lbs in all. This, together with the weight of the stewards, was and is an important factor in airline economics, bearing in mind that the value per annum of each pound of weight saved was reckoned to be about £20.

During the later 1940s and the 1950s a considerable amount of research was carried out in order to discover the effect of air travel on food and wine. On the whole, white wines were found to withstand vibration and differences of pressure and temperature better than red; and, of the red wines, bordeaux did better than burgundy; champagne fared best of all. Some foodstuffs, such as cream and mayonnaise, appeared to be adversely affected by the dry atmos-

phere of the pressurised cabin and were not included in menus until suitable airtight containers were developed.

One great advantage of the pressurised cabin from the caterers' point of view was that it removed most of the restrictions once considered necessary in planning meals for passengers whose digestion might have been impaired through shortage of oxygen. The main criterion for an aircraft meal is that it must not include dishes which are known to have only a limited appeal. Airline meals have to be as safe as possible, since the choice is always very limited, even in first class. The wider the social range of passengers became, the less adventurous in-flight meals had to be, although, in fact, the airlines have managed to change people's eating habits quite a lot over the years, by applying the results of a policy of stealth, constant market research and gradualism.

One of the difficulties the airlines have had to face and, if possible, over-come from the 1950s onwards has been that the feeding of passengers in economy class has been very strictly regulated by IATA. For meals other than breakfast, airlines are permitted to offer only the following:

137

One glass of fruit juice or one cup of soup or one canapé.
Bread, biscuits, butter.
Either one entrée and two vegetables, or one entrée, one vegetable and a salad.
One piece of fruit or one pastry or one piece of chocolate.
Cheese.

The quantity of bread, biscuits and cheese is not specified, and an airline which felt inclined to curry favour with its passengers in this way could legally provide great quantities of these commodities. What would, however, cause serious repercussions would be any attempt to serve both fruit juice and soup. In practice, 'one piece of fruit' is almost unknown. It is generally interpreted to mean a small quantity of tinned fruit salad, sometimes with ice cream, sometimes not.

It is only fair to note, however, that some airlines manage much better than others in serving attractive meals, while remaining strictly within the IATA rules. Some make a more satisfactory job of advertising their in-flight meals than of actually providing and serving them. The problem of eating any meal in the cramped conditions of economy class is a serious one. Unless the aircraft is providently half-empty, the food has to be transferred from tray to mouth with elbows tight against hips, to avoid knocking against the arm of one's neighbour, and this necessarily restricts the kind of food that can be offered. It has to be easy to divide into mouthfuls with a plastic knife and fork, and easy to pick up and lift in a reasonably foolproof manner. Much the safest and quickest way of going about the business, as experienced travellers know very well, is to return to one's childhood habits and use a spoon.

There are no regulations as to the meals which may be offered to first-class passengers, and consequently gluttony on a remarkable scale is encouraged in this section of the aircraft.

The airlines are restricted, too, in the size and position of the seats they provide for economy-class passengers. The exact details were laid down in 1957, in the first instance for the North Atlantic service, where the competition was fiercest and the potential greatest. What was prescribed, in order to prevent one airline treating passengers better than another, was:

A maximum seat pitch (the distance from the front edge of one seat to front edge of the seat immediately in front when both are in an upright position) of 34 inches shall not be exceeded except for technical or safety reasons.

The distance between the front edge of seats (measured in an upright position) facing a bulkhead and the bulkhead shall not exceed twenty inches.

The maximum possible number of seats abreast shall be fitted as calculated by taking a normal aisle and assuming the following seat widths, measured from edge to edge outside armrests: 1. single seat = 23 inches
2. double seat = 42 inches
3. triple seat = 61 inches[4]

----

[4] TWA Memorandum, *North Atlantic New Tourist Type Economy Service*, 27 December 1957.

The maximum pitch in first class is 42 inches, whereas in economy class it is 34 inches, but experienced passengers will be aware that neither are generous dimensions, and that five or six hours spent in one of these seats is a far from comfortable business. It is true that it is better to be cramped for five to six hours than for ten or twelve and that the steadily increasing speeds of aircraft have fortunately brought about a corresponding reduction in the length of the passenger's subjection. In this sense, the congestion of tourist or economy class (in the early days in the United States it was known, in a more genteel fashion, as 'coach class') probably matters less now than it did twenty years ago. There is, nevertheless, a certain mystery about economy-class seating. Few people travel with a tape measure in order to check up on such matters, but all seasoned travellers, especially those who, like the present authors, have long legs, know perfectly well that the seats on some aircraft and on some airlines do somehow give that extra inch of knee-room which makes all the difference between hell and a tolerable journey. And many people must have discovered that, on certain types of aircraft, the rows running between the emergency exits provide space almost equal to first class.

The regulations for seating, for meals, for drinks and for fares, voluntarily agreed by all IATA members, meant, in effect, that real competition between airlines could not exist. For personal and often whimsical reasons, passengers might prefer one airline to another, but it was not possible for them to be influenced by tempting promises of more leg-room or bottom-room, more elaborate meals or free wine, to say nothing of lower fares. It would be an exaggeration to say that, with the best intentions possible, IATA progressively killed enterprise, but there is, to say the least of it, something unreal about a situation in which competitors are not allowed to compete. They could, of course, attempt to get a bigger share of the traffic by choosing to operate better planes than their rivals or by earning a reputation for having better trained and more obliging staff, but beyond that they were unable to go, unless they happened to be Aeroflot, which has never been a member of IATA. He would be a bold man, however, who claimed that Aeroflot has been markedly more enterprising or innovatory than its IATA-chained competitors.

The truth is that, in the 1950s as in the 1960s and much of the 1970s, the airlines offering scheduled services were not greatly worried about competition between one another. What brought them close to panic was the proved and growing success of the private charter companies, which provided the public, under certain theoretically strict but easily avoidable conditions, with what it wanted and what IATA or no IATA, it intended, to have – cheap fares. The fear and, in some quarters, the belief was that charters diverted passengers from scheduled flights. For this there was extremely little evidence, but if someone had to be blamed for the airlines' poor economic showing, it might as well be the charter firms.

An aeroplane that came at the right time, the Vickers Viscount 813.

There was, however, considerable irony in the situation, since, by the early 1950s, the main operators of charter flights were the airlines themselves, who were able to provide better overseas airport facilities and sometimes lower rates than the private charter companies. An article in *The Aeroplane* in January 1951 noted:

Airline companies have recently become much more conscious of the non-scheduled potential and their attitude towards charters has changed from one of semi-indifference to one in which an all-out effort is being made to attract business. Immediately after the War, air lines' depleted fleets could barely handle the scheduled traffic offering, but today, with increasing supplies of new aircraft and competition getting keener on the routes, air lines are exploring all methods of earning revenue.

Often, an airline was able to offer a one-way charter, to avoid an aircraft travelling empty, and in general the policy was to regard charters not as

140

an expanding business but as a convenient method of covering gaps in a schedule. *The Aeroplane* concluded:

In the early post-war days it was undoubtedly true that private operators offered a better commercial service to charterers, a lower price and a more willing co-operation than the air lines could give. Today the position is rapidly being reversed and air lines are getting more and more willing to fulfil a charterer's every wish.

One all-important qualification had to be made to this somewhat optimistic statement; the airlines were co-operative only if it suited them to be. If a charterer wanted an aircraft for the Easter weekend or for a Saturday in August, he was extremely likely to be disappointed.

The private charter firms could certainly not be ignored, even in the 1950s. In 1950, for example, Fred Olsen Airtransport, a subsidiary of the Norwegian shipping line, ran four DC-3 charters from Britain to Norway at Easter and others for Scout and other youth organisations in July and August. Nothing similar was available from the airlines, and the passengers concerned would assuredly not have travelled on scheduled flights. This was additional business, not stolen business.

In the same year, Lanes (Air Charter) Ltd chartered a DC-3 to take a party of thirty-two from a London printing firm to Paris for Easter and bring them back four days later. The cost was £8 a head, which included road transport to and from the airport at both ends. BEA's own Easter excursion to Paris cost £10.

On 28 April 1950, Hunting Travel, a leading company in the charter market, took its first charter party from Dublin to Rome, using an aircraft chartered from Aer Lingus. During that year 12,000 pilgrims went to Rome from Ireland, and fifteen per cent of them went by air, which amounted to substantial business. The normal Dublin–Rome return fare at the time was £62 10s. Hunting did it for £37 a head.

What matters to any airline is how successfully it fills the seats on its scheduled flights. There are different ways of defining 'successfully'. It does not necessarily mean that all the seats on a particular flight are occupied. A few empty seats help to lessen the feeling of congestion and crowding and give the stewards a welcome chance to move difficult passengers somewhere else, if they are unhappy with their first position. Between two and five per cent empty seats would probably be close to the ideal, although no airline would ever deliberately keep any of its seats unsold merely to make passengers feel better or to make the stewards' duties easier. But to finish the year having sold only half one's available seats is clearly not good business. Something must have gone wrong with planning, marketing or salesmanship or with the airline's reputation, assuming that one is unable to blame the whole situation on the world economic position. With these thoughts in mind, here is the load factor – the percentage of seats occupied – for each transatlantic carrier in 1952 and 1955. The figures in each case refer only to scheduled flights:

	FIRST CLASS		TOURIST	
	1952	*1955*	*1952*	*1955*
Air France	76.7	61.9	71.9	70.6
BOAC	65.0	64.1	67.0	63.4
El Al	50.9	—	64.3	56.8
Iberia	—	28.7	—	43.6
KLM	71.1	62.2	71.4	60.1
LAI	45.2	41.5	76.5	53.0
Lufthansa	—	44.3	—	43.4
Sabena	54.7	57.7	66.0	57.0
SAS	62.0	64.8	70.8	62.7
Swissair	68.0	78.55	72.5	63.0
Total European carriers	66.3	59.9	69.5	60.7
PAA	68.7	71.4	68.5	64.9
TCA	63.1	72.9	85.5	76.7
TWA	67.7	71.6	76.8	70.55
Total North American carriers	68.1	71.5	74.2	68.3
Grand Total	67.2	65.3	71.8	64.6

Iberia began operations in the last quarter of 1954, Lufthansa in July 1955. El Al had no first-class seats after 1952. LAI was absorbed by the present Alitalia.

The reappearance of Lufthansa on the international aviation scene, after a gap of ten years, was a significant event, not least because it introduced a new and potentially powerful competitor into a market which was already experiencing considerable difficulties in filling the available seats.[5] With the approval of the Allied authorities, Lufthansa started in a comparatively small way – four Convair CV-340s for short and medium haul and four Lockheed L-1049G Super Constellations for long-distance routes. Only two months after its first services within Germany, Lufthansa went into the most highly competitive of all airline markets, the North Atlantic, and a few weeks later, in September 1955, it was back in the Near East. During the following months, its European services were continuously expanded, especially after the introduction of the Vickers Viscount medium-range propeller-turbine aircraft in 1956. In the first year of operations 74,000 passengers flew in Lufthansa planes. In 1959, the last year of the propeller age, the total was 786,000. There was, however, one big difference between the old and the new Lufthansa services. After 1955 Frankfurt, not Berlin, became Lufthansa's

[5] Japan had re-entered the aviation scene a little earlier. After her surrender to the Allies she had been forbidden to own or operate aircraft. This state of affairs lasted until the signing of the Peace Treaty in 1952, and the first JAL flight took place on 2 October 1952. At that time, the total fleet consisted of three DC-4s.

new base and its principal operational centre. Even today, in the political system set up by the Allies at the end of the war, German planes are not permitted to fly into Berlin.

A major French success. The Caravelle pure jet.

At this point, something should be said about the new aircraft which became available during the 1950s. Five were outstanding, the Vickers Viscount, the Boeing 707 and 727, the Douglas DC-6B and the Sud-Aviation SE 210 Caravelle.

The first production model of the Viscount flew in 1952 and entered service in 1953. It had forty-seven seats, three on one side of the aisle and two on the other. The first propeller-turbine aeroplane to operate a commercial passenger service, it was one of the milestones in civil air transport. It was the first British aircraft ever to be sold in any quantity in America and went into service with airlines all over the world.

The Douglas DC-6B was a development of the DC-6. It went into service in 1951 and remained in production until 1958. The DC-6B was a very economical aeroplane; it achieved lower costs per seat-mile than any other piston-engined aircraft. It had accommodation for between sixty and a hundred passengers, according to the seating density decided on by the airline.

The very important Boeing 707 was a pure jet. The prototype first flew in 1954 and by the end of the 1950s it was in service with many of the world's airlines. It was originally planned as a medium to long-range transport, but the first 707s were flown on the North Atlantic route with a reduced payload. Two classes, occasionally three, were carried in separate areas of the same aeroplane. To allow flexible ratios between first and economy class, the bulkheads between the two sections were made easily movable, so that the seating arrangements could be varied. But first class was always at the front

143

of the aircraft, next to the flight-deck, and economy class at the rear. There have been many modifications to meet customers' particular requirements, but a typical version accommodated 189 tourist-class passengers – this was the big aeroplane at last – cruised at nearly 600 mph and had a maximum range of about 6000 miles.

The 727 had a similar performance, but a shorter range. It could carry 119 tourist-class passengers.

The Sud-Aviation Caravelle, another pure jet, went into service in 1959 and proved to be one of the most successful, as well as one of the most beautiful, of all post-war airliners. It was designed for medium-haul work and had accommodation for eighty tourist-class passengers.

Two other aircraft, both British, need to be considered separately because, although they were technically advanced, they were both, for different reasons, commercial disasters. The de Havilland Comet came into service with BOAC in 1952, providing the world's first pure-jet flight with paying passengers, London–Johannesburg, on 2 May. It was fast and quiet and available several years before the first Boeing jet, but three accidents which occurred in quick succession during 1953 and 1954 destroyed world confidence in the aircraft. In two of the Comets, the cabin became suddenly depressurised and the aeroplane exploded into small pieces: G-ALYP blew up near Elba, with the loss of thirty-five people; and G-ALYY blew up in the Naples area, with twenty-one on board. G-ALYU was destroyed near Calcutta, killing forty-three passengers and crew. Pan American cancelled their orders and went over to Boeing 707s, and although BOAC, BEA and a number of other airlines continued to operate Comets until well into the 1960s, large-scale orders failed to materialise.

The propeller-turbine Britannias, brought into service by BOAC late in 1957, were big, roomy aircraft, but at this date the major airlines were thinking ahead entirely to jets for their long-distance routes and the Britannias stood little chance against the new generation of Boeings.

It is interesting to see how rapidly jets became fashionable, after the airlines, especially in America, had shown extreme caution while the early prototypes were being built and tested. 'Shall we build the industry on a sound commercial basis,' asked TWA's President, Ralph Damon, in 1950, 'or, listening to one and all, should we rush jets, cut forty-five minutes off the New York to Chicago flight time, have messed-up timetables again, perhaps Civil Aeronautics Board grounding orders, some near bankruptcies and possibly further drains on the taxpayer?' C. R. Smith, the President of American Airlines, made it clear, also in 1950, that his company had no intention of ordering jets for the time being. They were not, he thought, a money-making prospect nor sufficiently reliable. 'A good guess', he believed, 'would be that it would be around five years before you find jet aeroplanes flying on the scheduled airlines. The present aeroplanes are modern, fast, economical and reliable and they will be here for many years.'

Opposite above: Qantas old and new: the pioneering Avro of the Twenties dwarfed by a Jumbo of the Seventies.

Opposite below: The Boeing Model 80 was introduced in 1928 and carried mail as well as twelve passengers.

The last point was certainly true. Aeroplanes, in one respect, have been very like bicycles before the First World War and motor cars ever since. They are bought by the rich and move steadily down the social scale until they finally drop to pieces in the hands of the poor. DC-3s and DC-4s, Constellations and other aircraft of the same vintage were still in use and giving good service in many parts of the world thirty years and more after their original owners found them obsolete. Qantas, for example, found old Catalinas and DC-4s perfectly acceptable for its New Guinea and Pacific Islands routes long after the Americans and British had written them off as antiques. In areas such as this it was no commercial disadvantage to operate such aircraft, with no aviation Joneses to keep up with and conditions perfectly suited to an aeroplane which went at a sedate 150–200 mph and carried only forty or fifty passengers. When Qantas bought new de Havilland aircraft for work in and around New Guinea, the orders were not for Comets, but for the Drover, twelve passengers and 140 mph, or the Otter, eleven passengers, 127 mph.

With any form of transport, sensible passengers learn to make do with what is available. If one's need is to fly to the interior of Brazil or New Guinea, there is not much point in complaining that one has not been supplied with the speed and comfort of a 707. Similarly if, in January 1952, one was feeling

A good but unlucky aircraft. One of Middle East Airlines' de Havilland Comets at Beirut, 1961.

Opposite: Utility flying: a Qantas DHC Otter at Wau, New Guinea, 1959.

145

the need for a holiday in Madeira, as the actor, Brian Rix, was, then it was as well to accept the fact that a luxury flight was just not to be had on that route. It was an old flying-boat or nothing.

Mr Rix was taken from Southampton to Funchal by Aquila Airways, which had gone into the travel business with a number of old ex-BOAC Sunderlands of the type formerly used by Coastal Command. After several abortive starts, because icing on the wings prevented the plane taking off, the journey eventually began seven hours late, by which time the passengers were beginning to wonder why they had come. The Sunderland 'lumbered through the skies at about two hundred knots and at an altitude of about seven thousand feet. Not exactly speedy and not exactly comfortable on the old ears, for the cabins were not pressurised. Furthermore, the flight to Madeira took eight hours, so one had to suffer this discomfort for a long time. All right, I suppose, if you were warmly clad in flying boots and jackets, with the adrenalin keeping up the temperature as you chased Nazi submarines, but not so good for peacetime passengers.'[6]

During the twenty and more years following this flight, Brian Rix travelled a good deal on the most advanced aeroplanes, but, apart from the extra steadiness, quietness and, of course, speed, he found that little of real significance had changed. 'Nearly a quarter of a century later,' he philosophised, 'and with hundreds of miserable hours spent hanging around for Scheduled Flights and Charter Flights and Cheap Weekend Flights and Package Flights, we know things haven't changed very much.'[7]

The truth of the matter is that different types and generations of aircraft have made different demands on the patience and fortitude of their passengers. One kind of disadvantage has to be balanced against another. In the 1930s a journey to Australia took more than a week, but there were interesting and usually agreeable overnight stops, when one had a chance to relax and to see a little of the town. Modern jets with pressurised cabins fly above much of the weather and it is very rare for passengers to be sick. As late as the 1950s, however, they were often sick. Brian Rix mentions, with understandable pride, that, on his never-to-be-forgotten flight to Funchal, he was the only one not to need the sick-bags so thoughtfully provided by the airline.

By no means all the caution shown by the airlines during the early 1950s was due to technical wisdom or commercial canniness. The real problem was that jets were going to change the traditional pattern of airline operations and nobody knew how well passengers were likely to stand up to the new and very considerable demands that would certainly be made on them.

At the beginning of the decade Captain S. T. B. Cripps, with long experience of both flying and passengers, took a careful look at what was likely to be involved.[8] There would be, he was certain, a conflict between what was

---

[6] *My Farce From My Elbow*, 1975, p. 112.
[7] Ibid., p. 114.
[8] 'The Effect of Jet Speeds on Air Line Schedules', *The Aeroplane*, 1 May 1950.

An aeroplane that came too late. The Bristol Britannia propeller-turbine (turboprop) airliner entered BOAC service in 1959, when the first pure jets were in the final stages of development.

best for the passengers and what was best for the airline. The owners of the new and extremely expensive jets would want, above all, to keep them moving and earning money twenty-four hours a day. They would not be able to afford to have them sitting idle on the ground, eating their heads off and doing no work. They would demand what was known in the trade as maximum utilisation. But, thought Captain Cripps, 'on long-distance routes such high utilisation may not be acceptable to passengers, unless possibly some potent vitamin tablets are administered which will increase the average passenger's endurance to a point unknown at present'.

With this awful possibility in mind, Captain Cripps examined, in great professional detail, the way the London–Sydney service, operated jointly by BOAC and Qantas, was planned and run at that time. His charts and statistics showed that:

The present Qantas schedule outbound to Sydney requires an elapsed time of 87 hours, entailing two night stops and two nights airborne. This operation gives a percentage ratio of flying time to total elapsed time of 53.2 per cent, i.e. a flying time of 46 hours 44 minutes to the total elapsed time of 87 hours for the journey.

As this could be speeded up to 46 hours 44 minutes flying time plus 12 hours on the ground, i.e. a straight-through flight with six two-hour stops, giving 58 hours 44 minutes, it is apparent that both passenger comfort and fatigue requirements of the

147

present day necessitate night stops, and that there are limits to the extent of flying that the average passenger will undertake without a rest. Inward bound from Sydney, the Qantas schedule allows for three complete night stops and one night airborne.

At that point an important question arose:

Does a passenger want an express service to be developed which will take him to his destination in the shortest possible time, but in a fatigued condition, or does he want a service similar to the present Qantas operation, which gives him definite rest periods in bed overnight and also enables him to see something of the places of interest along the route?

If passengers want a comfortable service now, it is difficult to understand why they should change their opinions during the next ten years, or that places like Cairo and Singapore will become less interesting. How, therefore, will the travelling public expect to be served by the future high-speed aircraft? Will the same night stop time on the ground be expected, or will the prospect of reaching their destination quickly warrant passengers being subjected to even greater fatigue than is the case with the services in operation today?

Whatever may be the passengers' view, there is no doubt that the airline economist will be a hundred per cent in favour of straight-through services with a minimum of time spent on the ground. A jet transport of the future will have such a high revenue earning potential per hour, that any question of keeping such an aircraft on the ground for a ten- to twelve-hour night stop will be a matter of losing not hundreds but thousands of pounds' revenue per year.

As we now know, the accountants won the battle, as in the end they always do, and planeloads of passengers now spend twenty-six weary, cramped hours continuously in their seats from London to Sydney, while the flight-deck and cabin crews, whose unions rightly demand short working hours and a proper night's sleep for them in a proper bed, change four times along the route. In 1950 that would have been considered an unthinkable and intolerable state of affairs, as indeed it is.

Every effort was made, of course, to make the misery less intolerable. Four helpful little TWA innovations, all introduced during 1957, which seems to have been a vintage year for bright ideas, will show how deeply the airlines had their customers' needs and interests at heart. On the Polar Route, orchids were given to female passengers and, for those stopping off or stretching their legs at Frobisher, passengers of both sexes were offered either 'polar gear', which meant parkas, or 'foul weather gear', which added waterproof foot-wear to the parkas. On all routes, 'TWA's new electronic coffee-maker pro-vides, for the first time in the history of American aviation, a piping-hot cup of coffee brewed from select Mocha and Java grounds and constantly regulated by pressure and atmosphere'. Passengers were told that the new coffee machine was made by the Huggins-Young Company of Los Angeles, and, to make life easier, there was now the TWA Translator, which provided 'a new passenger service facility in seven languages'. This remarkable new facility was none other than a booklet prepared for cabin staff, to make

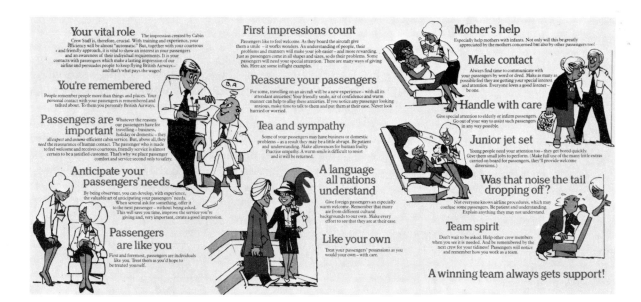

Guidelines for new flight attendants. From a British Airways training brochure.

possible what was described as 'simple communication' with passengers in German, French, Italian, Spanish, Portuguese and Greek, as well, of course, as English. Whether the cabin staff were required to memorise the contents of the booklet or simply to read aloud from it is not known.

But official provision could evidently not accomplish everything. In 1959 at Standiford Field, Louisville, Kentucky, a community service was brought into being for purely practical purposes, to meet people getting on and off flights, to arrange hotel reservations, to give information about bus schedules, and simply to answer questions.[9] The passengers whom the volunteers were asked to meet were occasionally described with creative imagination: 'You can't miss Aunt Susie,' someone might tell one of the helpers, 'she'll be wearing a hat like a pear tree.' Typical questions from the young were, 'Do they have comic books on the plane?' and 'Do they serve hot dogs and hamburgers on board?'

The scheme was organised by the Louisville Travelers Aid Society, which had been running information desks at the Greyhound bus station and at the Union railway station. 'We thought', said Miss Louella Jones, the Society's Executive Secretary, 'that we should shift scenes,' which was an interesting indication both of the number of people then using municipal airports in the United States and of the complexity and variety of their problems.

One of the most popular, if not exactly important, innovations of the 1950s – duty-free shops at airports – was certainly due, however, to European, not American enterprise. The world's first duty-free store was established in 1951, at Shannon, in Ireland. Le Bourget followed in 1956.

The beginnings of the duty-free system, however, are to be found much earlier than this, in the days of travel by train and ship. Duty-free allowances

[9] *Louisville Times*, 24 July 1959.

149

for arriving passengers originated as 'the unconsumed portion of travellers' sustenance' on international journeys. Standard allowances of alcohol, to-bacco and perfume were defined by the British Customs in the nineteenth century and similar arrangements developed in other countries. When one bears in mind the length of time needed to travel from, say, Paris or Brussels to London in those days, it is hardly surprising that bottles of wine or brandy were considered necessary equipment for the journey. The surprisingly gen-erous duty-free allowance of perfume which is given today also has its origin in those long, tedious journeys, when ladies felt the need of something to freshen themselves up with at frequent intervals.

People leaving a country were another problem. For a very long time, ships have been granted the privilege of selling Customs-free goods on the high seas. The practice gradually developed of allowing some purchases to be made duty-free at sea ports, the condition being that they were not for consumption in the country of origin. Shannon's achievement in 1951 was to extend this pleasant maritime habit to airports. The British Customs were characteristically cautious in permitting British airports to follow suit. In 1959 they conceded that liquor could be sold to departing airline passengers free of duty and shops were opened at both Heathrow and Prestwick that year. Two years later goods normally bearing purchase tax were added to the list of goods such a shop could sell, but at this stage tobacco was still excluded from duty-free shops.

In 1964, to carry the story a little further on, HM Customs agreed that duty-free shopping facilities should be permitted at any British airport which had 'appreciable international traffic'. This is not, of course, a precise term, but, with the tacit approval of the Customs authorities, it was taken to mean about 20,000 departing aliens each year.

Since then, duty-free has become an established international institution. Its practitioners have their own periodical and their own annual conference. Conditions vary somewhat from country to country but, in general, the system is for the airport authority to grant a private concern a concession to operate the store, in exchange for a proportion – usually a small proportion – of the turnover. Since the profits on a duty-free operation can be very sub-stantial, it is obviously in the airport's own interests to make sure that a store is well managed and that its sales are as high as possible. This involves a considerable measure of control, both over the range of goods sold and the prices charged. Experienced travellers know which airports' shops offer bargains and which to avoid. Amsterdam and Heathrow both have excep-tionally good reputations in this respect; the prices at other airports are no lower than those charged for the same goods in neighbouring city shops and in some instances they are noticeably higher. The enticing words 'duty-free' can be an effective trap for the innocent.

Many of the world's airports appear to run their duty-free shops in a half-hearted way, and unattractive clip-joints are unfortunately all too common,

The world's first airport duty-free store, established at Shannon in 1951. It was staffed by one girl.

but there can be no doubt about the vigour and enthusiasm with which the pioneer at Shannon has been developed. It has never been seen as a fringe activity. Shannon's Duty-Free Store proved to be the starting point for a chain of events which were milestones in the development of Ireland's now very important tourist industry and in the general promotion of Ireland and Irish exports.

The original duty-free shop consisted of a small kiosk staffed by one girl. Since then it has grown into what amounts to a large department store, with

The duty-free store at Shannon in 1978. It is claimed to be the world's biggest.

37,000 square feet of selling space and 120 sales assistants working round the clock. Nearly two-thirds of the total sales are of Irish-made goods, the most important line being Waterford crystal, for which Shannon Airport is the biggest stockist and seller in the world – about a million pounds' worth were sold in 1977 and 1978. Well over half the store's earnings are in dollars, mostly from tourists returning to North America from an Irish holiday.

The Irish tourist industry and Shannon Airport and its mammoth Duty-Free Store are so closely intertwined that it is impossible to decide which has been responsible for which. What can be said with some certainty, however, is that it was the Duty-Free Store, the great national shop window, which brought the jets down from the sky, by persuading their passengers that they would enjoy stopping in Ireland or at least stopping off there, instead of flying straight over it to the traditional tourist meccas further east.

SEVEN

Faster and Faster and Too Many Seats: the Story of the Sixties

People will persist in writing books and articles that make public relations departments of big concerns unhappy. The airlines are a case in point. After years of toiling to persuade the public that travelling by air was as easy and safe as travelling by train or boat, and a good deal safer than going by car, the PR men were far from pleased when George Johnson's brutal book, *The Abominable Airlines*, appeared in 1964.[1]

What hit the public on that occasion was a catalogue and analysis of recent American air accidents and near accidents which could hardly fail to make the flesh creep. There was, for instance, an incident near New York City on 16 December 1960: forty-three aircraft were in the New York area, getting in or out of Idlewild or LaGuardia. The forty-fourth was a TWA Constellation bound from Columbus, Ohio, to LaGuardia. It was cleared to fly at 5000 feet. A United Airlines DC-8 approached, en route from Chicago to Idlewild, at 20,000 feet. Air Traffic Control gave this plane a short-cut route to Preston Intersection, and told the pilot to be at 5000 feet on arrival there. This meant a steep dive to lose height and, as it unfortunately happened, one radio navigation receiver was not working. The United DC-8 hit the upper right side of the TWA Constellation, knocking it out of the sky on to Staten Island. The DC-8 continued on its way for eight miles and then fell in a street in Brooklyn, killing five people on the ground. The verdict of the enquiry was that the DC-8 had proceeded beyond its clearance limit and that high speed on approach had contributed to the collision, which resulted in a total of 128 deaths.

On 11 July 1961, a DC-8, once again of United Airlines, went out of control while landing at Denver, when two engines, both on the same side of the aircraft, failed to go into reverse thrust. Fire broke out. In the tourist section, sixty-seven passengers had only a $15\frac{1}{2}$-inch aisle available in order to pass to a single exit at the rear of the aircraft. The over-wing exits were ignored and those in the first-class section not used at all. Fifteen passengers died of carbon monoxide poisoning after surviving the crash.

[1] New York: Macmillan.

One of the engines and part of the propeller of the Eastern Airlines DC–7B which crashed at Idlewild (Kennedy) Airport on 30 November 1962. The tail section can be seen in the background.

On 30 November 1962, an Eastern Air Lines DC-7B was nearing Idlewild, New York, inward bound from Charlotte, North Carolina. It was told on approach that the conditions were one mile visibility, with ground fog. The weather was, in fact, far worse, the visibility being not one mile but nearly zero. The pilot tried to pull out, but hit the ground 500 feet to the left of the runway. Twenty-five people died in the crash.

Much worse, however, was to come. It concerned a TWA flight engineer named Miller, a man with fifteen years' service with the company. On 3 October 1962, Miller staged an exhibition at the George Washington Inn, in Washington DC, of certain photographs he had taken, for the benefit of a number of Congressmen and other interested persons. The exhibition had come about in this way. The Washington columnist, Jack Anderson, reported in his paper that pictures had been taken by a flight engineer of pilots 'snoozing at the controls, reading newspapers and cavorting with stewardesses in flight'. Reading this, the Federal Aviation Administration wrote to the President of the Flight Engineers' Union for further information. Not exactly trusting the FAA, the Union stalled.

Engineer Miller was on sick leave at the time and judged it prudent to retire to the Sierra mountains of California. He was, however, eventually persuaded to make the journey to Washington, with his photographs. Once there, he told a sub-committee of Congress that in 1956, the year in which the American Airline Pilots' Association voted that all flight-deck crew on jet aircraft should be qualified pilots, he had become concerned at the increasing number of mid-air collisions, and felt that most of them were caused by what he called 'care-safety laxity' in the cockpit. So he decided to produce documentation.

He bought 'a real cheap camera' and fixed it to the rear wall of the cockpit, with an extension control which allowed him to sit in his usual place behind the pilots and photograph their activities with the help of an infra-red flash bulb. In four years he took more than 300 photographs, of which 298 turned out to be clear enough to identify the pilots. Somewhat reluctantly he explained what a number of these photographs showed. The instruments contained in the pictures indicated that the pilot let the aircraft drift off altitude 400, 500 or even 600 feet for thirty minutes to an hour at a time, instead of disengaging the autopilot and flying the plane back to its correct cruising altitude. This, not unnaturally, made Miller nervous, because he knew that, with East-West traffic separated by only 1000 feet and altimeters incorrect by as much as 500 feet, a pilot who allowed his aircraft to drift 500 feet off its assigned level was asking for a mid-air collision. Miller showed the Congress sub-committee numerous photographs of pilots and co-pilots sleeping or reading or absent from their seats. One picture showed a stewardess sitting on a captain's lap and Miller commented, 'I've heard many times a request, almost a demand, that a girl get on his lap, and, since the girls are under his command, this puts them in a very difficult position.'

He also produced a picture of a donkey wandering about a plane in flight. The animal had been brought on board by a party of convention drunks, whom the pilot referred to, according to Miller, as 'just a bunch of good Joes'. 'The good Joes', he said, 'turned the donkey loose in the cabin, while they destroyed the furnishings.' While the aircraft was landing, the donkey fell against the door leading to the cockpit and was prevented from catapulting into it only by Miller's foot holding the door partly closed.

Miller was not suggesting, of course, that on every flight operated by an American airline there was a donkey or its equivalent roaming around in the cabin, nor that captains spent most of their time asleep on duty or dallying with stewardesses in the cockpit. His revelations, which the sub-committee had to accept, were merely George Johnson's star piece of evidence in his attempt to show that the public's trust in the airlines was not always well placed and that up-to-date equipment, so far from contributing to the safety of passengers, might well lead to their deaths, because it permitted air crew to be doing what they should not have been doing. From the beginning, the airlines had devoted a lot of time, money and effort to telling the public what selfless, responsible men pilots were, and any cracks in this particular façade were not likely to be good for business.

One interesting thread that runs through the history of passenger flying is

The varied duties of a stewardess. Marie Cref-Coeur shows off Mrs Barakat's newly-born son, which she has just delivered in a KLM aeroplane.

the nature of its hero-worship at any given time. Throughout the 1920s and 1930s, and certainly during the war years, there is no doubt that pilots had almost god-like status, both for what they did and for what they were. An examination of photographs of pilots of the past and of the reality of pilots of the present, as they walk along the airport corridors and to and from their aircraft, certainly suggests that, as a breed, they are good-looking much above the average, although quite why this should be so is difficult to say. Nowadays – it was not so in the 1920s and 1930s – their appeal may also have something to do with the money they earn. A distinguished income is a great help to a distinguished bearing and manner.

Psychologists have gone further and seen the pilot as an essential father-figure. As such, his strengthening, encouraging influence should be all-pervasive in the aircraft. If his first task is to fly the plane safely, his second is to reassure passengers that they are in good hands. Throughout the flight, the impression he must give us is, 'I know where I am. I know what I am doing. I know what is ahead of us. I have things under control. Relax and let me be concerned with the flight. I will keep you fully informed. Trust me.'

Only the word of the captain contains the assurance needed to reduce

156

passengers' anxiety to the fullest possible extent. If information had to be relayed, instead of coming directly in the voice of the father-figure, the communication should reach the passengers in some such form as 'Captain McGregor says that we will be in Paris in about an hour and that the sun is shining there.' The ritualistic use of his name is essential if the message is to have its maximum effect. Or so the theory goes.

If the pilot is father, the stewardess is mother, waiting on her children hand and foot, listening and watching to see if one is crying or unhappy, always at hand with comforting words and an understanding smile. A steward cannot have this function. He is no more than an airline servant in uniform, and his usefulness is limited to efficiency.

However, the pilot and the stewardess can only exercise their magic within the aircraft. Outside it, they have no power to remove fears. There are, unfortunately, no substitute figures within the airport, where tension can build up to an appalling extent, and where release not infrequently takes the form of physical assault on check-in girls and other wholly innocent members of the airlines' ground staff. The problem is made worse by the fact that, in order to overcome their fear of flying, a surprisingly large number of people drink heavily either at the airport or before arriving there. The airline passenger is by no means always the cuddly, friendly animal he sees himself to be.

The Johnson findings were only a symptom of the consumerism that began to be very noticeable in the air travel world during the 1960s. Today we take criticism of airlines and airports for granted, but, on a large scale, it was something new in the 1960s.

It is never easy to decide if criticism is fair. The angry person may have struck a good airline on a bad day and the happy person the reverse – the airline may have been bad, but this particular flight, by some fortunate miracle, remarkably good. So, in the spring of 1965, one enterprising journalist decided to make a round-the-world trip by air, economy class, to gather experiences and make comparisons. He wanted, in his own words, 'to sample as many airlines and aircraft as possible'.[2]

The London–New York flight was by TWA and went well. 'The "in-flite" movie,[3] *Goodbye Charlie*, was hardly an award winner, but it was a wonderful way of breaking up a long and tedious afternoon,' and the captain was pleasantly talkative.

Captain Flanaghan kept us fully in the picture, and warned that there was a one in fifty chance that we should wind up at Washington instead of JFK; that we should probably get stacked (which we didn't), and his final words were: 'It's blustery out there, so when you get off, hold your hats and, you country girls, take hold of your skirts.' The last engine (better known at TWA as the 'dynaJet') was switched off some ten minutes before the scheduled arrival time.

[2] 'Phileas', 'Around the World Economy Class', *The Aeroplane*, 25 May 1965.
[3] In-flight films first hit the travelling public in 1965, the pioneer being Pan American.

Five internal flights within the United States produced a good impression on the intrepid traveller, who noted some nice and unfamiliar touches, such as a do-it-yourself seat-selection chart, an in-flight announcement, 'By Papal dispensation Roman Catholic passengers on United Airlines' flights are not obliged to the Church law of abstinence,' and, above all, unfailing helpfulness and politeness on the part of ground staff – 'The brusqueness which one meets so frequently in other American "public servants" does not extend to the airlines.'

The stage from San Francisco to Tokyo was by Pan American, and there was nothing to complain of about this. Free champagne was served, contrary to IATA regulations, even to economy-class passengers.

An impressive feature of this Pan Am flight was the careful safety briefing and the suggestion that seat belts should be kept loosely fastened even when the sign was off. As with all the flights beyond San Francisco, there were no empty seats, and conditions were somewhat cramped.

On internal flights in Japan, he noticed that 'the ordinary Japanese citizens were using aeroplanes like buses, buying tickets and joining flights until the doors were closed'.

Osaka to Hong Kong was by Cathay Pacific.

The Convair 880 was fifty minutes late, and there was some confusion over seat numbers, so that the less fortunate passengers were still milling around in the aisle as the aircraft left the ramp, bound for Hong Kong. The cabin crew made a valiant effort to overcome the unfortunate start by distributing a vast meal and a wallet full of odds and ends, including a Chinese fan and a potted history of the company.

A trolley full of duty-free liquor appealed to the fifty-four alumni of some American college who were on an inclusive tour, but was rather less popular with those who were trying to fight their way to the lavatory.

Qantas took over from Hong Kong to Sydney.

The service and meals on Qantas was excellent, and the only snag was that the passenger sitting immediately in front seemed able to trap me when he reclined his seat completely. The seat pitch was thirty-four inches, but the back pivot point seemed to be unusually close to the floor.

Ansett-ANA provided a thirty-eight-inch pitch from Sydney to Melbourne, together with the most fetching stewardess encountered throughout the trip. Unfortunately, the trip was thirty-five minutes late, and there was no whisper of what had happened until six minutes after the scheduled departure time. Otherwise one gained a general impression of a slick, well engineered routine. No 'usherettes'; simple, minimal ground equipment; a 'time and motion study' approach in the terminal; all added up to a cost consciousness which is sadly absent from British airports.

Qantas returned for the crossing from Melbourne to Johannesburg. The aircraft was an Electra.

Qantas made the trip as pleasant as it could be. There was an almost continual drizzle of hot towels, orange juice and cups of coffee, in addition to the main meals. All

SAS hostesses keep in trim.

were welcome; so were the captain's lectures on economic geography as we approached the various islands. The Electra seat seemed to be more roomy than those seats in the Boeing, even though the pitch remained at thirty-four inches.

The last leg was by BOAC VC10 from Johannesburg to London. BOAC should have made sure that none of its competitors get hold of those superb seats; and the captains deserved a standing ovation for their landings. Cabin service too was excellent. An extra 'unofficial' cup of early morning tea was especially appreciated.

Unhappily the ground organisation along the route was not so good. At Johannesburg the traffic staff were swamped with work by the almost simultaneous departure of three other large jets and several local flights. It appeared that a little work study might help. Passengers had to attend three airline desks as well as the Customs and Emigration. And nowhere else was it necessary to check the passengers' names again at the gate. The result was a half-hour delay in take-off.

Although this was partially regained in flight – the VC10 really is 'triumphantly swift' – time was lost again by a cargo loading fumble at Nairobi. The captain announced eventually that the freight was 'so bulky that it cannot be got on'. Finally at Rome BEA lost a passenger, and so the aircraft landed seventy-five avoidable minutes late at Heathrow.

The trip as a whole revealed two major snags about flying economy:

Diamonds in The Sky

The first is that inevitably many of the passengers are very occasional travellers. The sad truth is that many of them do not mix well with their more travelled brethren. This sort of atmosphere causes people to think twice about flying economy class. On some routes, it costs an extra eighty-two per cent to escape into the first class: and some of us cannot justify such a large premium.

Secondly, six-abreast seats on a thirty-four-inch pitch are not good enough for an overnight journey if one has to work on arrival. During this trip I managed to get sleep only once – in the five-abreast thirty-eight-inch pitch seats, en route from Chicago to San Francisco. Although there are IATA style economy seats on some domestic US jet flights they are the lowest class of four available on some routes. On IATA services, a twenty per cent premium would cover a five-abreast layout; the VC10 seat solves the legroom problem; and the Australian airlines demonstrate that the roomier seats don't have to be in a special cabin.

In the following year, 1966, R. E. R. Johnson took the measure of twelve American local-service airlines, by means of a Visit USA fare, which for 150 dollars gave the foreign visitor unlimited travel over a period of 21 days. 'More than half of the locals,' he reported, 'have now introduced jet aircraft, and all but one has turboprop aircraft in service or undergoing conversion. Eight of the thirteen locals, however, are still DC-3 operators, and it is still just possible to fly from coast to coast exclusively on DC-3s.'

He was very favourably impressed, especially by the good timings, by the absence of delays due to technical faults and by 'the usual North American minimum of fuss'. His first flight was by Mohawk. It was simple, but acceptable.

I had not flown in a piston-engined aircraft for some time and was pleasantly surprised that the noise was not as deafening as I remembered. Service on board was on the rudimentary side, but this was general throughout the trip. Food served was never more than a packet of biscuits, or in one case a sandwich. Cabin announcements were extremely thorough on the safety side, but a little sparse as regards flight times and so forth.

There was occasional trouble with seat reservations. Computers and computer links were not what they are today, and misunderstandings could occur. At an intermediate airport on the St Louis to Chicago flight, 'a large party joined the aircraft and when all were seated the tour conductor found that there was no seat for himself. This was despite the fact that I had only booked on the flight at short notice and had been assured that there was no space problem.' Frontier Airlines, based on Denver, operated a scheme which guaranteed passengers a seat on the next flight, if their first choice happened to be full. Their Convair 580s were so reliable that 'a disgruntled motel owner told me that the Convair 580 was unpopular with him because of the lack of delays causing connecting passengers to be delayed overnight.'

The general impression was that, like American aviation as a whole, the American local airlines were brisk, businesslike and efficient and that passengers regarded them as useful, no-frills, long-distance buses, which indeed they were.

Opposite above: The workhorse of the airlines: a Pakistan International Airlines DC–3 at Chitral, NW Pakistan, on a proving flight on 18 February 1962.

Opposite below: An Indian Airlines DC–3 at Trivandrum, S. India.

160

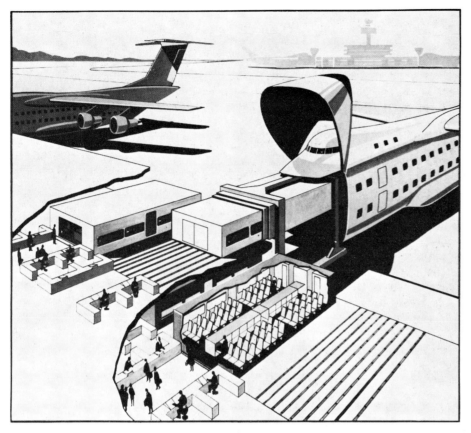

Passengers in bulk. Design for Krupp's not-yet implemented unit transport system, 1970. Passengers would be loaded into their containers at the town terminal and unloaded in the same way on arrival at their destination. The containers would be transported to and from the aircraft, either by rail or road.

But however efficient any airline, big or small, might be on the operations side, forward planning remained a nightmare throughout the 1960s and a number of airlines came close to bankruptcy. The problem was very similar to the one with which pig farmers are all too familiar – the cycles of demand and production refuse to coincide, no matter how ingenious and thorough one's research techniques seem to be. The farmer finds himself over-producing pigs for a market which should have continued expanding, but which, for some perverse and inexplicable reason, decided not to. The airline operator orders new aircraft to cater for the additional passengers which he is assured will need his services, but who, to his horror, are not there when the aircraft are delivered and have to be paid for.

The root of the trouble was, and is, that even the hardest-headed businessmen can be the most incredible optimists and romantics. When prospects look good, every airline orders more aircraft, hoping or convinced that the empty seats will be on some other company's planes. The optimism is usually shared by the authorities with the power to award airlines additional routes and services. By 1958 there was competition on 348 of the 400 most important domestic routes in the United States. Between 1955 and 1958, the number of routes with three or more carriers increased from 38 to 115. 'Such duplication', said the understandably worried President of American Air

Opposite above: One of Lufthansa's Boeing 707s being serviced at Cologne airport.

Opposite below: Pre-war image making: the entrance to the Victoria Air Terminal in London.

161

Lines in 1961, 'is increasingly dangerous, as the airlines have acquired some of the fixed obligations of older utilities, like water and power. Unused airline capacity has steadily grown more costly. Just as there can be too much competition, there can also be too little.'[4] To improve the situation, there were, in the opinion of most American operators, only two remedies; un-economical services should be pruned away and bodies like the Civil Aeronautics Board should keep closely in mind the industry's need for a minimum $10\frac{1}{2}\%$ annual return on investment and award new routes only when there was no doubt whatever that there was a public need for them.

During 1961, United States domestic trunk airlines recorded a net loss of $30 million, the first deficit since 1948. The main reasons for the failure of revenue to keep pace with expenses, according to the Air Transport Association, were what it euphemistically termed 'the decline in passenger growth' – the brutal truth was that fewer passengers were carried in 1961 than in 1960 – and a big swing away from first-class travel. A US Government directive to civil servants, always big users of the airlines, to use coach-class travel wherever possible led many private companies to issue similar instructions. This was a case of the new technology biting the hand that fed it. With jet aircraft available on most of the important routes, coach travel no longer involved sufficient hardship to justify the first-class fare. As one airline president commented, 'Our coach passengers today look like the blue book of industry.' And the experience of the European airlines was very similar. What was happening in the United States was happening everywhere.

The long-haul situation was little better. On the North Atlantic routes the figures issued by IATA for the second quarter of 1961 were as follows:

	Total	Change over 1960
Scheduled passenger flights	8029	$+18\%$
Seats offered	994,989	$+47.3\%$
Revenue passengers	500,277	$+4.5\%$
Passenger load factor	50.3	-20.6%

The lesson was obvious. There were simply too many seats and the situation was apparently getting worse. But, as it happened, 1961 turned out to be the bottom of the trough so far as the 1960s were concerned, and during the next few years there was a steady annual increase both in the total number of passengers carried and in the number of passengers per aircraft although, since the average size of aircraft was increasing all the time, these statistics need interpreting with care. What can be taken at its face value, however, is the fact that the total number of passengers carried on scheduled flights throughout the world more than doubled during the decade. The number of passengers killed in accidents did not, fortunately, increase in proportion. On the contrary, it was no higher in 1970 than it had been in 1960. What was

[4] *The Aeroplane*, 27 April 1961.

162

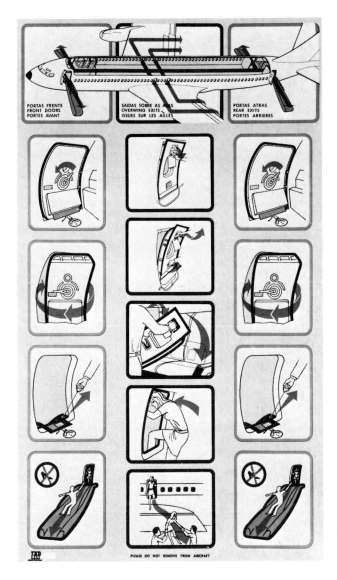

TAP shows passengers
how to use the emergency
exits.

disturbing, however, was the increasing number of accidents due, or thought to be due, to sabotage.

Attempts have been made to develop an efficient system for detecting explosives hidden in cargo and in passenger baggage but so far without a marked degree of success. If this trend continues, freight may have to remain in ground storage for a fixed period and passenger bags subjected to scrutiny before being carried.[5]

It was an intelligent forecast of what was to come. But for the passengers, fortunately the great majority, who survived the saboteurs' bombs, the mid-air collisions and the other hazards of air transport, there was no end to the

5 *The Aeroplane*, 3 January, 1968.

reasons supplied by the airlines as to why this company was so much to be preferred to that. This was particularly marked in the case of the North Atlantic services, where the competition was fierce. By the mid-1960s there were no fewer than seventeen major North Atlantic operators, each trying to find some way of getting the edge on its rivals.

The first line of attack was by means of the passenger's palate and stomach, at least in first class. In 1967 Olympic Airways, the record-holder, offered its first-class customers a ten-course meal. Qantas and Air France were runners-up with eight courses, while BOAC, Lufthansa and Air Canada could do no better than seven. Swissair was the only company which gave its first-class passengers the opportunity of choosing the dishes of their main meal before boarding the aircraft.

There was a wide range of not very imaginative giveaways. Air Canada provided playing-cards and BOAC stationery compendiums. Qantas posted letters free of charge. Air Canada, Lufthansa, Olympic, Qantas and TWA all offered baby-care needs, games and toys. Socks, slumber shades, leg rests, toilet water, toothpaste and toothbrushes could be had from most airlines, provided one had a first-class ticket, and from TWA there was a choice of four kinds of aspirin. Although no evidence was ever forthcoming that all or any of these things influenced a person's choice of airline in the slightest, the operators themselves clung tenaciously to them, knowing that once they went nothing whatever in the way of personal identification would remain. An airline was, so to speak, its socks and toys. If TWA had four sorts of aspirin on offer, the only way to be significantly different was to offer either five sorts or none at all.

Air-India paid a lot of attention to this matter of identity. The stewardesses and pursers were told that their task was to make every passenger 'feel like a Maharajah'. In 1966, a spokesman for the company explained this approach in some detail.

From the moment of embarkation when our stewardess welcomes the passenger with the traditional Indian *namaste* greeting she does her best to make the passenger feel like a guest in her home. Her Bangalore silk sari is the first impression of the peaceful atmosphere of India created by us. The Indian décor with its soothing green and gold colour scheme reflects the beauty and serenity of India. Indian dance motifs in subdued colours are on the side panels and there is a tracery design in ivory and gold taken from the old Benares brocades decorating the cabin interior.

Throughout the flight the stewardess must move quietly and elegantly up and down the aircraft attending to the needs of all the passengers. On a recent flight of ours one of our girls wore a pedometer and she walked $5\frac{3}{4}$ miles to New York from London. It should not be necessary for a passenger to ask for another drink or to request that his martini glass be taken away before lunch is served. Despite the amount of work that the stewardess has to do during the flight she must be prepared to converse with the passengers who may want to talk to her. Here, however, it is important that she can strike a happy medium and not talk to one passenger for too long, thereby becoming a bore to him, or appear to other passengers to be spending too much time with any one

Rajastani uniform worn
by hostesses in the
Maharajah section of
the Air-India 747B.
Photographed in the Air-
India Maharajah lounge
at Heathrow.

person. Many passengers want to know more about India and our stewardesses and flight pursers in their initial training are given instruction about all aspects of India.

Indian, like Japanese, stewardesses do, without question, give an airline more than a touch of the exotic and in that way help to give the airline an identity which it would otherwise lack. Companies like JAL and Air-India are well aware of this and use their cabin staff as an advertising weapon, year in and year out. Air-India was assuring its potential customers in the early 1970s:

They have the kind of training other airlines only wish their girls could have. It starts at birth. Indian girls are brought into a world where it's a woman's job to make life easier for people. As soon as they can walk they're taught how to serve, so by the time they're old enough to go to our training school it's practically second nature.

Our training school takes young ladies and turns them into air hostesses. We teach them about flying, airport procedure, passenger relations, in fact everything they couldn't learn at mother's knee. And despite the fact that many of our girls come to our school with degrees, this takes about six months.[6]

Air-India had a very strong card here. It is a very long time since educated English or American girls were brought up to respect the idea that a woman's job is to make life easier for people, 'people' meaning, of course, mainly men

[6] Advertisement in *The Economist*, 6 March 1971.

and, for many of those who have had to accustom themselves to a different and more egalitarian kind of relationship between the sexes, the Air-India approach and raw material might well have a certain nostalgic attraction!

Some airlines appear not to have made the most of their opportunities where stewardesses are concerned, including, very surprisingly, the usually exceedingly astute El Al. Most of the El Al girls have been Army officers, something of which no other airline could boast. They apply to join El Al immediately after completing their military service. There has always been great competition for the job, because, in a country where foreign exchange is difficult to get, it is one of the few ways of making trips abroad.

What El Al does do, however, is to emphasise the airline's Jewishness. Jewish dietary laws are strictly observed on every flight. It does not serve pork or pork products, meat from carnivorous animals and birds, shellfish or fish without scales or fins. Meat and milk must not be cooked together and it is forbidden to eat meat or meat products with milk or milk products. On the ground and in the air there are separate kitchens, utensils and cutlery for meat and dairy food. For religious reasons El Al flies only 306 days a year.

All this, like the Air-India hostesses, makes El Al different. One cannot confuse it with its competitors, and that is good for business. The task has been much more difficult for the American and European airlines.

United Airlines pinned their faith to 'in-flight entertainment', i.e. films and taped music. They were frank about the problems this involved.

Experience has shown that even though passengers may not like in-flight movies or approve of certain films, they exhibit a preference for carriers offering the service.

Inclusion of IFE in a carrier's passenger service would seem to imply responsibility to furnish entertaining films in good taste and not offensive to a mixed passenger group. Yet few current film productions can be considered suitable for captive airline audiences. Passengers of different ages, religious faiths, ethnic groups, sexes and moral outlooks understandably view films from different points of view.

To compound this enigma, film distributors tend to delay release of their best films to airlines. They evidently feel airline showings downgrade prime productions and thereby reduce theatre box office revenues. It might be suggested that in-flight showing of *good* films before theatrical release would act as a promotion of the film and serve to increase box office revenues.[7]

Apparently, and fairly obviously, in-flight entertainment was an attraction and a selling-point only if one's competitors were not offering it, or not providing such good fare. As soon as it was on the menu of all the companies operating transatlantic routes, a point which did not arrive until the early 1970s, the sales value, the mark of identity, lay in not offering it. At this stage, the airline which offered total freedom from in-flight movies was very likely to find itself pulling in customers from other airlines.

The Russians, secure in the bosom of their state monopoly, could afford to

[7] *The Aeroplane*, 24 November 1966. Supplement on Passenger Service.

smile at such childish goings-on. The growth of Aeroflot was certainly remarkable: 2,524,000 passengers in 1955, 16,032,000 in 1960, 42,070,000 in 1965.
What kind of service all these people were getting is another matter, and so,
too, was the accident rate, on which the Soviet Union, never a member of
IATA, has been careful to preserve a discreet silence. Nothing, either, is
known about such important matters as punctuality, unsold seats and the
ratio of revenue to costs. And, most regrettably of all, we have no record of
what Soviet passengers thought about their air services. There was no competition and, of necessity, they took what they were given. What we do know,
however, is that they were travelling longer and longer distances. During the
1960s the average distance per passenger on air journeys within the Soviet
Union increased by about a third.

One question which the layman may very well think reasonable is: 'If
planes were getting bigger and the number of passengers was not growing
fast enough to fill all the seats available, why did airlines refuse to do the
obvious thing, drastically reduce the number of services at least temporarily,
so that one new big aeroplane did the work of two old small ones, so saving
landing fees, fuel costs and manpower?' The matter was, alas, not so simple as
that. Once a service had been given up, it was exceedingly difficult to get
permission to put it back. In any case, combining services was a tricky
business. If, say, Alitalia's 8 am and 11 am flights from Rome to London had
both been flying with half their seats empty, it did not follow by any means
that the abolition of the 11 o'clock flight would mean a full aircraft at
8 o'clock, or vice versa. Passengers might decide that the Air France flight
at 9 am or the BEA flight at 10 am suited them better, so that whichever
Alitalia flight survived could still be flying only half full.

In most cases it was safer to regard empty seats as one of the more unpleasant kinds of growing pain and to see what savings and extra business
could be found in other directions. One solution often adopted with considerable success during the 1960s was to hold on to some at least of one's older
planes, instead of disposing of them to a market which was becoming increasingly glutted, and to use them either for charter work or for freight. The cost
of the aircraft would already, in all probability, have been written off, and
their new functions could consequently become very profitable.

Alitalia did precisely this in the early 1960s. Four of the company's DC-7Cs
were converted into freighters by Douglas, at the very reasonable cost of
$350,000 each, and put on regular runs to Tripoli, Beirut, Tehran and New
York, and other places with a good freight potential. In addition to this, a new
subsidiary company, Societa Aerea Mediterranea, was formed. Three of
Alitalia's unwanted DC-7Bs were transferred to SAM, which devoted them
entirely to charter flights, so benefiting both Alitalia and the Italian tourist
industry.

One very successful independent operator, Britannia Airways, followed
quite a different policy. It bought new Boeing 737s solely in order to operate

Preparing in-flight meals at the SAS central kitchen, Copenhagen, 1970. Boxes containing special kosher meals can be seen on the extreme left of the picture.

holiday package tours. In his 1968 Brancker Memorial Lecture, given in London to the Institute of Transport, J. E. D. Williams, a member of the Board of Britannia Airways, explained the philosophy behind his company's operations. It rested on the conviction that, in order to extract the maximum profit from a holiday package, every element in that package – airline operator, hotel operator, tour operator – should be controlled by the same concern – vertical integration. When this type of system was well organised, the effect on costs was spectacular. Williams illustrated the savings in two ways. During the winter of 1966–7, Sky Tours, the company with which Britannia Airways was associated, offered a seven-day winter holiday in Palma, the cost of which to the company was less than half the BEA/Iberia return fare.

At this date, integration between the airline and the tour operator was already well established in Europe, although it took different forms in different countries. Britannia Airways was integrated with Universal Sky Tours, under the umbrella of the Thomson publishing organisation. Other British airlines, including British United and Channel Airways, had interests in tour operating companies. On the Continent, the pattern was different, with the tour operator owning the airline. In Sweden, for instance, Transair was owned by Nyman and Schulz and in Denmark the Tjaereborg Rejser travel organisation was the sole shareholder in Sterling Airways.

This situation came about in a curious way. In the early 1960s Eilif Krogager was pastor of the Evangelical Church in the West Danish village of Tjaereborg. As a hobby, or perhaps one should say a sideline, he set up a travel company, with the aim of giving people much cheaper holidays abroad, firstly by cutting out the travel agent, whose commission averages ten to twelve per cent, and secondly, by owning and operating aircraft instead of chartering them. The company prospered remarkably, with Krogager showing great skill and energy in combining the two jobs of managing director and pastor. In 1967 he turned the business into a foundation. There are no shareholders and no dividends. All the profits are given to charity.

The headquarters have remained in Tjaereborg, but there are now offices in Finland, Sweden, Germany and London. Tjaereborg Rejser owns twenty-two jet aircraft and, nearly twenty years after it was founded, it claims, route for route and holiday for holiday, to be 9.8 per cent cheaper than any other travel operator, which suggests that, under good management, vertical integration is an efficient system.

In the case of British Eagle and Sir Henry Lunn Ltd, the link between the two branches of the tour was a man: Harold Bamberg was chairman both of the Eagle group of companies, which included British Eagle International Airlines, and of Travel Trust, of which Sir Henry Lunn Ltd was a part. Eagle-Lunn concentrated on providing holidays in the Caribbean and were in for a different kind of marketing. They realised that the passenger who was willing to pay £200 or more, a lot of money in the 1960s, for a holiday in Bermuda or the Bahamas was not the type who went with the herd on a typical package holiday to the Costa Brava. So the emphasis was put on the image of the airline, rather than that of the operator, with mention of 'regular flights by British Eagle', and of the high standard of cabin service.

It was possible to offer real bargains in this way. For a fourteen-night stay in the Bahamas, Eagle Lunn charged £157 and the BOAC consortium £216, at exactly the same hotel.

In the search for new ways of bringing down the cost of air travel, one enterprising British operator, Eric Rylands, hit on the clever idea of what he called coach-air. During the late 1940s, Rylands was inspired by the arrival of coachloads of holidaymakers in Blackpool from all over Lancashire and Yorkshire. He persuaded the organisers of these trips to sell a single ticket for bus and air travel, so that the coaches could drive straight on to the tarmac at Blackpool airport and then embark the passengers on his three de Havilland Dragon Rapides for holidays in the Isle of Man. The service prospered and eventually Rylands sold it off to Silver City Airways, bought a company called Skyways and, at the same time, an airfield at Lympne, on the Kent coast.

Having made arrangements for his planes to use a former German fighter base at Beauvais, Rylands began his London–Paris service in 1955, at a return fare of £7 14s., off-peak. The service, coach from London to Lympne, plane from Lympne to Beauvais, coach from Beauvais to Paris, was an immediate success, carrying 47,000 passengers in the first year. To begin with, Skyways used four DC-3s, fitted out as 36-seaters, which was exactly the capacity of the coaches. In 1962, however, new Hawker Siddeley 748s were brought into service and the DC-3s were converted to freight handling.

The biggest problem Rylands had to face was the fall-off in traffic during the winter months. To compensate for this, he chartered out his planes and their crews all over the world during the slack period and looked for every other possible way of earning revenue. Great efforts were made to sell duty-free goods on board the aircraft. His methods in this field were original and highly successful. In Paris, passengers were able to order what they wanted in advance, before leaving for Beauvais, and their orders were then telexed through to the airport and made up in parcels for handing over on board. This produced a much higher level of sales, and therefore of profit, than the traditional system of using harassed stewardesses to sell the goods during the flight.

What emerged quite clearly in the 1960s was that, for the majority of Europeans, if not Americans, flying meant cheap flights and packaged tours once a year when they went on holiday. The growth of this type of traffic and its potential market were much bigger than for scheduled traffic, a fact which was underlined by J. E. D. Williams in his Brancker Lecture, when he referred to 'the real dilemma which underlies most controversial issues in air transport'. This, he said, was 'What are airlines for?' The only possible answer was, 'For people who want to fly,' and that involved a further and all-important question, 'Which people?' The major task which the 1970s had to deal with was to find the answer to that question.

EIGHT

The Developing World

As we have said earlier, flying, in such regions of the world as Brazil, the Soviet Far East and much of Africa, is not merely a convenience. For half a century it has been a necessary tool of economic development. Without aeroplanes, many areas of the world would have continued to get along much as they had done for centuries. It is possible to believe that, in such countries, aviation has brought more evils than benefits, and this point will be considered in the last chapter. Here, however, the task is to survey what has happened and to show the chain of events which the aeroplane is capable of starting.

The best way of doing this seems to be to explore two widely separated areas in some detail, and we have selected for the purpose New Guinea and Brazil. We could equally well have concentrated on Mongolia and the Congo, or on Siberia and the Sudan.

In 1955 Brazil's President, Juscelino Kubitschek, announced a competition for the planning of a new capital city, to be built in the empty heartlands of his country and to be called Brasilia. The winning designs, by the urban planner Professor Lucio Costa, laid out the principal streets and public buildings of the city in the shape of an aeroplane. Whether this was deliberate or not, the symbolism could hardly have been more appropriate; only in the age of air travel could Brasilia function as a capital city and only with the help of the aeroplane could it have been built where it now stands.

At the outset there were no ground communications whatever, and until roads were built everything came in by air – machinery, steel, concrete and bricks, as well as many of the workers and their provisions. Now that the city is built, and the futuristic drawings of Professor Costa and the architect, Oscar Niemeyer, have been transformed into a teeming administrative centre, not everyone likes the new capital. Many would agree with the legislator who has to live there and said that there are only three good things about Brasilia: 'The skyline, the clean air and the plane to Rio.' Even that sour remark confirms the importance of aviation: that Brasilia could only have been conceived in a country and on a continent where the aeroplane had

A Junkers F13 of the
Brazilian airline,
Syndicato Condor Ltda,
founded in 1927.

long been established as the only way to defeat the vast distances and the terrible terrain.

Distances within Brazil are hard to grasp. To say that it is almost as large as the United States, twice as large as Western Europe and the fifth largest country in the world, is not to say nearly enough. To sit in a modern jet aircraft and to fly, hour after hour, over the monotonous dark green of the rain forest, broken only by rivers and streams, with not a road or any other sign of man's activity, is just the beginning of understanding what distance means in Brazil. Two-thirds of the country has a population density much below the national average of twelve per square kilometre. The Amazon basin in the north and west occupies more than half of the land but includes only four per cent of the population. It is in the context of this desolation that one has to look at the development of air travel in Brazil and in the neighbouring countries of South America, where conditions are similar.

Brazil's national airline, VARIG, was set up, as we have said earlier (p. 51) in 1927. Its early years were extremely precarious, despite the obvious potential for aviation in Brazil. The airline's second President, Reuben Berta, managed to extract enough money from the sale of VARIG's own postage stamps and special covers to buy each of the four staff a decent meal every second day and a haircut twice a year. They named these hard times 'the bearded period'. But business gradually improved and routes were steadily

172

extended to include many destinations in the south of Brazil. The effect of these new air links is recalled vividly by Gotz Hertzfeld,[1] who joined VARIG in the 1930s and who is now Director of Aircraft Maintenance. He points out that before the aeroplane, many of the small towns were totally isolated in the wet season, that even the huge wooden wheels of the ox-carts were unable to negotiate the mud, and that when the weather was good it would still take days or weeks to make a modest journey. Although Brazil is networked with great river systems, most of them flow north and south and, apart from the Amazon itself, provide few lines of communication from the coastline into the interior. Consequently, the obvious rule for the aeroplane was to provide routes running east to west, linking the north to south river systems.

This is precisely what happened and the economic and social benefits were soon evident; but in the long term, the political consequences were perhaps even more profound. In a country where communities are divided by great distances and by strong racial and cultural differences, nation-building is not easy; the turbulent history of Brazil demonstrates that problem exactly. But in recent years, improved communications have played their part in creating a more cohesive modern state.

Despite the early difficulties, the history of VARIG and its domestic competitors in the post-war period has been a vigorous and largely conventional tale of growth and rationalisation. But in one important respect it differs from many other airline stories. In Brazil, the aeroplane has been the tool of the pioneer; it has been used to open up and develop large areas where there were – and in some cases still are – no other means of transport. Its impact, therefore, could be reasonably compared to that of the railways in North America in the middle of the last century.

In this connection, the following quotation is instructive:

Here is an enormous, an incalculable force, let loose suddenly upon mankind; exercising all sorts of influences, social, moral and political; precipitating upon us novel problems which demand immediate solutions; banishing the old, before the new is half matured to replace it; bringing the nations into close contact before yet the antipathies of race have begun to be eradicated . . . yet, with the curious hardness of a material age, we rarely regard this new power otherwise than as a money-getting and time-saving machine . . . not many of those . . . who fondly believe they control it, ever stop to think of it as . . . the most tremendous and far reaching engine of social change which has ever either blessed or cursed mankind.

Those words could so easily have been written about the impact of the aeroplane on our world, and particularly on a country like Brazil, where air travel has made possible the violation of so much virgin country. In fact, they were written in 1868 by Charles Francis Adams Jr, as the first transcontinental railway was nearing completion in the United States. In responding to Adams's criticism as it might apply to the coming of the

---

[1] Conversation with Julian Pettifer, 3 November 1978.

aeroplane to Brazil – to his assertion that we never stop to think about this 'most tremendous and far reaching engine of social change' – it is fascinating to see what has happened in recent years to the city of Manaus.

Manaus awoke from its sleep after John Dunlop invented the pneumatic tyre in 1889. At that time, the biggest known reserves of rubber trees were growing wild in the forests of Amazonia. Almost overnight the sleepy little town of Manaus on the banks of the Rio Negro became the centre of the richest part of Brazil, and its new millionaires spent much of their wealth on raising extravagant monuments to their own good fortune. Many of the new buildings were erected by British contractors. Across the Atlantic and up the Amazon came an elaborate market building of wrought iron, a new customs house and what was then the world's largest floating dock. Manaus became the first city in South America to install trams, electricity and telephones. So wealthy were the rubber barons that it is said they sent their laundry to Europe to be washed. But certainly their most daring gesture was to build the now famous Opera House. The Teatro Amazoñas was a jewel of the Belle Epoque set in the jungle, a flamboyant and ill-judged gesture of confidence in the continuing prosperity of Amazonia. No sooner had it been completed at astronomic cost than Manaus began its catastrophic tumble; and it was Perfidious Albion, having profited handsomely from the boom times, that was responsible.

The British imported rubber tree seedlings from Brazil, nurtured them at Kew and at their new Botanic Gardens in Singapore, and then launched a massive planting programme in their Malay States colonies. Rubber from these sources easily undersold that produced by the inefficient Brazilian operation with its itinerant workers tapping the wild trees. Manaus descended into romantic decay.

The rebirth of Manaus has been spectacular. The town has been restored to prosperity by a development programme in which aviation is playing the leading part. Since the Brazilian Government launched Operation Amazonia in 1966, a poor, depopulated and isolated city has been transformed; its population has soared from 150,000 to 700,000 in a decade. Investment has created thousands of jobs and Jumbo jets fly into the new International Airport directly from Europe and the United States. Manaus, so recently a forgotten backwater, is now first port of call in Brazil, both for an Air France service from Paris and a Braniff service from Miami. In addition, Surinam Airways has just inaugurated a further service which will provide a direct link to Amsterdam with KLM. This is quite apart from all the international links provided by the domestic carriers.

In trying to discover how this transformation has been achieved it is difficult not to get lost in an Amazonian forest of acronyms. Governmental development agencies abound with names like SUDENE, SUDAM, SUFRAMA, FUNAI, INCAH, IBRA, BASA, PROTERRA and many more. Of these, the only one that need concern us is SUFRAMA (the Superintendancy

for the Manaus Free Trade Zone). At the heart of the Brazilian Government's development strategy has been the creation of a huge Free Trade Zone centred on Manaus but covering a total area of 10,000 square kilometres on the banks of the Rio Negro and Amazon. Unlike other Free Ports, Manaus does not lie on the crossroads of international trade. On the contrary, it lies deep in one of the most isolated corners of the globe and this has forced SUFRAMA to do two things – to put Manaus on the map by creating new roads and airport facilities to supplement the traditional waterways, and then to offer the most generous incentives to attract the tourist and the investor. To woo industrial investment, these incentives include complete exemption from income tax for ten years, exemption from import duties and financial and technical assistance in getting established. The bait has been taken. As of January 1978, 225 manufacturing projects had been approved and 189 were in full production. More than 40,000 jobs had been created with thousands more in the pipeline.

The tourist development of Manaus has been almost equally remarkable. It has centred on the Tropical Hotel, which advertises its package tours as offering 'an Amazonian adventure'. The 358-room Tropical Hotel stands on the banks of the Rio Negro a few miles from where it joins the Amazon. The entire complex is in the middle of thousands of acres of Amazon forest. While the surrounding area is a magnificent example of untouched nature, the hotel itself provides every conventional convenience imaginable – sauna, disco-

Manaus, Brazil. A rubber metropolis brought back to life by the aeroplane.

thèque, swimming pools, tennis courts, shopping arcades, restaurants and cafés, and, of course, conducted tours.

On a river boat trip visitors are offered 'Amazing Amazonia' in several languages, none of them readily comprehensible. The origin of the curious English spoken by the guide remains a mystery until one learns that he is a Bengali, brought up speaking Spanish in Colombia, and that his Portuguese is just as strange to the Brazilian ear as his English is to ours. However, he is not lacking in confidence in any tongue, and the public address system on the tour boat crackles with Amazing Information:

Everyone knows the Amazon is big, but how big is big? Its basin measures 2.7 million square miles, more than twice the size of India, and the river contains one-fifth of the world supply of fresh water. How much water is that? Our visitors from the United States will like to know that in one day the Amazon pours enough water into the Atlantic to keep New York in water for nine years, and scientific tests show its chemical purity is greater than most tap water in the United States. More kinds of fish live in the Amazon than you could possibly imagine – 700 have been classified and some are very strange. Everyone knows about the mean little Piranha, but have you heard of Anableps Tetropthalmus? He has four eyes so that he can see below and above water at the same time. But when nature gives, it also takes away. This same species have genital organs that can function only on the left or right side – so that a 'left-handed' male cannot mate with a 'right-handed' female.

This last piece of information is greeted disapprovingly by an elderly American lady. It is clearly not the sort of intelligence to be found in the *National Geographic Magazine* that she refers to from time to time, as if to verify the evidence of her eyes. But it is the sort of information that is being used to sell the Amazon. The guide is quoting directly from a brochure published by VARIG to publicise its Tropical Hotel, Manaus.

Like many other airlines, VARIG has invested heavily in hotels. Ten have already been constructed and three of them are in areas that were formerly quite isolated and where the tourist had rarely strayed. In selling these hotels the advertisements are full of phrases like 'awesome Amazon', 'untouched nature, abounding with flora and fauna', and 'Amazon adventure'. Generations of travellers' tales, both truthful and fictional, have left us with a thrilling and romantic vision of Amazonia that is now being used by VARIG's marketing men to sell package holidays. The problem is that what the advertisements promise is very hard to deliver. It is, of course, difficult to decide how much people expect on a package deal that gives them three days in the Tropical Hotel, Manaus, as part of a two-week swing round South America. Though the advertising suggests that the visitor might, if he cared to, indulge in a little jungle-bashing, with the chance of a face-to-face confrontation with a jaguar, the fact is that the only animals he is likely to see are in the hotel's own zoo. The tour programme also includes a 'visit to a native village and the opportunity to see rubber trees being tapped'. The reality of this is a half-hour stop during the river boat trip, at a souvenir shop on the river bank, where a

Opposite: Air France tries the appeal of elegance on a menu card in the Seventies.

PARIS
ORLY
08.70

WHAT IS THIS "KOSHER"?

Put very simply, "kosher", or "kasher" means "fit" or "proper". It applies to all the daily requirements of Jewish ritual life. "Kosher" is also the popular name for the Kashruth dietary laws—a discipline of the Jewish faith set forth in the Old Testament. The laws of Kashruth are concerned with the fitness of food for the Jewish table. Their observance has enriched Jewish life and helped to preserve Jewish identity for thousands of years. To the anthropologist, these laws indicate an ancient knowledge of health principles. However, in the traditional Jewish interpretation of the Bible, spiritual, not physical or national health is the sole reason for their observance. The Kashruth laws, as part of Judaism, help to keep the Jewish people aware of their obligations to their God, to their fellow men, and to themselves.

Instant tourism on the packaged Amazon.

much scarred rubber tree is further mutilated and many piranhas, stuffed, mounted and rouged, are purchased as gifts for the boss or the boyfriend back home.

It was that most perceptive traveller, Dame Freya Stark, talking on the subject of travel by air, who remarked regretfully that 'there are fewer nice white places on the maps these days; there is less of the unknown, and the unknown is fundamentally the pleasure of travel'. Ever since its discovery by Europeans, Amazonia has been one of the most challenging and alluring of these 'nice white places on the maps'. It has attracted travellers and explorers like few other corners of the world. Men like Alfred Russell Wallace, Henry Walter Bates and Richard Spruce left a legacy of scholarship and real-life adventure that is even richer and stranger than the fictional Amazonia of R. M. Ballantyne's *Martin Rattler*. Add to this huge bibliography the never-solved mystery story of Colonel P. H. Fawcett's ill-fated expedition of 1925, and it is easy to see why Amazonia has had such a firm grip on the collective imagination of the 'developed' world.

But now, like so many other places on the map, Amazonia is becoming a little shop-soiled. As roads have been built and as the aeroplane has criss-crossed its blank spaces with more and more routes and stamped them with more and more airports, the grandeur and the romance of the term 'Amazonian adventure' has been downgraded to the level of an advertising copy-writer's slogan. Every three-day stopover at the Tropical Hotel, Manaus,

Opposite: El Al explains on-board kosher.

177

Ripe for tourist development. The Rio Negro prepares itself for the future.

with its four-hour cruise down the Rio Negro, its zoo and disco and sauna and its international cuisine, is now an 'Amazonian adventure'. The fact that the experience thus described is about as venturesome as a choirboys' outing is perhaps inevitable and probably what the customer wants. Yet, in so thoroughly devaluing the mystery and wonder and excitement of the Amazon, one cannot help wondering whether those who are selling it – and that is principally the airlines – are not destroying their most precious asset. Once the bubble reputation is burst, it is as if it had never been. And that moment may be closer than the promoters of 'Amazonian adventure' think.

In our consideration of the coming of the tourist to this hitherto little visited part of the globe, there is an interesting fact about the Tropical Hotel, Manaus, that does not find its way into the glossy brochures. According to a local social scientist, within one year of its opening seventy-five per cent of the chambermaids employed by the hotel had become pregnant. In the view of our informant, the local girls simply did not like to say 'No' to the important visitors from the outside world, and he went on to say with some satisfaction that it was highly likely that several of the gallants who had impregnated the girls would have flown out of Manaus taking with them a local strain of venereal infection which does not respond well to antibiotics. Whether one shares his rather apocalyptic view or not, this misfortune does draw

178

attention to what epidemiologists are calling 'airline-transmitted diseases'.

Professor A. W. Woodruff of the London School of Hygiene and Tropical Medicine has been doing some arithmetic, and coming up with some alarming conclusions. He has calculated that in 1978 there were at least 600,000,000 airline passengers, and that about a third, i.e. approaching two hundred million, were intercontinental travellers. 'Through London Airport alone there pass some 23,000,000 passengers a year, of whom it is estimated that at least four million arrive in London from the tropics and subtropics, including the Mediterranean . . . [these figures] indicate that one in thirteen to eighteen of the people in this country [Britain] has been exposed in the recent past to disease in tropical or subtropical regions.'[2] Professor Woodruff goes on to comment on the ignorance of many of the new and inexperienced travellers about the health hazards they may face and the precautions they should take. 'The information given in the brochures issued by the tour operators is inadequate and misleading . . . a result is that serious disease and death is encountered with significant frequency among those who travel in these regions.'

Another source of information on this subject is the BBC's Medical Unit. Every year hundreds of camera crews and reporters make thousands of journeys to every corner of the world. When Dr Frank Zino decided to screen returning film crews and other staff he found that seventeen per cent were suffering from some sort of tropical or subtropical disease, and that in some patients more than one pathology was present. It is true that many of the complaints diagnosed were of a trivial nature, but there are several transmitted diseases that are causing great concern, and not only to the BBC.

Dr Anthony Turner, the Senior Overseas Medical Officer for British Airways, is particularly worried about malaria. He points out that since the early 1970s the number of cases reported each year in Britain has risen steadily from about 100 to almost 2000 in 1978. Other Western European countries are experiencing the same phenomenon. The World Health Organisation reports the strange case of two military recruits who had never visited malarial areas, but who were stationed close to the Zurich International Airport, and who both contracted malaria. 'It is likely that the two soldiers were bitten on the same night by the same infected anopheline [mosquito]' is the conclusion reached. And the account continues gloomily, 'Aircraft arriving from tropical areas have been reported to have carried large numbers of mosquitoes and . . . cases of malaria have occurred in the vicinity of [other] international airports in Europe.'[3] Although the danger of airline-transmitted disease is only just beginning to send alarm signals among the general public, in scientific circles it has long been a matter of concern. In 1933, the Medical Officer of Health for the City of Coventry, Dr

[2] *Journal of the Royal College of Physicians* Vol. 12, No. 4, July 1978.
[3] *WHO Weekly Epidemiological Record*, 1978. Vol. 53, pp. 337–344.

Diamonds in The Sky

Arthur Massey, published a monograph entitled 'Epidemiology in Relation to Air Travel'. In the preface he warns:

Speedier transport is equivalent to the reduction of distance. This was shown when steamships superseded sailing vessels. It is demonstrated more forcibly today by the events of civil aviation. Among the momentous advantages . . . born of this development, there is the disadvantage that countries affected by certain major infectious diseases are brought nearer to countries which ordinarily enjoy freedom therefrom.

Dr Massey's work shows that even forty years ago doctors were aware of the threat of the spread of several diseases, including malaria, and he describes experiments carried out to discover the survival rate of mosquitoes inadvertently carried on aircraft.

But in the very recent past, perhaps the most alarming findings are contained in a paper published in 1978 and summarised as follows in the *British Medical Journal*. 'Apparently most of the sporadic outbreaks of cholera in Europe between 1970 and 1975 were beneath the flight path of airline services from Calcutta.' In the latest *Journal of Hygiene*[4] investigators at the London School of Hygiene and Tropical Medicine have put forward the theory that the source of infection may have been discharged from aircraft. Hand-washings and the overflow from sewage-holding tanks could, they say, contain enough cholera organisms to originate outbreaks, especially if infected droplets fell into fluids which 'would promote rapid bacterial growth. Never again will Minerva feel entirely happy eating out of doors in a Mediterranean setting.'

Despite the slightly flippant tone of that summary, it was based on a serious piece of research and presumably further investigation will follow. In itself, it is enough to raise uneasy reflections on the pandemics that swept Europe in the Middle Ages, and of the detention for forty days of the ships, crews, travellers and cargoes (hence 'quarantine', or *quaranta giorni*').

According to Dr Anthony Turner of British Airways, even those who take the rosiest view would agree that air travel has contributed to the present scourge of venereal disease and to the rapid spread of the various types of influenza. Unfortunately, the more we move around, the more our bacteria and parasites move around with us – or even without us. They are the new generation of stowaways.

In the case of Amazonia, the aeroplane has certainly brought in more disease than it has carried out, and when one looks at its total impact on the area, it is all too easy to see this 'engine of social change' as something largely dangerous and malevolent. That is because aviation has played such a central role in a total development programme that many scientists view with apprehension. The fact is that the aeroplane has made it possible to develop more rapidly than was previously thought possible large areas that some ecologists believe should not be developed at all. The rain forest of the Amazon is one of the world's most ancient, enduring and complex ecosystems.

[4] Vol. 81, No. 36, 1978.

It is also known to be one of the most fragile. The evidence of fossils suggests that it may have existed almost unchanged for sixty million years. Now, in the course of a couple of decades, it is threatened with interference of all kinds. Most anxiety is expressed for the conservation of the soil, once it is stripped of its tree coverage. It is feared that the subsequent erosion and leaching of the soil could cause the whole of Amazonia to become a desert or an area of poor scrubland, able to support only subsistence farming. These fears begin to gain some credibility when one sees what is already happening in the remote territory of Rondonia. Ten years ago the entire area, which is twice the size of England, had a population of only 100,000. The Brazilian Government sought to double that figure by 1980 and encouraged the flow of settlers. To begin with, the only way for them to reach the territory was by air or a circuitous riverboat route, but they were not deterred. The flow has turned into a flood, and the population of Rondonia is already more than half a million. Seen from the air, what these settlers are doing to the countryside is frightening. From horizon to horizon, forest fires consume the timber as the land is cleared for homes and ranches. By day the smoke is so thick that it even makes flying dangerous. Familiar landmarks are totally obscured and pilots are quite disorientated in the rapidly changing landscape. Optimists see Rondonia as a tropical California, which later this century will bring great agricultural wealth to Brazil. Critics say the soil may be ruined in a generation. That ecological debate is far beyond the scope of this book, yet it must be said that many of the difficulties would simply not exist if the aeroplane had not opened up this virgin territory to farmers, ranchers, prospectors and lumber men. It is said that there are pioneers all over Amazonia who can fly a plane and ride a horse, but who cannot drive a car. Certainly there are plenty of communities, including substantial towns like Cruzeiro do Sul which, for most of the year when the river waters are low, are totally isolated except by air.

But perhaps the most threatened part of the Amazonian ecosystem is its native human population. There are thought to be 80,000 Indians living in Amazonia and their interests are protected by the government agency FUNAI, the Fundacão Nacional do India. Throughout the world and particularly in the Americas, the history of the impact of the European immigrant on the primitive native population has been sad and shaming. Despite the efforts of the Brazilian Government, some anthropologists fear that the Amazonian Indian will inevitably be wiped out as a distinct cultural entity. Unfortunately, the aeroplane has been used against the Indians as a tool of intimidation and oppression. Areas that settlers wished to clear of their native populations have been 'bombed' with sticks of dynamite and in other cases clothing infected with smallpox has been dropped into Indian villages with predictably horrifying results. It is a melancholy fact that the aeroplane, which has proved to have been all too sufficient a means to persecute these simple people, has been quite inadequate to protect them from the incoming settlers. Many *fazendas* are hundreds of miles from administration centres and virtually self-governing. In this frontier country, gun-law still prevails and with the best will in the world the occasional police patrol in a light aircraft cannot possibly prevent abuses. In one case a landowner had succeeded, with the help of an unscrupulous missionary, in holding an Indian tribe in conditions of slavery. Eventually the authorities learned what was happening and put a stop to it, but not soon enough to prevent dreadful suffering.

The story of the aeroplane in one of the last of the frontier lands is much more complex than its history in the developed world. In Europe and North America, it is a tale of steady technological and commercial progress, of winning a place within an established communications system and of the subsequent social and economic adjustments that had to be made. In Brazil and in other frontier areas the picture is more dramatic and drawn in high relief: both the benefits and the dangers of aviation are more obvious and pressing. Yet, however alarming the changes it may help to bring, it is quite certain that air travel will play an indispensable part in the future of those remaining 'white patches on the maps', and those who talk as if they would like to turn back the clock and banish aircraft from the skies should perhaps take note of another reflection of Charles Francis Adams Jr on the coming of the railways:

. . . perhaps if the existing community would take now and then the trouble to pass in review the changes it has already withstood, it would be less astounded at the revolutions which continually do and continually must flash before it; perhaps also it might with more grace accept the inevitable, and cease from useless attempts at making a wholly new world conform itself to the rules and theories of a bygone civilisation.

In New Guinea, the jump into the late twentieth century has been even bigger and more rapid. Consider a day in September 1978, an entirely typical day. At the end of a steep and grassy clearing, high in a range of impressive mountains, what looks like a Stone Age raiding party has gathered. The men are short, heavy-featured and dusty-black. They carry a large assortment of businesslike weapons: across their backs they wear cloaks of beaten bark and around their waists thick sporrans of dried grass. Nearby is a group of bare-breasted women and naked children. They are members of the Anga tribe of the Highlands of Papua New Guinea and the grassy clearing is an airstrip. They are waiting for the arrival of a scheduled flight from Goroka, the capital town of the Central Highlands district. These men, women and children are part of the world family of air travellers. Their grandfathers – and probably their fathers too – were certainly head-hunters, and perhaps cannibals.

When the little aeroplane arrives, it becomes evident that the hand luggage of those on board is bows and arrows and that their more substantial baggage are their heavier weapons, clubs and axes, all neatly labelled. When this tribe was first contacted by Europeans forty years ago, its people had not even

182

discovered the wheel, yet for the past few years they have travelled regularly in a sophisticated machine which must be even more magical to them than it is to the rest of us. They call that machine in pidgin English *'balus'*, which means 'bird'. We call it a de Havilland Twin Otter. As part of that immense fellowship, 600,000,000 people, who every year travel somewhere by air, these primitive tribesmen share the same advantages and excitements of flying as the rest of us, and probably the same fears and irritations. They are the improbable continuation of that story which started sixty years ago, when the first fare-paying passenger boarded the first daily scheduled flight from London to Paris. What is even more improbable is that aerial services in New Guinea followed hard on the heels of those in Europe and by the early 1930s had so far overtaken them that the two busiest airports in the world, by a very long way, measured in terms of take-offs and landings, were both located in this remote and backward country.

Fifty years ago, most of Papua New Guinea was unknown, unmapped, unsurveyed. This is a country where everything stands in the way of the road and railway builder – coastal swamps, great rivers that never keep their course for more than a year or two and, above all, the mountains, a switch-back of steep and jungled ridges rising to a towering central spine dominated by the 15,000-foot peak of Mount William. A further discouragement to the traveller, particularly in the Central Highlands, was the aggressive nature of the inhabitants. For all of the clansmen warfare was a way of life and for many cannibalism a customary practice. If ever there was a need to fly

Men and women of the Anga tribe on the airstrip at Marawaka in the Central Highlands.

over the difficulties rather than struggle through them, surely it was in New Guinea, particularly when there were such considerable rewards waiting for the early explorers. In 1922 two prospectors, William 'Sharkeye' Park and Jack Nettleton, struck gold on the Bulolo River. The New Guinea gold rush was on, and the aeroplane entered a new phase of its development.

It is probably true to say that only the lust for gold could have provided the impetus – and the capital – for the extraordinary achievements of the pioneer aviators in New Guinea. In the early 1920s, when the gold rush started, air transportation was still a feeble and tentative business and many doubted if it had any future at all. Yet, in that distant river valley, still peopled by Stone Age tribes, progress was so rapid that more air freight was lifted to and from the Bulolo goldfields in the late 1920s and early 1930s than was flown by all the rest of the world's airlines put together. The explanation is simple. Hundreds of gold-fevered prospectors were landing on the coast: to reach the goldfields was an eight-day walk inland, through thick jungles and up razor-back ridges, with a real danger of attack by the hostile tribesmen, who were very upset by all these strangers making their way through their territory. To build a road was far too costly and time-consuming, and the only way to bring in supplies was on the backs of unwilling native porters, and that was hopelessly inadequate. If there were fifty porters, twenty-five of them would have had to carry food for the others, which was a wasteful, expensive operation. It was soon realised that the aeroplane, primitive though it was, was the only answer.

By the end of 1927 there were four aerial services operating between Lae on the coast and Wau in the goldfields. There was a wide variety of aeroplanes in use, but some of the entrepreneurs were convinced that, to meet the real needs of the goldfields, they needed something more robust than the light string and fabric biplanes. The purchase of the first all-metal aircraft, the Junkers W 34, was a great advance, but its payload was still only 2000 lbs. A more efficient Junkers, the G 31 tri-motor, was already in service in Germany, and with this aircraft Charles Banks planned to do something in aviation that had never been attempted before. He wanted to operate steel dredges weighing between two and three thousand tons and he had the fantastic idea of flying them in, piece by piece, and assembling them in the goldfields. The evidence of his success is still there, rusting away in the jungle; skeletons of the great dredges towering over the tops of the trees are clearly visible from the road that now carries heavy trucks up from the coast. The machinery was designed and built in sections, all of which were within the 7000-lb lifting capacity of the Junkers G 31. As well as the dredges, a complete small town, generating gear and sawmill were flown from Lae to Wau. Four Suffolk Punches, transported at the bargain price of £35 each, were probably the world's first airborne horses. In one month in 1931, the fleet of four Junkers carried more freight into the Bulolo goldfields than the combined air fleets of the world had flown in the previous twelve months.

The breakthrough was not just a matter of shattering freight records, although every one of them was demolished time and time again; it involved learning how to do things with aeroplanes that had never been attempted before, of achieving high standards of efficiency and safety under great difficulties. The greatest hazard in New Guinea was, and still is, the weather. By the standards of the 1930s the Junkers was a powerful aircraft, but its flying height and rate of climb were limited, especially with a load. When the clouds suddenly closed in, a pilot would find himself flying blind down a valley, wondering if he would ever find his way out of it. He would do up to seven trips in one day, according to the weather, starting early in the morning and pressing on until the clouds rolled in.

But despite the problems and the dangers, the Guinea Airways pioneers achieved excellent safety standards. As well as flying record volumes of passengers and freight, they established an impressive row of 'firsts'. They were, for instance, among the first to provide insurance for their passengers, but only for Europeans. Native labourers were regarded as freight and were transported by weight at a rate of a shilling a pound. But, whether they were regarded as cargo or as human beings, the aeroplane was transforming the world of the native New Guinean, not only in the goldfields, but in the Highlands, where it was employed as the tool of the prospector and explorer.

Before 1975, when the country gained independence, Papua New Guinea

Papua New Guinea. Gold-mining equipment brought in by air.

was administered by Australia and it was her policy in the 1920s and 1930s to establish a government presence everywhere in the territory. The police patrols that set off on foot to explore the central plateau were often accompanied by prospectors and supported by aircraft. In 1933 a patrol officer, Jim Taylor, and a prospector, Mick Leahy, made the first major expedition into the interior of New Guinea to be supplied entirely by air. Before entering an unexplored area on foot, Taylor used to fly over it several times, to perform an aerial survey but also to warn the people that something unusual was about to happen. He recalled:

When we made contact with them on foot they were ready for fighting and carried shields and weapons. We walked up towards them and as soon as I got into what I thought was a favourable position, I put my arms out and made a humming sound and pointed to the sky. They were ready for that and they all came forward and shook hands and threw their arms away and said in sign language, we all know you, we heard and saw you go by a week ago.[5]

Once the foot patrol had established camp, the help of the tribesmen was enlisted to make an airstrip. After clearing the bush, they were encouraged to perform their traditional dances: the shuffling and stamping proved to be a most effective way of flattening the ground. Then came the day when the first aircraft would make a landing at the new base. Taylor recalls the arrival of one of the most famous of the pioneer pilots, Ian Grabowski:

When the 'bird' landed, the people saw Grabowski emerge, looking as if he might have been a Martian in his white regalia (he always wore a white flying suit) and they went to bow down. Shortly after, the chief made a speech lasting one and a half hours. No one spoke except him, and if anyone looked as if they were likely to speak, he had his battle-axe and he looked towards them and they didn't say anything. They thought we were the dead returned and they admired us for coming. One man tied himself to the machine so that he could be taken up to see the other world. Another came to us and said, 'You know, all my relatives are dead, let me go with you.'

Andrew Strathearn, Professor of Anthropology at London University, has spent a great deal of time talking to older members of the Highland tribes. He says:

Those men who are old now still remember very clearly and vividly the times when the first aeroplanes arrived, and one in particular has given me a lengthy account of this. He describes how he was sitting by the river along with the older men practising the art of making stone axes. They heard the first noise of the aeroplane up above. They looked for it and at first they thought it could not possibly be in the sky. It must be on the ground below, so they searched for it there, thinking it was some particular new kind of wild animal. Finally they looked up and they saw it was a bird. But the real interest they took in the aeroplane was after it had landed and the explorers and administration officers emerged and began to show the types of wealth they had.[6]

Professor Strathearn also discovered that in the areas where the people

---

[5] Conversation with Julian Pettifer, 1 March 1978.
[6] Conversation with Julian Pettifer, 4 June 1978.

were not cannibals, 'they assumed that the Europeans *were*, because they came out of the sky in this extraordinary thing and therefore must be a type of sky spirit and in their mythology the sky spirit is cannibalistic'. Since the aeroplane was taken to be a living thing, it was naturally assumed to perform all the natural functions. There are many accounts of tribesmen attempting to feed it on bananas and even live pigs, and crawling about underneath it to determine its sex.

A typical Highlands village whose main contact with the outside world is by air.

The culture that produced the aeroplane is so very far from the Stone Age world it encountered that it is amazing to see how quickly flying has become a commonplace experience in New Guinea. But according to Professor Strathearn, 'It is a quality of the Highlands population that they very rapidly get used to new things and become keen on them.' Apart from flying, 'there was no other way in which they could get down to the coast and begin working for cash on the plantations; there was no other way they could get to hospital, or to school, before schools were established in all the local areas. So for more than twenty years before roads were built, the aeroplane became something that was part of everyday experience for these people in a way that it isn't for most ordinary people in England.'

One pioneer recalls meeting a Highlander off a plane and taking him for a ride in a truck. After a few minutes bowling down the road his passenger asked anxiously when they would take off. For him, all machines were flying machines.

187

Diamonds in The Sky

The construction of airstrips in the deep bush, started by the patrol officers in the 1930s, has continued to the present day. New areas are still being rescued from isolation by the aeroplane. For the first-time visitor, landing at places like Marawaka, where the strip is short and steep, is a hair-raising experience; yet, primitive though it is, it has a twice-weekly scheduled service and a twice-weekly government charter to serve the administrators. Before the airstrip was opened, the people of the Anga tribe who live nearby were still largely untouched by Western influence. They were extremely warlike and are still much feared by their neighbours, not without reason. They always go armed, and the spears, bows and arrows and clubs they carry are not just playthings. Hardly a day goes by without a report of interclan fighting and killing, and even occasionally cannibalism somewhere in the Highlands. And yet they have this scheduled air service which brings them – as well as the opportunity to travel – oil for their generators, books for their school and, to many people's regret, beer for their bottle shops.

It has also brought them another influence, almost as profound as alcohol, the Christian religion. Making regular appearances on the airstrip are the little planes bearing the logo of MAF. The Missionary Aviation Fellowship is only one among several aerial services run by the numerous Christian missions, and no account of aviation in Papua New Guinea can ignore their work. They carried on where the early government patrols left off. According, once again, to Professor Strathearn, 'The influence of the missionaries supported by the aerial network which they separately built up for themselves was enormous. They stayed for a long time in the area, got to know the people fairly well and sometimes learned the language. They were often established in places where no road has been built and probably never will be built.' But perhaps the most valuable work is the aerial ambulance service. The missions are often prepared to fly to destinations and in weather conditions that might deter commercial operators.

Nevertheless, the role of the flying priest is declining and many of the airstrips carved out of the bush by the missions are now served by commercial operators. The biggest of these is Talair. Talair is what is known in the aviation world as a Third Level Operator, which sounds patronising and is sometimes meant to be, but there is nothing third-rate about Talair. It operates sixty aircraft, flying to 134 destinations, which makes it the biggest Third Level Operator in the Southern hemisphere, probably accomplishing more take-offs and landings than big international operators like Pan American and Lufthansa.

Tep-Tep is a good example of a kind of Talair destination. Even on the finest of days, landing on airstrips like Tep-Tep can cause anxiety, with the spiralling descent through a narrow gorge onto the steep and grassy strip. 6700 feet up in its spectacular bowl of mountains, Tep-Tep was totally isolated until 1973 when the airstrip was put in. Before that, it would take a week to walk to the nearest town on the coast.

In the six years since the aeroplane came to Tep-Tep progress – or at least change – has been rapid. Several tin-roofed buildings brought in by air have taken their ungracious place among the thatched roofs. Inside one of these new structures a teacher flown in from the provincial capital provides the first generation of local children to receive *any* education with a course of elementary studies that includes English. It is all very impressive, except for the sad fact that, while learning a foreign language, many children are forgetting their own.

In Papua New Guinea one can see in microcosm and very sharply focused what is happening worldwide – increased mobility is very quickly wiping out cultural differences. This can be seen not only in language, but in dress, customs, religious beliefs, crafts and music: the whole culture is breaking down, and this is largely due to the mobility of people. Closely related to this is the introduction of the cash economy, people doing things for money rather than in a co-operative spirit.

What has happened at the village of Karamui shows how the cash economy has developed in the Highlands since the introduction of air services. Although it is only twenty minutes' flying time from Goroka, the only way to get there – except by air – is on foot over jungle paths and that would take weeks. Piled beside the airstrip are sacks of coffee-beans waiting to be flown to market. Each sack will bring the growers about £170, which is a great deal of money for a people who until recently never handled money at all. Until the aeroplane came they were subsistence farmers: they grew enough to eat and that was the end of their labours. Now, all over the Highlands, they grow coffee and cardamom seeds and raise cattle. In Karamui, the beginnings of their herd, like everything else, came in by air, and when they have stock to sell, the calves will leave by the same route. But not everything that has found its way into these Highland fastnesses can be counted a blessing. The newly-established clinic and its medicines are welcome, to be sure. But what of the diseases that were previously unknown here? The tuberculosis, the influenza and recently the epidemic of venereal disease that has swept the Highlands? And despite the fine new cash economy, malnutrition is still serious among children because money earned flying out coffee is spent on flying in, not food, but beer.

Of course, Karamui was bound to change. Sooner or later all the people of the Highlands would have been rescued from their isolation and joined the rest of the world. It is just that the aeroplane has allowed a great deal to happen in a very short time. And there are certainly more surprises to come. The foreign tourist is only just beginning to make himself felt in Papua New Guinea, but already the Prime Minister, Mr Michael Somare, is concerned about future developments. He wants to see tourists, but not too many. Perhaps it is a little late for the Prime Minister to be worrying on that score. Although the number of tourists is small, some of them are pushing into the remoter parts of the country and causing no little stir.

Karawari Lodge.

'Amboin International Airport', says a crude wooden sign at the end of a remote missionary airstrip now turned over to the works of Mammon. Every few days, an aircraft lands at Amboin with a group of about twenty tourists, mostly Australians and Americans. They are on their way to spend a few days at the Karawari Lodge, a resort hotel on the Karawari River where they are promised, among other things, an intimate glimpse of the private lives of the locals. Their journey has brought them from Port Moresby to Mount Hagen in a Fokker Friendship of Air Niugini and thence to Amboin in a Talair Twin Otter. For the next stage, they scramble down the muddy bank of the Kara- wari River into a flat-bottomed river boat that roars off on a forty-minute ride to their final destination. When the hotel comes into sight, it looks very much like one of the villages scattered along the river bank. The buildings are local timber and thatch constructions and include a traditional *haus Tamboran* or spirit house, which is the hotel's main dining-room and bar. The visitors are conveyed up a fearsomely steep hillside to their lodgings in a wooden trailer drawn by a skeletal truck that is clearly long beyond retire-

190

ment age. The driver, a bearded young New Zealander, is the manager and the only white man at the hotel. Karawari Lodge was built by a former Government Patrol Officer who had the ambitious idea of operating it as what can best be described as a Jungle Bunny Club. He hoped to attract a male clientele from Port Moresby or even Australia to spend a few days in a specialised establishment where they were promised the kind of diversions that would tempt a jaded appetite. The project failed because of fierce opposition from local fundamentalist missionaries. The nature of the attractions that were offered is clearly indicated by the works of art still adorning the hotel – phallic figures vigorously carved by local craftsmen support the great roof beams and sprawl across the walls. Today, blue-haired ladies from Ohio examine them circumspectly and assume they are just local fertility totems, which is the less interesting part of the truth.

After the visitors have been shown their rooms, each of which is provided with hot water from solar panels, they gather beneath the rampant caryatids in the dining-room to hear their itinerary for the following four days. They are promised 'a glimpse of local village life *au naturel*'. In this part of East Sepik Province, the people are not even subsistence farmers, they are gatherers and fishermen. The tourists will be shown how they extract the starchy grains of foodstuff from the wild sago palm and how they set their fish traps.

These are everyday activities, and obviously they can be seen in any village at any time, but when visitors are also told that they will be able to witness initiation rites, one begins to wonder how it is done. Since the turnround of visitors at Karawari Lodge is very rapid, it is obviously impossible that each arrival coincides with a spontaneous local event, so there are contracts with a number of local villages to stage their intimate rituals specially for the tourists. The climax of the four-day stay at Karawari Lodge is a two-hour river trip to a village where the tourists see the re-enactment of a headhunting raid of the kind that undoubtedly took place there thirty or forty years ago. One wonders how long it will be before the villagers of the East Sepik have become as commercialised as the famous Mud Men of the Highlands, who are now on contract to a travel agency and will enact their charming myth only for money.

Whatever inhibitions the Prime Minister, Michael Somare, may have about promoting tourism, they are certainly not shared by Bryan Grey, General Manager of the state airline, Air Niugini, who believes 'that the majority of the people desire tourism because the money and the employment that can stem from tourism is very important to them in an area where unemployment is high'.[7] He is also unreservedly rapturous about the total impact of the aeroplane. 'There's no doubt at all that aviation is responsible for the entire development of Papua New Guinea. The first wheel that most of these people actually saw was the wheel of an aircraft.'

[7] Conversation with Julian Pettifer, 2 March 1978.

Martha Handu of Air Niugini in her home village.

However one judges the broad benefits conferred by the aeroplane, Air Niugini itself is still staffed, at least in most of the technical and managerial positions, by foreigners, mainly from Australia; but the airline is proud of the progress made in training locals to take over these top positions. In 1978 it had its first black captain, and others will certainly be promoted in the next few years. In this connection, an article in the American magazine, *Ebony*, is instructive. According to *Ebony*:

Black pilots are such strangers to most travellers that it is still not unusual for passengers in a terminal to mistake him for a baggage handler. Most whites are shocked to see a black face in the cockpit. While more than a hundred black pilots [in the US] may seem a lot, they are only a minute percentage of the 40,000 commercial pilots flying for scheduled airlines today.

Passenger prejudice against black pilots is a fact of life and in a late-developing country like Papua New Guinea the problem is particularly troublesome, but by the state airline at least it is confronted head-on. If you fly Air Niugini you may well find yourself in the hands of a black pilot; you will certainly be served by black cabin staff, by a girl like Martha Handu, who somehow manages to live in two incredibly different worlds. When she visits her family in their mountain village she still sometimes wears the *Tupa* (beaten bark) skirt and the shell beads that her mother and sister wear. At work, she appears in the trim tailored Air Niugini uniform. While her grandparents never travelled outside the valley in which they were born, she flies off to Hong Kong and Australia. The generation of Martha Handu have flown three thousand years at record speed and, considering the toughness of the trip, they show remarkably little jet lag.

Opposite: The Central Highlands, Papua New Guinea, from the air.

192

NINE

The Wide-Bodied Seventies

The 1970s were ushered in by the entry into service in 1970 of Boeing's 747, the Jumbo Jet. Pan American led the way and within a few months the big new aircraft was to be seen at many of the world's major airports, in the livery of Lufthansa, JAL, and all the other airlines who had so much to fear from being left behind.

It was the largest commercial aircraft ever to fly. It carried twice as many passengers as any previous plane, it flew faster, the tip of its tail was as high off the ground as a six-storey building, a tennis court could be accommodated easily on each wing, the aeroplane in which the Wright brothers made their original flight would have fitted inside the passenger cabin with plenty of room to spare – the airlines competed with one another in the exciting business of finding new ways of describing the monstrous size of their latest acquisition.

The advantages to the passengers were equally remarkable, or so the publicity people said. JAL put it this way:

The Economy Class cabin of our new 747 can accommodate 320 passengers. And yet you'll never experience the sense of being crowded into a long tube. To begin with, you'll seldom see more than a third of your fellow passengers because the entire cabin has been divided into three sections by upholstered bulkheads. And the 'tubular' atmosphere has gone completely, because the entire interior of this new plane has been re-shaped with an almost flat ceiling and only slightly curved walls. These features, combined with the muted colours and delicate patterns traditional to Japanese décor (each of the three sections having its own floral motif), have been arranged to give you the feeling of being in a tastefully designed living-room, rather than in the Economy Class cabin of a futuristic jet plane.[1]

It may be so, although 320 guests are surely rather a lot for anyone's living-room, however tastefully designed. The 747SP has arrived meanwhile. Pan American put the 747SP into service in 1977, the first airline to do so. This aircraft is shorter and lighter than the 747 and it can fly 1500 miles further. In the words of the proud operator:

[1] *The Garden Jet – JAL's 747*, Japan Air Lines, 1970.

Opposite above: An aircraft of Tal Air on the airstrip at Marawaka.

Opposite below: The terrain of the Central Highlands has made the aeroplane the only means of transport.

Although considerably larger, the control cabin of a 747 is less complex than that of a 707. The major portion of the instrumentation in a 747 control cabin is identified in this picture of a Trans World Airlines superjet cockpit:

1--Overhead switch panel
2--Standby compass
3--Navigational radio selector
4--Autopilot engage switch
5--Navigation mode selector
6--Speed mode selector

7--Airplane registry no.
8--Map, panel light knobs
9--Central instrument warning lights
10--Approach progress indicators
11--Inertial navigation warning lights

12--Thrust reverser indicator lights
13--Pitch trim controls
14--Clock
15--Mach/airspeed indicator
16--Gyro horizon
17--Electric altimeter
18--Radio altimeter

19--Navigation marker beacon lights
20--Total air temperature
21--Gear down/locked indicators
22--Microphone switch
23--Autopilot disengage
24--Nose gear tiller
25--Chart holder
26--Pilot's control yoke
27--Horizontal direction indicator
28--Vertical speed indicator
29--Standby altimeter
30--Engine pressure ratio gauges
31--Lowspeed engine comp.
32--Exhaust gas temp.
33--High speed engine compressor RPM
34--Fuel flow indicator
35--Flap position indicator
36--Static air temp.
37--Turn and bank indicator
38--Flight control position indicator
39--Annunciator light panel
40--True airspeed indicator
41--Landing gear control handle
42--Radio magnetic indicator
43--Instrument switches
44--Reserve brakes
45--Speed brake handle
46--Thrust levers
47--Inertial navigation controls
48--Brake pressure
49--Water injection control
50--Computer selector switch

51--Weather radar scope
52--Rudder pedal
53--Manual stabilizer trim levers
54--Go-around switches
55--Flap lever
56--Pitch trim
57--Parking brake latch
58--Parking brake light
59--Engine start levers
60--Stabilizer trim cutout switches
61--Seat arm, down position
62--Weather radar control panel
63--Automatic direction finder
64--Air traffic control transponder
65--Very high frequency radio
66--Ultra high frequency radio
67--Aileron trim
68--Rudder trim
69--Warning horn silencer
70--Seat positioning controls
71--Pilot's handset for intercom and passenger announcements
72--Seat arm, up position

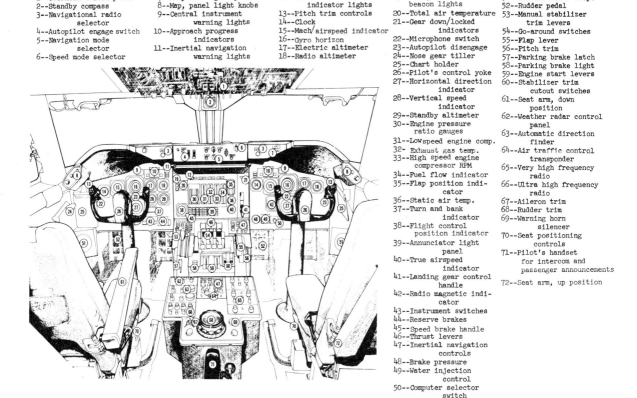

Key to the 747's controls.

The longest range commercial aircraft ever flown, the SP enabled Pan Am to re-draw the world's air routes: for the first time passengers could fly non-stop between New York and Tokyo, New York and Bahrain, Los Angeles and Auckland, San Francisco and Hong Kong.

Over distances like this, it might certainly be comforting to be able to feel that one was in a tastefully designed living-room, rather than an aeroplane. But, sitting-room or aeroplane, one is stuck with it for the length of a full working day, with nothing but the clouds, one's fellow passengers and the in-flight movies to look at. There are times when the old-timers on the London–South Africa service strike one as having been immensely privileged.

It is interesting to wonder what the aviation historians of the future will make of the 1970s. What will they see as its significant features – wide-bodied jets, supersonic travel, hijackings, computerised information systems, camping out on the pavement for five days to get a Laker seat to New York, waiting at an airport for thirty-six hours and more for a holiday flight to Palma? What

194

balance will they strike between the technical achievements and the human miseries?

They could usefully start with the miseries, of which there is a plentiful contemporary record, written while passengers' sufferings were still fresh in their memories. A useful beginning, since few worse instances of callousness and mismanagement would be likely to be encountered, might be an account of an incident that happened in Russia in 1973. The story, as it emerged during an attack on the responsible authorities printed in the Soviet weekly paper, *Literaturnaya Gazeta*,[2] concerned a scheduled flight from Moscow to the Far East. The aircraft was only half full at take-off, so, in a sudden fit of thriftiness, Aeroflot cancelled the flight and told the unfortunate passengers to relax in the packed terminal building. They waited there all night and all the next day. Most of them, understandably, were asleep or dozing when finally an announcement was made that the plane was leaving at last. When these sorely tried passengers had roused themselves and attempted to check in again, they were required to pay an additional twenty-five per cent of the fare as a fine for missing the second flight.

The West might find it difficult to beat that, but there would be runners-up in fair abundance. Some of the most fearful of these horror stories would certainly concern the effects of the go-slow perpetrated by French air traffic controllers during the summer of 1978. One of the victims was Magnus Linklater, News Editor of the London *Sunday Times*, who was attempting to return from Palma with his family. They eventually arrived at their destination thirty-seven hours late and after spending fourteen hours in the aircraft, first waiting in the queue to take off and then in flight. He reported:

By seven o'clock last Sunday night the main charter departure lounge of Palma Airport was beginning to resemble something out of the Gulag Archipelago. Harsh overhead lights revealed a sea of apathetic humanity welling over the rubbish-strewn floor. Some lay, contorted, on hard plastic benches. Others shuffled forward in endless queues for food. Behind the bars waiters were charging outrageous prices for sandwiches and warm beer without raising more than the faintest protest from their defeated customers.[3]

Mr R. J. Wilkins never got abroad at all. With his wife and three children he was booked to go to Majorca on 30 July. After waiting $26\frac{1}{2}$ hours they gave up: the flight eventually left $35\frac{3}{4}$ hours late.

This was completely outside our tolerance level and the whole experience was a nightmare. During all this time the airport was absolutely filthy, catering facilities were completely overwhelmed, it took $1\frac{1}{2}$ hours queueing to get anything to eat or drink and the only place we found to sit or lie was on the floor.[4]

The Wilkinses were lucky to have a floor and doubly lucky to have a roof over

[2] Summarised in *The Times*, 27 November 1978.
[3] *Sunday Times*, 3 September 1978.
[4] *The Times*, 8 August 1978.

The delights of flying. Waiting for Laker seats to New York outside the terminal at Victoria Station, London.

their heads. Large numbers of people, trying to return to the United States on one of Laker Airways Skytrain services, had to make do with the pavements around Victoria Station in London.

Skytrain, which began in 1977, allowed people to cross the Atlantic for £59 one way. It was a great triumph for the owner of Laker Airways, Freddie Laker, who had battled against British Airways, Pan American and the other transatlantic operators for years in order to run this kind of service. Laker insisted that there was a large potential market that had not been so far tapped, simply because the existing fares were too high, and once Skytrain was off the ground he was very soon proved right, so right indeed that all his former critics immediately made plans to follow his example. It was Laker, virtually single-handed, who broke up the established IATA-supported Atlantic fare structure. What he offered was very basic. Seats could not be booked in advance. They were obtainable only on the day the flight departed from London, New York or, later, Los Angeles. In New York, Laker sold 530 seats a night on two planes. Of these, ninety were obtainable at the company's two Manhattan offices, the rest at Rego Park, halfway between Manhattan and Kennedy. Queueing began at Rego in the small hours and selling started at 4 am, for planes leaving for London at 11 in the evening. Meals could be obtained on board, but they had to be paid for.

196

It is a spartan way of travelling, but it is very cheap and large numbers of people, mostly young, are willing to put up with hardships for the sake of the price. And Laker Airways makes an excellent profit on these services. The overheads are low, the planes usually full, and, most valuable asset of all, Laker is regarded as the people's friend, on both sides of the Atlantic, the man who caters for ordinary people and for nobody else. 'Better Laker than never' has been their motto and, so far from resenting the long queues, the Laker public shows every sign of being grateful that the service exists at all. It is a remarkable social phenomenon and Freddie Laker's knighthood was well earned.

The trouble in July, August and September 1978 was caused by one simple fact. During May and June, thousands of passengers had been ferried across the Atlantic by Laker and at standby fares by other airlines. When they wanted to go home again, all the airlines were at their busiest time of the year and there were simply not enough seats available. So the passengers piled up in enormous human traffic jams. Many of them had little more than their fare left. What happened was briefly but skilfully described by a London journalist who devoted special attention to these strange happenings:

Lakerville, that instant shanty town in the streets around Victoria Station, London, continued to grow yesterday as the summer, nearing its height, unleashed a second day of torrential rain on the flimsy shelter of its two thousand inhabitants.

The Queue, as it is affectionately known, edges slowly towards its goal: the Skytrain office in the station where each day, several hundred people pay £59 for a one-way ticket to New York, by courtesy of Sir Frederick Laker. While they wait, and it may be for as long as four or five days, Lakervillians build, erecting makeshift homes of tarpaulin, plastic sheeting, polythene and tents against the iron railings and walls of the neighbourhood, keeping them together with string and good humour.

The queue is split into ten sections, each with about 250 people, and all sections have their own queue leader (a voluntary post) who takes down the names, nationalities and passport numbers of its members, issuing them a number that will dictate when they can buy a ticket. In this way nobody can jump the queue, which remains orderly and friendly, in spite of the weather.

Each section is divided into groups of eight people and each group must at all times have at least two members on duty to keep its place and deal with any difficulties. Occasionally a section is moved on by the police because of complaints from local (permanent) residents, but a new home is quickly found and the queue settles down again.

Many nationalities are represented, but young Americans returning home, frequently with no more than the fare in their pockets, predominate. People while away the hours, reading, playing cards and games, strumming guitars and gossiping.[5]

There were similar scenes outside the airline offices, although not on such a large scale. During the summer months, between 250 and 500 people were queueing outside British Airways' Victoria Terminal at 6.30 in the morning to

[5] *The Times*, 3 August 1978.

buy the day's allocation of standby tickets to the United States. They were not looking for a comfortable journey; all they wanted was something cheap. 'I would travel to London on the kitchen chair,' said one Australian woman, 'if it saved me dollars.' She was reflecting an attitude which created a greater upheaval in the airline industry during 1978 than all the problems of the North Atlantic over the previous twenty years. The airlines somehow have to adjust themselves to the results of this marketing explosion without committing suicide.

The dismantling of the IATA regulations that allowed the introduction of highly-competitive cheap fares on international routes was matched within the United States by an equally dramatic move towards de-regulation. The Carter Administration promised to free the airlines from many of the economic controls and restrictions, and to do this Professor Alfred Kahn, the futurologist, was appointed to the Civil Aeronautics Board. Within a very short time the American airlines found they were free to cut fares and compete on new routes, a development that was greeted enthusiastically by some and with deep dismay by others. One of Professor Kahn's greatest supporters was Richard J. Ferris, the President and Chief Executive of United Airlines. United serves 110 cities throughout the USA, has more than 50,000 employees and carries an average of 130,000 passengers a day, which makes it not only North America's largest domestic carrier, but, with the exception of the Soviet Union's Aeroflot, the largest airline in the world. Little wonder that Richard Ferris welcomed de-regulation and that many of his smaller competitors were nervous; in a no-holds-barred contest United seemed to be in a strong position to overwhelm the opposition.

In short, Dick Ferris expected United to thrive in a climate of free competition, but even he was astonished at the success of the new discount fares. 'If last year [1977] somebody had come along to us and said that next June you are going to grow by thirty per cent, I tell you we would have locked him up and thrown away the key because we never would have believed him.'[6] Why, one wonders, were the airlines so surprised at the success of the cheaper fares?

And who were these new passengers who were filling the aircraft? According to Monte Lazarus, who handles United's relations with the Federal Government, 'People who never flew before are having the opportunity to fly. How do I know? Very simple . . . Ask our aircraft cleaners, they will tell you that passengers are taking things off aircraft that they never took before; they are taking souvenirs like cocktail stirrers, napkins and safety instructions. It didn't happen before, so we know they are first-time fliers.'[7]

Behind that observation lies the heart-warming fact that a seat in an aeroplane is now within the means of a far wider public and that many of the new passengers are what the airlines term 'VFR' (visiting friends and re-

[6] Conversation with Julian Pettifer, 4 August 1978.
[7] Conversation with Julian Pettifer, 12 November 1978.

latives). Everywhere, families separated by great distances are being brought together by the aeroplane.

So, in 1978, the image that airlines in the United States were selling was no longer elegance and service or even punctuality; it was value for money, and every major airline was marketing a discount fare with names like Chicken-feed, Peanuts, No Frills and even Super No Frills. That these special offers meant fuller aeroplanes and higher profits there is no doubt, but they also presented the operators with enormous and unprecedented problems which they had not expected, and which overwhelmed their systems and procedures. Nothing, they realised, was ever going to be the same again. Mass travel had arrived in a way which surprised even the Americans. What happened to United Airlines was entirely typical.

'We are', reported Kay Lund, of Consumer Affairs at United, 'receiving more complaints per 100,000 passengers boarded than ever before.'[8] The complaints came both from experienced and new passengers. The first were irritated and frequently infuriated, the second confused. Reservations could not cope with the unprecedented number of enquiries, there were ever-longer queues at the check-in desks, flights were missed and late, baggage was delayed and lost, standards of service declined seriously and rapidly all round.

A letter received from a businessman who had flown with United for thirty years indicated why the airline was worried:

Cut rate fares have certainly filled up your planes and this probably makes you feel good, but I can tell you that the full fare businessman who is really supporting the airlines now has to put up with many inconveniences. I can tell you, I hate to fly any more. I intend to keep my flying to a minimum.

That, of course, is precisely the kind of message the airlines do not want to receive, but its exact significance can be argued about. On the one hand it may mean that the industry has simply got the forecasts wrong and that in a year or two it will have learnt how to deal equally well both with the business travellers who expect reasonable comfort and convenience and with the mass of people who are prepared to put up with anything if the price is low enough.

But – and this is an equally real possibility – it may mean that the old airline world has come to an abrupt end. Kay Lund has put the point neatly. 'Air travel', she believes, 'is not the big thing it used to be. It has become the bus service of the nation.'[9] And many people, especially those in positions of power and influence, dislike travelling by bus and waiting at bus stops.

The United States is probably under greater pressure than other countries to get this particular problem sorted out quickly. There are two reasons for this. In the first place, America depends on its air services, needs them, to an extent which is not paralleled elsewhere. As Monte Lazarus, put it:

[8] At a meeting filmed by the BBC in November 1978.
[9] Conversation with Julian Pettifer, 12 November 1978.

Airport coach at Chicago fitted for business meetings, to use every possible minute of a highly-paid executive's day.

In the United States, as nowhere else in the world, we rely on air transportation and the private automobile as our primary forms of transportation. The airlines of this country carry seventy-five per cent of the inter-city common carrier traffic and we burn about four per cent of the fuel consumed.

In other words, if the French, Germans or the British dislike what their airlines are giving them on the domestic routes, they can always try the train. The Americans, on the other hand, have allowed their railway system to wither away. For long distances, it is now, except for those with a taste for adventure, the air or nothing.

The second difference has been plainly expressed by the President of United, Richard Ferris: 'I believe that in Europe fifty per cent of everything that moves in the air moves on charter service, fifty per cent on scheduled service. In the United States, ninety-five per cent of everything that moves is on scheduled service.'[10] This is another way of saying that, if the scheduled services are overwhelmed, there are no charter services as a safety valve. But, and this is the most important point, Richard Ferris was entirely opti-

[10] Conversation with Julian Pettifer, 4 August 1978.

200

mistic. He was sure the problems can be solved and will be solved. Asked to forecast the next ten years, he stressed better, computer-based, ways to 'improve the flow through the airport facility'. The whole problem, in other words, was, he thought, entirely technical.

In trying to make commercial sense[11] of the new situation, the airlines had to recognise two particular problems. One is that they must somehow continue to make profits and accumulate reserves large enough to allow them to replace obsolescent aircraft and in other ways to keep themselves technically up to date. The second is that they had to cater, in the ordinary course of business, for very large numbers of passengers who have no intention whatever of travelling by Laker Airways or on standby, who are going to continue to demand the traditional facilities and amenities, and who are willing and able to pay for what they want. In these circumstances, what at all costs has to be avoided is the slightest hint that passengers who pay the full fare are in any way subsidising those who travel under a standby scheme.

European airlines are frequently criticised for the high level of their fares, the comparison being usually with what is charged per mile in the United States. An examination of the facts, however, suggests that British Airways, SAS and the rest are not the unscrupulous rogues they are alleged to be. It would be fairer to say that they are the victims of the small size and fragmentation of Europe. European routes are nearly all, in aviation terms, ultrashort and the situation is bedevilled by every country having its own airline, with staff and overheads to match. Europe runs air travel, for nationalistic and prestige reasons, in just about the most labour-intensive and expensive way possible.

The details are remarkable. In 1976–7, scheduled air travel within Europe produced eleven per cent of the total world 'ton kilometre capacity' but it required forty-five per cent of the total world's fleet to do so. It generated no less than fifty-five per cent of the world's aircraft movements. This type of short-haul operation, quick up, quick down, necessitates twin-engined or narrow bodied tri-jets, which account for ninety-three per cent of total provision, compared with 2.5 per cent for the rest of the world. As a result of this, the low seat cost as experienced on long-haul routes because of the use of wide-bodied aircraft, such as the Boeing 747, has not been passed on in savings to the customer.

The typical full-fare passenger, either first or economy class, does not exist, but there are some useful clues in the life-style of someone who one most certainly cannot imagine spending days on the pavement until her turn with Laker came up:

---

[11] A fairly desperate situation. In its 1978 publication. *Reason in the Air*, IATA said: 'International aviation is presently facing serious problems. The world's airlines are in trouble – they are losing money. The thirty-year-old regulatory system is foundering.'

In 1978, IATA had eighty-nine active members and eighteen associates. The Soviet Union continued to be outside the fold.

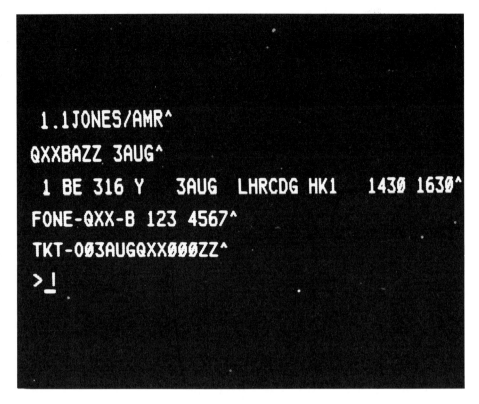

What the computer tells the ticket counter assistant:
Passenger A. M. R. Jones has an economy-class seat on Flight BE316 on 3 August from London, Heathrow, to Paris, Charles de Gaulle, holding confirmed for one seat (HK1), departing at 14.30, arriving at 16.30. It is a business reservation (QXX), made at British Airways' West London Terminal (ZZ). The ticket was issued on 3 August. The business telephone number at which Mr Jones can be reached is 123 4567.

I clocked in at 10.15 am at the National Airlines desk at Heathrow Airport for my flight to Florida. Then I was directed up to their first-class lounge where I was able to make two rather important telephone calls in comfort. . . .[11]

These preliminaries having been accomplished:

Soon the time came for boarding and I went straight to my front window seat on the DC-10, which had very kindly been reserved for me. I settled down very comfortably, then one of the stewardesses came round with a tray of champagne or orange juice, both of which I refused, and I asked for some Perrier water, as I wanted to drink this all through the nine-hour flight. I knew in advance that on my arrival in Palm Beach I had a cocktail party and a dinner ahead of me, so I decided to eat very little, drink plenty of Perrier or any mineral water, and sleep as much as possible. My plan worked out well and I arrived feeling as fresh as the proverbial daisy. The National Airlines flight to Miami, which runs daily, is one of the most comfortable and easiest of trips to make. For those who enjoy eating and drinking when they are travelling, there was the most sumptuous menu, offering a wide choice of food, a large variety of drinks, and the service throughout was excellent.

Her host and hostess met her at the airport.

We drove up to their new home on Tradewind Drive where we arrived around 7 pm. I

[12] From 'Jennifer's Diary', *Harpers & Queen*, May 1978. The author was the magazine's Social Editor, Betty Kenward.

had the quickest possible bath and changed into evening dress and we were off again in around forty minutes.

We went first to a party being given by Van Cleef and Arpels . . . From here we walked on the very short distance to the famous Everglades Club, where we met our charming and attractive dinner hostess . . . When I got home, I unpacked and settled myself in comfortably, and then had a wonderful night's sleep.

Two comments might be made on this fascinating piece of autobiography. The first is, of course, that we are presented here with a lady of quite remarkable stamina, for whom the twenty-hour day, with a transatlantic flight woven into it, means nothing. The second point of particular interest is that we have here a passenger who really does understand the rigours and temptations of flying and who knows how to look after herself. One way of doing this – a method available to both first and economy class – is to get oneself enrolled, as a loyal and regular traveller, in one of the airline clubs run for people who fly a good deal. Pan American, for example, has its Clipper Clubs at many of the larger airports and British Airways its Executive Clubs, Aer Lingus its Tara Circle and Sabena its Business Club. The privileges available to club members include special lounges, quicker check-in, later and safer Final Calls, and, it is rumoured, a good chance of getting a seat when the plane has been declared full. In some cases lower rates at hotels are also available. Members are given special cards to identify them at check-in desks and, in the case of Aer Lingus, the computer puts 'Tara' after the passenger's name when the reservation is made so that from that moment on officials recognise that he is not as other men.

The larger airports have two other kinds of special lounge, those for Commercially Important People – CIP lounges – and those for Very Important People – VIP lounges. Heathrow is particularly good at this side of the business. It has five VIP lounges, together with a separate Royal Family lounge, which is used only by heads of state. Competition for VIP facilities is fairly sharp and closely governed by protocol. This can and does lead to delicious incidents. In August 1978, for instance, Lord Ramsey, formerly Archbishop of Canterbury, was travelling to Rome in the company of the Bishop of London in order to attend the funeral of Pope Paul. He was not admitted to a VIP lounge at Heathrow, on the grounds that, although Archbishops were VIPs, former Archbishops were not. There was an indignant correspondence in *The Times*, in the course of which it emerged that it was not the airport but government departments which decided, well in advance, who should be given VIP treatment. Equally important, it was these departments, not the airport or the airlines, which paid for refreshments, telephone calls and the other generously provided facilities.

Air-India's Maharajah lounge at Heathrow is generally considered by connoisseurs to be the most luxurious, but what is provided for Concorde passengers both here and in the United States runs it fairly close. Cosseting is on a lavish and even slightly ridiculous scale. On arrival at the Concorde lounge, one's coats are placed on movable hanger-frames, which are pushed out into the aircraft before departure. All manner of refreshments are offered, with a standard of service that must surely rival that of Imperial Airways at its best in the 1930s. The same service is a marked and agreeable feature of the flight, where the temptation to over-eat and over-drink during the three and a half hours over the Atlantic is almost irresistible. Everything contributes to make the passenger feel that he is a very privileged person, which indeed he is, and, having paid so much more than the ordinary first-class fare, certainly should be. His one criticism, especially if he happens to be on the bulky side, is that the seats are distinctly narrow. One is travelling, not in a Rolls, but in a very high-quality sports car, and in sports cars the seating usually does take second place to other technical features.

Concorde, which first went into service in 1976, is unmistakably the symbol of the rich in the air, just as Skytrain is the symbol of the poor, and much of the hostility that has been generated about the aircraft has certainly been due to precisely this, although it has always been presented in environmental terms – 'Concorde is too noisy,' 'Concorde produces sonic booms which shatter windows and crack walls,' 'Concorde is a super-polluter of the atmosphere.' What is really being said, however, is 'Concorde is an élitist aeroplane.' It could also be said that Concorde is a technical marvel which makes no economic sense. Its development costs, heavily subsidised by the British and French governments, were astronomical, its fuel consumption is extremely high, and so far it makes a handsome operational loss each year for both Air France and British Airways, despite the fact that it is now, after a shaky start, quite well patronised. Seats on the New York services are difficult to obtain and on the other routes seat-occupancy is rather better than it was on the normal Atlantic flights before the days of cheap fares. Perhaps the greatest boon for passengers, however, is that Concorde, the most pampered of all aeroplanes, has an extraordinary record of punctuality. Other planes may be kept waiting, but not Concorde. During their first year of operations, 92.8% of all Air France Concorde flights arrived within five minutes of their scheduled time, a record very rarely before achieved by any airline anywhere.

How is one to assess Concorde? Is it a rich man's toy, a technological masterpiece or a flying test-bed? Does it belong to yesterday or to tomorrow? Should it have been killed off early? Has it been a victim of the determination of Boeing to go one better in ten years' time? What does 'being fair to Concorde' mean – and that question is nearly as impossible to answer as 'What does this poem mean?' or 'Should diamond necklaces exist?'

The present writers are prepared to take their courage in both hands and, just for once, tell the economists and the environmentalists that the supreme value of Concorde is that it has brought colour and excitement to a dreary world which needed this kind of tonic very badly. The thought of going from London to New York in three and a half hours would have set everyone's

pulse racing in the 1920s or 1930s and so it should today. One day, probably in the early 1990s, there will be much bigger and more comfortable Concordes crossing the Atlantic in two hours as a matter of course and almost certainly with a different form of propulsion, using different fuel. When that day comes, the French and British teams whose skills produced and operated Concorde will be praised as pioneers, not cursed as spendthrifts and enemies of the human race. Meanwhile, there has to be a place in this particular book for a sentence which says plainly and simply that Concorde is a very beautiful, satisfying object to look at, both on the ground and in flight, and to have flown in it is a milestone in anybody's life. Economically it may be absurd, poetically it is superb.

Concorde may eventually be seen by historians as a plane out of its time, a memorable freak, a flying laboratory. It has also represented one more addition to an international fare structure which has become crazier and more baffling each year. The 1970s will assuredly be remembered as the period when fares went really mad.

The new problems affected domestic and international flights equally. In November 1977 American Air Lines, in its Fare Summary issued to the public, gave particulars of thirty different fare codes, each with its own regulations and restrictions. There were seven different fares between Washington and El Paso, eleven between Washington and New York, nine between Philadelphia and Albany. Only one of these in each case was first class. The other possibilities were coach, economy, off-peak economy, super coach, military reservations coach, de luxe night coach, night coach, night economy individual tour coach, forty-passenger group, inclusive tour coach, ten-passenger group coach, four-to-nine-passenger group coach, child's four-to-nine-passenger group coach, twenty-passenger group coach.

Each airline has produced its own recipe for providing cheaper fares and so of attracting more passengers. The Pan American solution was especially interesting. Called Budget Fare, it was a planned attempt, with US Government approval, to meet the threat presented by Laker's Skytrain, a novelty which caused all airline managements many sleepless nights. Budget Fare allows a customer to select the week he wants to fly, although Pan American picks the actual day of the flight. In this way the Budget Fare passenger to, say, London has a confirmed reservation and receives exactly the same on-board treatment as a regular economy passenger. Pan American has the advantage of being able to assign seats which would otherwise fly empty, thereby achieving a higher seat factor and an increase in 'realised revenue' per aircraft mile.

The New York–London return Budget Fare was $256. A standby ticket cost exactly the same. Although the price was a little higher than Laker's, it attracted a lot of new business. Pan American estimated that sixty per cent of the people who went Budget Fare during its first year of operation represented new traffic, people who would otherwise not have flown at all or who would not have chosen Pan American. The introduction of Budget Fare was significant in another way for Pan American. Its success accelerated the company's withdrawal from charter flights, a field in which it had for a long time been one of the world's major operators.

Budget Fare and the like may have filled the planes, but these schemes made the full-fare economy passengers a little touchy and since they, the prized business passengers, were by far the most profitable, something had to be done for them. In the autumn of 1978 all the major airlines brought another class into their aircraft, the Full Fare class, and gave them special treatment. The existence of the Boeing 747s, the DC-10s and other big jets made this comparatively easy to do.

British Airways decided to call their Full Fare passengers to the United States 'Club Class'. It was to be, their advertisements told the world, 'British Airways' new Elizabethan Service'. Club Class has special check-in facilities, a free bar, 'open almost from take-off to touch-down', free music and films, and, as the major bait, 'a menu based on authentic Tudor dishes, similar to those served in Royal residences and Noble houses in Elizabeth I's day'.

Pan American's 'Clipper Class', with its echoes of the grand old days on the flying-boats, offers 'upgraded service for the same full economy class ticket that you're buying now'. This includes, of course, a special check-in desk, and in addition, use of the first-class lounge at San Francisco, New York and Seattle. As with British Airways, drinks and in-flight entertainment are free and, to compensate passengers for not providing roast swan and other Elizabethan delicacies, there is 'a special choice of entrées'. TWA's straightfor-

wardly named Full Fare Coach section gives much the same extra facilities as Pan American's, but with the extra advantage of 'seat selection for both outward and return trips up to twenty-eight days in advance'.

Long before the crunch came in 1978, however, Pan American had instituted their Frequent Traveller Scheme. These extra-prized passengers had a special identification card, luggage tags and stickers, all to make sure that they were immediately recognised by members of the Pan American staff. A special section on all 747s was reserved for them.

Frequent Travellers roughly equal business passengers, and there is no doubt that all the airlines want them badly. Lufthansa reckons business travel is one of its strongest points and it does a number of interesting things in order to obtain and hold it. Its efforts in this direction range from a worldwide booklet on 'doctors who may be consulted with confidence', to Profitours, i.e. industrial and commercial study tours in Germany, lasting up to three weeks. British Airways has responded with a special magazine, *British Airways Executive*, and, a very brilliant stroke, Executive Think-ins, 'in some quiet spot abroad'.

The delights of flying. Waiting for delayed flights at Terminal 1, Heathrow.

207

A big effort is certainly being made to make businessmen and other regular travellers feel that the airlines still value their patronage. As yet, however, no practical use seems to have been made by any airline of the disturbing fact that people are getting bigger all the time and that yesterday's seats are no longer adequate, if indeed they ever were. Research carried out by the McDonnell Douglas Company[13] shows that, if present trends continue, by 1990 men will be $1\frac{1}{2}$ inches wider at the shoulders and women almost one inch wider than when measurements were last taken in 1955. Hips will have spread 0.7 of an inch and 0.4 of an inch respectively.

But, Clipper Class, Club Class and the rest notwithstanding, first class remains and the airlines do their best to fill it. The basic approach was laid down many years ago, that better people deserve better treatment, and it is constantly being re-interpreted and re-presented to suit changing styles of living.

So, for first-class passengers, wider and more comfortable seats, more leg room, sumptuous meals and free everything. Year by year each airline racks its brains to try to discover some new form of first-class luxury that its rivals are not yet providing – foreign language phrase books, in-flight television, exotic national foods, separate bar-lounges and all the rest. Ironically, two of the most recent innovations, beds and dining-rooms, are merely a revival of what was once common practice and are presented to the travelling public as such.

In 1972 a Pan American advertisement for its dining-rooms went like this:

1936 The China Clipper had a dining-room seating 15. The Clipper – Pan Am had 3 – was a Martin M 130, with a cruising speed of 130 mph. She seated 32 – 15 to 20 on long journeys. Her range was 2400 miles.

1972 Pan Am's 747 goes at 625 mph, with a range of 6700. The dining-room takes 15 of the 38 first-class passengers.

Six years later Japan Air Lines made much play with its in-flight beds. These were introduced on the London–Tokyo flights in October 1978. Each 747 now has five beds in the upper first-class cabin. The cost of a bed is £75 and, for modesty and privacy, each bed is curtained off.

'Beds', the JAL advertisements pointed out, 'were installed in some long-distance services up to the 1950s. With the coming of jets, they were given up as uneconomic.' They are still, in fact, completely uneconomic.

In attempting to sum up the contribution that aviation has made to gastronomy we could say that some airlines have certainly provided a consistent standard of food. If we adopted a Michelin system of grading them in reverse, the maximum number of black stars would perhaps go to Aeroflot for its reliably uneatable rubber chicken legs, which must surely be carved from a special breed of durable fowl. Airline kitchens *do* make special demands on

Opposite above:
Something for the passengers to look at: a Canadian Pacific 747 over the Rockies.

Opposite below:
Dulles International, Washington, DC. Two Concordes congratulate one another.

[13] Reported in *The Times*, 19 May 1978.

their provisioners and it is in this area of food technology that we must look for aviation's major contribution to gastronomy.

The most important considerations for the flight caterer in seeking ingredients are freshness, appearance and standard size and quality. The need for freshness speaks for itself: the possibility of bringing a Jumbo-load of passengers down with gastro-enteritis in flight has imposed on flight kitchens the most stringent standards of hygiene, which in some less developed parts of the world have not been easy to achieve. For fear of food poisoning, members of the flight crew usually eat different meals and on some airlines shell-fish is forbidden them. Modern aeroplane galleys are miracles of compactness but in order to function properly, the contents of the meal tray must be exactly the same size; the over-large tomato or apple will prevent the tray sliding into the trolley, hence the demand for food products of standard size and quality. In the case of the egg, the solution has been ingenious. If you ever glance at the other trays of those around you on an aeroplane, you will notice there is nothing to arouse your envy: everything is identical, even down to the diameter of the slice of hardboiled egg. Whatever happens, you may wonder, to the sharp ends of the egg? The answer is that there are no sharp ends to the airline egg. Your slice has been cut from a factory-made sausage of extruded egg-white and yolk that provides the standard portion for everyone. Modern market-gardening methods have also been able to provide the standard size tomato and apple. In areas like the Middle East where fresh fruit and salads are in short supply, the demands of flight kitchens have stimulated the growth of hydroponic farming. In the Sultanate of Oman, a group of British entrepreneurs and scientists have established a flourishing farm on the totally arid desert sands beside the Gulf. Using de-salinated water from the sea, enriched with chemical nutrients, Gulf Growers are now producing lettuce, tomatoes, capsicums, herbs and fresh flowers of standard high quality. The first customers were the airlines, closely followed by the hotels, and now they are also supplying the local market.

Looking to the future, one can only suppose that the needs of mass travel will lead us ever further in the direction of mass catering, or even no catering at all. Laker has already established the pattern: his Skytrain service provides meals as an optional extra, and those who decline them can and do take their own coffee and sandwiches, or in some cases something more elaborate. One English pop-music star climbs aboard with his own hamper from Fortnum and Mason. His logic is impeccable: 'The aeroplane seat is the same whether you fly on Laker's DC-10 or on any other airline. The food is never as good as Fortnum's on any of them.'

Serious food writers infrequently turn their attention to airline catering and perhaps that is just as well for the airlines, because when they do they invariably dip their pens in vitriol.

Airline food has managed to encapsulate the underlying depressing quality in flying. We readily accept that men on the way to the moon should get their nourishment from

Opposite above: Consumer appeal: the interior of the Air France offices on the Champs-Élysées, Paris.

Opposite below: Spirit-lifting architecture at Los Angeles International, 1978.

pills, and, once in a plane, we also shy away from anything tasting like earthling's grub. We eat canned fruits embedded in a kind of astral plastic aspic, the colourless amber of life above earth. When it is time for hot dishes we obediently put away the laughable imitations of down-there dishes: Tournedos Rossini, Sauté de Veau Marengo, Chicken Chasseur. They have no distinguishing taste. They are symbolic only. Despite the fact that it would be perfectly possible to assemble a fine picnic and take it with one onto the plane, remarkably few people do so. They need the partitioned trays, the plastic cutlery, the polythene glasses, the salt and pepper packaged like tiny Tampax, because they realise that flying is not something that comes naturally to man and the food must in the end betray the fact. That is, anyway, my generous view of why airline food is so horrid and will never get better.[14]

On the airlines as elsewhere, death is the great leveller and there have been some very unpleasant accidents during the 1970s, made worse by the sheer size of the aircraft. In 1919 a crash might have killed the pilot and perhaps three passengers; in 1978 it is likely to end the lives of three hundred or more. The figures show that the safety record of airlines has deteriorated during the 1970s. Between 1950 and 1970, with the exception of two particularly bad years, flying became progressively safer, but in 1971 the trend was reversed. In 1972 2124 people were killed, almost double the number in the previous year. The details for the first six months of 1978 illustrate the pattern.

Date	Operator and Aircraft Type	Passengers and Crew	Location	What Happened
Jan 22	Royal Jordanian Airlines Boeing 707	173 killed 33 survivors	Kano, Nigeria	Crashed on landing – runway collapsed
Jan 29	Egyptair Ilyushin 18	37 killed	Cyprus	Hit mountain while approaching Nicosia
Feb 19	Aeroflot Tupolev 154	66 killed 34 survivors	Prague	Crashed on landing – stabiliser locked
Feb 21	Urruca DC-3	19 killed 5 survivors	Panama	Crashed en route
Feb 21	Libyan Arab Airlines Boeing 727	108 killed 6 survivors	Sinai Desert	Shot down by Israeli fighters
Feb 28	Merpati Nusantara Twin Otter	13 killed	Nabire, W. Irian	Crashed en route. No details released
Mar 3	Bulgarian Airlines Ilyushin 18	25 killed	Moscow	Crashed on approach
Mar 5	Iberia DC-9	68 killed	Nantes, France	Mid-air collision, 99 people on board the other aircraft survived

[14] Fay Maschler, *Punch*, 9 May 1979.

Mar 5	Aviaco Caravelle	3 killed	Madeira	Crashed into sea during approach
Mar 19	Air Vietnam DC-4	60 killed	Ben Me Thuot	Crashed on approach
Apr 10	Invicta Vanguard	105 killed 40 survivors	Basle	Hit mountain during approach
May 29	Air Gaspe DC-3	4 killed	Rimouski, Canada	Hit mountain
May 31	Indian Airlines Boeing 737	48 killed 17 survivors	Delhi	Crashed during approach
Late May	Aeroflot Tupolev 104	100 killed (estimated)	Siberia	Crashed during gunfight after hi-jack attempt
June 1	Servicos Aereos Cruzeiro do Sul Caravelle	23 killed	Sao Luiz, Brazil	Crashed on landing
June 5	Transportes Aereos de Nayarit Beechcraft	11 killed 1 survivor	San Juan, Mexico	Crashed on take-off
June 9	Varig Boeing 707	72 killed 2 survivors	Rio de Janeiro	Crashed on landing
June 20	Aeromexico	27 killed	Puerto Vallarta	Crashed during approach
June 22	Transair	3 killed	Miami, Florida	Crashed on take-off
June 30	Aeroflot Tupolev 134	9 killed* 75 survivors	Amman, Jordan	Hit houses during take-off

It will be noticed that a high proportion of these accidents occurred while the aircraft were making their final approach or landing, and that the great majority of the victims were passengers on scheduled services.

With air casualties as with road casualties, one must, of course, make some allowance for the annual increase in the number of people travelling and, in the case of airlines, for the number of miles flown. It remained true, even so, that in 1973 the risk of being killed on a scheduled flight was twice as high as it had been three years previously.

After BEA's Trident, 'Papa India', crashed near Heathrow in 1972, killing 118 people, a statement issued by Captain George Stone, and signed by forty-five other pilots, set out what they believed were the root causes of the deteriorating safety record. Captain Stone was a pilot of thirty-one years' experience and his report was prepared before the Trident crash. There were, in his opinion, two fundamental problems: the pilots' hours of duty were too

*7 of those killed were in the houses struck by the Russian aircraft.

long and the proportion of young, inexperienced pilots, requiring constant supervision by the captain, was too high.

In an attempt to squeeze the last farthing of profit out of the new and very expensive jets, the tempo of the work had greatly increased. In the piston and turboprop days, everything went at a slower pace. There was time to relax in the air and, with ground stops of an hour or more, it was possible during a long day to leave the aircraft and relax for a little while. Captain Stone said:

Nowadays, with high-speed jets, the whole operation is one long mad rush, turn-arounds are as short as thirty minutes and it is not unusual for the crew to remain on the flight deck for consecutive sectors (legs) of a flight.

It is quite normal these days to find oneself rostered for duty days of eleven hours or more of nonstop duty, including eating one or more meals on one's lap on the flight deck, operating four sectors with a change of aircraft at the halfway point, with all the rechecking of equipment this entails.[15]

BEA and BOAC denied that their pilots worked excessive hours and, during a fierce controversy in the press, it was suggested that pilots became tired mainly as a result of having so little to do. Two Scottish psychiatrists said Captain Stone and the British Air Line Pilots' Association had over-simplified the problem. There were other things to look at, besides allegedly excessive hours of duty. These included 'flight-deck and social boredom, excessive warmth, dehydration, physical confinement, exposure to toxic agents, inappropriate relaxation, emotional detachment, unpleasant hang-over, neurotic and physical illness, and time-zone changes affecting biological rhythms'.[16]

The principal medical officer with BEA/BOAC said[17] at a conference in Edinburgh in 1972 that human error had certainly been to blame in almost half the accidents during the past sixteen years, in which 148 passenger-carrying jets had been destroyed. It was difficult to prevent human error, but the situation had certainly been made worse by what were politely called 'airfield deficiencies', that is, by trying to operate modern aircraft from airports with antiquated facilities. The Aerospace Correspondent of the London *Financial Times* wrote:

Air safety is a vast and complex field, ranging from the intricacies of the design and airworthiness of aircraft, through to crew training, en route navigation and the provision of radio, lighting and other aids on the ground.

The pilots' pressure for improved landing aids and better airfields is one major area where much more needs to be done, and much more money spent, but it is only one aspect of an overall global problem which requires much more concentration by all – manufacturers, operators, airport authorities and government and international agencies. As the size of aircraft rises, so the number of deaths in each accident will tend to rise. The 400–500-seater jet is already here; the 750-seater and 1000-seater are not many years away.

[15] *The Times*, 3 January 1973.
[16] *The Times*, 15 December 1972.
[17] *The Times*, 26 May 1972.

Barring catastrophe, these developments are certain. In October 1978 Boeing announced that it was in a position to develop a 600-seater to be ready to enter service in 1985, and that it had long-term plans for a 1000-seat, double-deck Jumbo. There is no reason to suppose that Douglas and the Russians are not thinking in similar terms. If the concept seems fanciful, it could be pointed out that the size ratio between a 1000-seat Jumbo and the little planes which began the London–Paris service back in 1919 is very similar to that between the *Mayflower* and the *QE2*. But the comparison fails at one very important point. Passengers in the *QE2* have a reasonable chance of survival if the ship should happen to catch fire or hit an iceberg; there would be no survivors or, at best, very few if one of the Boeings were to crash. The conclusion, as the *Financial Times* saw it, was clear.

As aircraft grow in size, so ought the level of attention given to, and the money spent on, the aviation safety infrastructure rise with them.

For it will not be reasonable to expect passengers to fly in aircraft whose development has outpaced the environment in which they are employed.[18]

In 1977 Funchal, Madeira, was revealed to the world as a perfect example of an airport which had been allowed to become dangerously obsolete. There were two very serious accidents there in a month and the moral was clear. At that time – certain improvements have taken place since then – Funchal was similar to many other airports in the world whose hinterlands have become centres for package holidays. Its facilities were being used by more and bigger jet aircraft than could ever have been envisaged when the airport was built. In many such cases the traffic has outstripped the technical devices installed at the airports to ensure the safety of aircraft and passengers. Good weather for most of the time at places like Funchal lulls the aviation authorities into a false sense of security, so that too often what funds are available have been spent on items such as new and luxurious terminal buildings designed to impress the newcomer rather than on a new and updated instrument landing system and the training of the staff to operate it.

But it is not only the newly popular tourist countries such as Madeira which are at fault. Although British Airways have been developing blind landing equipment on board their airliner fleets for nearly two decades there are still far too few airports in Europe, usually considered an advanced aviation area, which have installed the complete ground equipment with which the airborne equipment has to interlock if it is to be of any use. And very few indeed of the big-city airports in the world, most of which pride themselves publicly on being right up to date, have ground surveillance radar which picks up moving aicraft and vehicles on a foggy day.

He would be a bold man who said that the problem of 'airfield deficiencies' had, by the end of the 1970s, been put right. There are still many airports in the world where both equipment and personnel are still far from adequate by

[18] 13 August 1973.

No survivors: the end of
an American Airlines
DC–10 at Chicago,
25 May 1979. An engine
fell off soon after take-off.
This accident led to the
temporary grounding of
all DC–10s in the summer
of 1979.

today's standards and about which pilots have been complaining for years,
without any marked progress having been made.

They have not been very happy, either, about the measures taken to deal
with that other great flying menace of modern times, hi-jacking.[19] During the
ten years between 1969 and 1978 there were over 400 attempted hi-jacks,
involving 75,000 passengers. In the same period there were at least seventy-
five instances of shots being fired or explosive devices detonated inside
aircraft, in flight or on the ground, sometimes with disastrous consequences.

After a wave of hi-jackings in the United States between 1968 and 1972 – 159
aircraft were hi-jacked and eighty-five of them flown to Cuba – the authorities
in that country introduced full baggage and body-search procedures for every
domestic and international flight originating from an American airport. This
meant dealing with 14,000 domestic flights daily and over 150 million passengers a year, but it soon proved its worth. In the following two years, there
were only three hi-jack attempts on planes which had taken off in the United
States, and all failed.

[19] The first post-war recorded hi-jacking took place in 1948.

214

Since then, the problem has mainly involved terrorists representing Japanese and Palestinian groups, although various other national units, such as the German Baader-Meinhof gang, have also played their part. It has become clear that there can be no final solution to hi-jacking so long as so many airports, especially in the poorer and developing countries, continue to be content with such lax security procedures[20] and until every nation in the world refuses to harbour hi-jackers. It is also necessary to refuse under all circumstances to give in to the hi-jackers' demands. The only country to have consistently followed this policy has been Israel, where the hard line has included, if necessary, the sacrifice of passengers' lives.

Crashes and hi-jackings present not only individual airlines but the whole aviation industry with serious public relations problems. The product has, so to speak, not matched up to the customers' expectations of it. In such circumstances, and indeed in perpetuity, the only thing to be done is to emphasise and re-emphasise the pleasures and advantages of travelling by air, in the hope that these will be seen to outweigh the dangers and unpleasantness, as they assuredly do.

It depends, in any case, on how one regards danger. The Americans have always placed great emphasis on flying their passengers safely and their airlines have a safety record unequalled anywhere else in the world, except, possibly, in Australia. But safety costs money and the sad truth is that some countries – and not always the poorest – begrudge this kind of expenditure. Between 1971 and 1976, US carriers averaged more than two million flights for every fatal accident. Put another way, one of their passengers could reckon to fly more than 300 million miles before having an accident, which does not sound, on the face of it, like a very serious risk. And, in any case, accidents or no accidents, flying has become so much part of the American way of life that one can hardly imagine it disappearing for almost any reason short of a major holocaust. In 1977 sixty-three per cent of all Americans over the age of eighteen flew at least once. This figure represented sixty-seven per cent of all adult men and fifty-nine per cent of all adult women. Fifty-two per cent of all air journeys were made for business reasons: the rest were for what the industry terms pleasure.

But one should certainly not allow the airlines to get away with the idea that they do no more than provide transport. They are far too tightly in-

---

[20] Effective equipment for security checks costs a lot of money. The International Aeradio Rapidex, typical of the new generation of equipment, includes a baggage screening system with a remote-controlled X-ray camera, able to pan, tilt and zoom, with a high definition screen. An explosives detector is also incorporated into the system. There is also a metal detector gallows, through which passengers walk, and a hand-held detector for special body checks. Seventeen of these units are now in operation at Terminal 3, Heathrow. Concorde has had one from the beginning of its services. But – and it is an important but – each unit, in 1979, cost over £500,000, which many, perhaps most, airports in the world are likely to consider beyond their purses. They will probably continue to rely on old-fashioned methods of frisking and visual inspection, which are unfortunately by no means foolproof, especially where explosives are concerned.

May 1978. Passengers
being searched for
weapons at Aberdeen
Airport.

terwoven with the tourist industry as a whole to make any such suggestion reasonable. And the tourist industry makes its money by selling a profitable, carefully manufactured commodity called leisure travel, the true nature of which was indicated recently by a leading travel agent, when he said that 'leisure travel by air is rapidly becoming more showbiz than travel'. And there is no doubt that the airlines have, willy-nilly, become involved in precisely this. They are showbiz organisations as well as travel organisations.

Of course, there has long been a strong element of theatre in the travel business. The great ocean-going liners had everything from the comedy of manners of the Captain's table to the low farce of the Crossing the Line ceremony, but that was very different. That was a way of diverting people, of passing the long days and nights during a journey that might take several weeks. Today the element of theatre actually aboard the aeroplane is minimal: flying itself is a serious business and, apart from in-flight cinema, very short on fantasy. Today the charades begin when the traveller arrives at his destination. The tourist brochures have set the scene. On a visit to Bangkok or Singapore, for example, they have *promised* that in the 'Mysterious Orient' the visitor will find 'a heavy mixture of cultures and strange customs, a street life that will thrill you with its colour and variety; as you watch the snake charmer in the market or wonder at the skill of the "mahout" as he works his elephant in the teak forests, you will experience at first hand the world so vividly described by Maugham and Kipling.'

That promise would be hard, but not yet impossible, to keep in the 1970s, but one would need weeks to find the ingredients and make the journeys. To deliver the goods to the forty-eight-hour stopover passenger in Singapore or Bangkok would be totally impossible. To begin with, Singapore has rapidly abandoned most of the trappings of the mysterious Orient in the past twenty years and has enthusiastically turned itself into an industrialised, Western-ised city state. And yet that does not stop Singapore promising and provid-ing in its own way at least some of these story-book experiences. It supplies them, processed, as a happening called 'Instant Asia'. In the space of an hour and a half, in a theatre, the visitor is shown half a dozen acts, including Chinese and Tamil dancers, a Muslim wedding ceremony and a snake char-mer who hangs serpents round the necks of shuddering volunteers from the audiences. Likewise in Bangkok, in an outdoor setting near the city, the beautiful country of Thailand is reduced to a non-stop variety show, called 'Timland', where bored elephants roll logs at each other to no purpose and even more bored dancers go through the motions of a court ceremony. Asia is not alone in providing these pre-digested cultural meals. Ireland has its medieval banquets in candle-lit castles, where 'wenches' serve 'traditional fare' on 'wooden platters' while 'minstrels' carol from their 'galleries'. Hawaii has a tourist village where traditional craftsmen are employed to perform their 'age-old' role of making baskets and ornaments.

The longer one examines the balance sheet of air travel, the more one may feel that the greater number that fly, the less there is to fly for, and that not only should the nomadism cease, but its upward trend might profitably be reversed. To many people this will certainly seem an élitist view, overlook-ing, as it does, the vast majority of mankind which has never had the opportunity to travel anywhere. Thinking the matter through to its logical conclusion, however, logic demands either that one accepts the élitism as an inescapable fact, with the corollary that one may oneself remain a part of an even smaller élite or, if that view is rejected, that the only alternative in a free society is for the individual, even if he is financially able to travel, to stay voluntarily at home, to foreswear travel altogether. There are a few, a very few, who have taken that extreme view and acted accordingly. Even to a great adventurer like Dame Freya Stark, it would not seem an unreasonable decision to take today. She put it in this way:

There is less of the unknown today and the unknown is fundamentally the pleasure of travel. You can be a traveller in your own garden. When everybody travels it will make it awfully pleasant to sit at home.[21]

Perhaps the poet, Alfred de Vigny, felt the same way when he wrote:

> Distance and time are vanquished.
> Science traces around the earth a straight and tedious road.
> The world is diminished by our knowledge of it.
> And the Equator is no more than a too tightly fitting ring.[22]

The truth of those lines, as the airlines and travel companies well know, is likely to impress only the relatively few people who, willingly or unwillingly, have travelled extensively. It is much easier to renounce something when one has already had a great deal of it and, so far as flying is concerned, that point has not been reached for most people. This year's holiday may be a disappointment, perhaps, but next year's could well be better.

So much of the present and future of air transport are so closely related to leisure travel that it is instructive to look at what the predictions are for tourism over the next couple of decades.

In 1978, says the World Tourist Organisation, there were approximately 1200 million international and domestic tourist arrivals and, according to the same authority, we can expect to see 3000 million arrivals by the end of the century.

In 1978 the revenue from international tourism alone amounted to US $65,000 million, an increase of 24 per cent over the previous year and over 5 per cent of the total earnings from *all* world trade. If these trends continue, by the end of the century tourism will form one of the major activities of the world economy; already, in revenue turnover, it ranks second only to oil and well above major industries such as iron and steel and armaments. With over four million people now working in the accommodation sector alone, tourism is also an increasingly important employer. Unless there is some extraordinary international crisis, it seems likely that these growth trends will persist because everything suggests that tourism is a high priority activity for which many of us are willing to sacrifice other luxuries and even some necessities. A sample survey carried out after a recent tourist season revealed that faced with hard times, only six per cent of those interviewed would be willing to forgo holidays, whereas nine per cent would be willing to cut down on home comforts, fourteen per cent on food, sixteen per cent on other recreational activities, twenty-seven per cent on car travel and twenty-eight per cent on clothing.

All this must gladden the hearts of tour operators, airline executives and aircraft manufacturers, but it is not a totally appealing prospect either for the travellers or for those who will play host to them.

Inevitably some established tourist areas will become saturated with visi-

---

[21] Conversation with Julian Pettifer, 12 May 1978.
[22] *La Maison du Berger.*

Thomas Cook caters for the sun-seekers.

tors and as a result, new destinations will be developed. According to Spain's Secretary of State for Tourism, Señor I. Aguirre, parts of his country are already approaching this saturation point.[23] Speaking of the island of Majorca, he noted that:

At Sanjuán airport at Palma . . . some 12,000 aircraft landed and took off during the month of August, an average of one flight every two minutes.

And he went on to explain that:

Spain receives roughly ten per cent of all international travellers and if we relate the size of my country to the unsubmerged area of the globe, we realise the great disparity between its share of the world tourism market and its percentage of land area, [furthermore] we find that this ten per cent of the international tourist flow 'piles up' along a narrow strip of the mainland and island coasts.

Señor Aguirre concludes quite bluntly that 'if present conditions of distribution remain unchanged, we shall soon have reached genuine saturation of the traditional tourist areas'. And to achieve the 'redistribution' that will relieve the problems of countries like Spain 'new and non-traditional areas will have to be promoted and have their image created by means of suitable publicity campaigns . . .' Of course, what Señor Aguirre is talking about is happening already and it is likely to be happening at an ever-increasing tempo. More and more 'non-traditional' areas, mostly in the developing world, find themselves playing host to more and more tourists, mostly from Europe, Japan and the United States.

[23] Address to International Conference on Tourism and Air Transport, Mexico 1978.

Diamonds in The Sky

Which parts of the globe have the privilege of being developed first depends very little on the desires of the traveller. Today's tourist is not much motivated by the wish to discover a particular foreign destination; most, perhaps the majority, are cleverly persuaded by the well-devised publicity and promotion of the airlines and tour operators. The airlines alone spend $240 million a year on destination advertising and national tourist authorities at least as much. So with the saturation of the traditional resorts we find the tourist being persuaded to travel to some novel and curious places.

The Gambia is a tiny West African State that few Europeans had ever heard of until very recently. The Gambian people lived in peaceful obscurity on the banks of their mighty river, until the chance arrival in the late 1960s of a Swedish lady called Mrs Britt Wadner. Mrs Wadner had been running pirate radio stations off the coast of Denmark, Sweden and Great Britain, but when that sort of piracy became unprofitable she migrated with her radio ship *Cheeta* down the coast of West Africa and anchored in the mouth of the Gambia River. There she was permitted to operate her broadcasting station legitimately. But in a small and backward country the economics of the undertaking were such that Mrs Wadner was forced to look for other commercial openings. As well as peanuts, there is one thing that the Gambia has in abundance and that is sunshine; better still, it has winter sunshine; a very saleable commodity in Mrs Wadner's native land. In the winter of 1965–6 three hundred charter flight tourists from Sweden arrived in the Gambia. By 1978–9 that figure had risen to 25,000 from several Northern European countries, including Britain; and by that time Mrs Wadner was running her own large tourist hotel, the Wadner Beach, as well as operating Radio Syd.

By world standards 25,000 tourists is an insignificant number – London in the same year had eight million – but for one of the smallest countries in Africa it was an invasion amounting almost to a takeover. The Gambia is a tiny sliver of land that lies on the banks of the Gambia River and forms an enclave in the Republic of Senegal. On the Atlantic Ocean it has a short seaboard stretching about thirty miles and it is there that these 25,000 tourists are to be found; or to be more precise, they are to be found on a six-mile stretch of that beach near the capital, Banjul. The total population of the Gambia is only half a million and that of Banjul 50,000; so already, in the capital during the four-month winter 'season', the ratio of visitors to residents is high – and it is going to get much higher. Already tourism is the most dynamic sector of the Gambian economy; in 1967 there were two hotels with fifty-two beds; now there are thirteen with over 2000 beds and it is planned to increase this number by five hundred beds a year until 1985. If the number of visitors increases as expected, then the Gambia will soon have to cope with over 100,000 arrivals a year. At present – and presumably in the future – many of the tourists will come from Scandinavia on package air tours and this goes part of the way to explain why many Gambians are becoming worried about the harmful effects that the proposed large-scale tourism will have on their society.

The Gambia is a relatively poor agricultural country, predominantly Muslim and with conservative values. The Scandinavians fly in from the richest individual societies in the world, characterised by outstandingly liberal values, even by European standards. On the beautiful West African beaches the clash of cultures resounds deafeningly. In a society where women cover their legs and arms with loose flowing garments, the sight of topless – and sometimes bottomless – Swedish women provoked at first shock and disbelief but then, inevitably, among the young Gambian males, curiosity. This curiosity did not go unrewarded. It soon became apparent that many of the middle-aged women – the predominant age group among tourists – were anxious to 'have the whole Africa experience', or in the words of a cynical hotel operator 'to purge their third world guilt'. Whatever the reason for their behaviour, to young Gambians it must have seemed astounding; not only were the visitors free with their favours but they were also prepared to pay handsomely for the young men's attentions. According to one report:

While female prostitution is common, male prostitution among young Gambians is rampant. Middle-aged Scandinavian women . . . openly solicit and the potential rewards for the young men concerned are not limited to the payments they receive. Many young Gambian men have been enabled by these women to travel to Sweden and elsewhere in Europe . . .[24]

Let it be said at once that seen from the 'liberal' Scandinavian point of view, there is nothing much wrong with these relationships and to condemn them might sound prudish or racist or both. But if our instinct might be to say 'Good luck to them,' that is not how traditional Gambian society looks at it. Prostitution of this kind is seen as another disturbing symptom of profound social and cultural disruption brought about by tourism.

Truancy among school children has reached alarming proportions because the youngsters are on the beaches begging from tourists. Theft has greatly increased and armed robberies are becoming more common. While such crimes are common in many parts of West Africa, they have not been so in the Gambia.[25]

Even the economic consequences of tourism in a developing country like the Gambia are far from being one hundred per cent desirable. Erik Holm-Petersen, in his case study of the Seychelles and the Gambia, points out[26] that where the host country has to import many of the goods that the visitors consume (as in the Gambia) then tourism will have an adverse effect on the trade balance. In fact, he concludes that the Gambian trade deficit was

[24] B. E. and D. L. Harrell Bond, Paper delivered at Congress of African Studies, Kinshasa, December 1978.

[25] Ibid.

[26] 'Consequences of Mass Tourism in Developing Countries', Case studies of the Seychelles and the Gambia, Copenhagen, 1978.

directly attributable to tourist consumption. Inflation too is another consequence of tourism:

> . . . this is due to insufficient supplies . . . meaning that the extra demand from the tourism industry which is ready to pay relatively higher prices, can lead to a marked upward movement. An example of this might be meat prices in the Gambia and fish prices in the Seychelles.

Despite all these disturbing trends, it is unlikely that new tourist destinations, like the Gambia, will be able to resist the forces that are urging them to open their doors and their airports ever more widely. The Gambia has just invested heavily in enlarging her international airport and although Gambian Airways at present have no aeroplanes, that seems likely to change. The President, Sir Dawda Jawara, is obviously keen that his government should share some of the profits now being made by the airlines. But how keen is he to accelerate further the changes that the aeroplane is already bringing to his country? He is certainly not unaware of the dangers but, like so many leaders of developing countries, he is torn between the economic orthodoxy that demands 'modernisation' and change and on the other hand the forces of conservatism and tradition. How he balances these two influences will be of the greatest importance, as events in Iran have so strongly underlined.

The fact that aviation can perform economic miracles for the remotest and most inaccessible places has unfortunately led to the belief in the developing world that it can always provide the answers: that all you need to do to transform a poor agrarian economy is to carve out an international airport and sit back and wait for the money to roll in. Such delusions are both pathetic and dangerous, particularly when they threaten a place like Tonga.

A signpost stands outside the visitors' bureau in Nuku'Alofa – the capital of the Pacific Island Kingdom of Tonga – and that signpost tells us clearly just how remote these islands are: 13,000 miles from London; 2000 miles from Sydney; 5000 miles from San Francisco; and even neighbouring Fiji is 500 miles away. In the age of the aeroplane, Tonga remains a relatively difficult place to get to, and ever since Captain Cook set foot on the principal island of Tongatapu, this inaccessibility has seemed to many Tongans – and to others – to be a great good fortune. In many respects the world has passed Tonga by, and all the better for that, it is argued. But if the King of Tonga gets his way, those happy days off the beaten track of tourism may be numbered. His Majesty King Taufa'ahau Tupou IV rules the last Polynesian kingdom, a pattern of 150 islands scattered over 50,000 square miles of sea, and His Majesty is determined to rescue his 100,000 subjects from obscurity. It might be argued that the King's mother, Queen Salote, did all that was possible to put Tonga on the map when she endeared herself to the crowds at Queen Elizabeth II's coronation. That spectacular appearance and the almost certainly apocryphal Noel Coward joke about it fixed the name of Tonga in the minds of a generation:[27] but now Queen Salote's son is attempting to follow his mother's act with something more daring and, some would say, fool-hardy.

He plans to construct a 12,000 foot runway and an international airport in the belief that by turning Tonga into an anchored aircraft carrier in mid-Pacific he can transform his coconut-kingdom into another Singapore. The King of Tonga is an even more imposing figure than the late Queen, and equally genial; his whitewashed palace, built like an English seaside villa, seems too insubstantial to accommodate such a huge and regal person as, enthroned on the balcony, he discourses on his ambitious schemes. He points out that at present Tonga's airport can only take BAC1-11 and Boeing 737 aircraft, and that if he can raise the money to upgrade its facilities to accommodate wide-bodied intercontinental jets, then many intercontinental airlines will wish to make use of it. The King insists that in his travels around the world, the bosses of no less than a dozen airlines were falling over themselves to put Tonga in their flight schedules. Unfortunately, His Majesty may be unaware that in a world where there are not too many kings remaining, there may be a tendency among commoners to tell royalty what they imagine royalty want to hear. In other words, those who know the aviation business well are extremely doubtful if more than a couple of airlines would want to use Tonga's international airport, and even if they did, the benefits might be very limited. They point out that, quite apart from raising a loan and servicing the debt, the financial burden of running a large airport would far outstrip the likely income; that since many expatriates would have to be employed in specialised jobs, the salaries alone could upset Tonga's precarious balance of payments. The King, however, is convinced not only that the air traffic would come, but that it would bring prosperity; he sees his country both as a tourist destination and as a centre for light industry: 'Electronic components will be air-freighted from Japan and the USA to be assembled by our inexpensive work force.' Maybe. At present there are enough hotels to support only a very modest tourist industry, and even if more beds could be provided, the benefits of mass tourism in a place like Tonga are questionable. The King perhaps too easily discounts the experience of other Pacific islands; what has happened to the once beautiful islands of Hawaii may not be entirely relevant, but he can hardly overlook what has occurred in neighbouring Fiji.

For some years Fiji has had a major international airport at Nadi. During the early jet age it was an essential technical stop for trans-Pacific aircraft, and as a result its development as a tourist destination began fifteen years ago. The industry has grown steadily in importance ever since, until today, in

---

[27] It seems that at one stage the Queen of Tonga was accompanied at the Coronation by the Emperor Haile Selassie, and when asked to identify the towering brown woman and the diminutive brown man the Master is said to have replied: 'That is the Queen of Tonga, and the small person is her breakfast.'

terms of gross expenditure, it leads the field. But many Fijians are worried by their dependence on such a volatile source of income. They point out that already the new generation of long-range jets can – and do – over-fly Fiji, and that already several airlines have pulled out of Nadi. Surely if aircraft no longer wish to stop in Fiji, where there is a long-established airport and good hotels, why should they wish to stop in Tonga, which has so much less to offer? The King has no adequate answer to that question except to insist that Tonga would be not just a technical stop, but a tourist destination in its own right. But if the Fiji experience is anything to go by, the tourist market in the Pacific area is both limited and unreliable. Because air travel from almost anywhere is so long and costly, most visitors to Fiji come from Australia and New Zealand, and these are both quite small markets. Even though Fiji manages to attract about 30,000 tourists a year, mainly from Australasia, much of the money they bring into the country goes straight out again. Of every tourist dollar earned, only twenty-five cents remains in Fiji; the rest is exported in profits or to pay for goods consumed by the tourists. One of the supposed advantages of tourism is the stimulus it gives to local industry, yet in the fertile tropical islands of Fiji, the visitor will be fed on meat and salads from New Zealand and canned orange juice from Australia. Somehow local farmers have been unable to adapt to the demands of the hotels, and the only recourse has been to buy from abroad.

Just as the economic picture is a clouded one, we find once again that the social consequences of tourism in Fiji are causing dismay. Children are playing truant from school to act as 'guides' to shoppers; prostitution flourishes and inflation burgeons, but perhaps the most alarming consequence for those who knew Fiji twenty years ago is the growing dislike that some Fijians now display towards their visitors. In the past, these beautiful islands were famous for the friendliness and hospitality of their people; today that natural goodwill has become a marketable commodity, heavily advertised in every holiday brochure, and inevitably it has become devalued. In Fiji, as in London, as in Palma, as in any other tourist destination, one encounters contempt for the visitor, which sometimes develops a surprisingly bitter tone:

. . . today, travel, far from broadening the mind, is actually contriving to shrink it. Along with the benefits of efficiency and labour-saving that the package tour concept has brought, with it comes the concomitant danger of stultifying sameness. As our people in Fiji go about their daily tasks of serving the visitors we see an endless succession of the same little old ladies, with the same blue hair rinses, spending the same life insurance money and speaking in the same accents of the same things which have penetrated their similar perceptions. And what of the little old ladies? As they climb in and out of their same cars, their same planes, their same hotel beds, as they eat the same foods, drink the same drinks and buy the same souvenirs is it to be wondered at that many cannot tell from one day to the next which country it is that they are presently visiting? These people travel the world like registered parcels,

Opposite above: Cosseting for the world's élite on a British Airways Concorde.

Opposite below: In-flight service with Japan Air Lines

blindly unaware of the local population, their aspirations, problems and tragedies. Instead of promoting mutual understanding they promote mutual contempt.[28]

Even if it is felt that the writer of that piece has overstated his case, the King of Tonga should perhaps think twice about his international airport. He has had difficulty raising money for the project, but latest reports suggest that Libya's Colonel Gadafi has lent a sympathetic ear to his request for aid.

If it is true that what America does today the rest of the world does eight years later, then the 1980s seem destined to become the decade during which flying becomes, at least for the industrialised nations, as normal an activity as celebrating Christmas. What other forecasts could one reasonably make, on the basis of present trends?

One is that something will have to be done about airports, which are at present probably the least satisfactory aspect of the flying business. Part of the trouble is that although a number of projects are on the drawing board and even under development nobody knows what the aircraft actually operating in the 1990s are going to be like – how big they are likely to be and how high off the ground, and where the wings will be – and, since it takes from ten to fifteen years to design and build an airport, every airport is at best obsolescent the day it is opened. In any case, there is no real agreement as yet as to what an airport is supposed to be for. Is it primarily for stranded or delayed passengers or for passengers moving briskly from surface transport to aircraft? Is it a social centre for meeting friends or relations? Is it a shopping centre? Is it intended to be an efficient place or an agreeable place? Can it satisfactorily be both at the same time? Dulles, Washington DC's beautiful international airport, is extremely agreeable, but, handling very few flights, extremely expensive to run and therefore inefficient. If the extra traffic were miraculously to materialise, the mobile lounges, taking passengers from terminal to aircraft, would almost certainly have to be abandoned in exchange for some more speedy system of loading and unloading. Charles de Gaulle in Paris, an architect's dream and a passenger's nightmare, is beautiful and utterly confusing and, with its rail connection added on as so much of an afterthought that a bus had to be provided to go half a mile from air terminal to rail terminal, is already something of an absurdity. Kennedy in New York and Heathrow in London are so straggling, overloaded and exhausting that passengers even now do everything possible to avoid them. It is difficult to see how they can survive the 1980s in their present form.

The kind of question one always needs to put to oneself when trying to assess the merits of an airport is, 'How easy would a Portuguese au pair girl find it to make her way from the aeroplane to a bus taking her to the city terminal?' or 'What sort of experiences would an elderly lady, who had never flown before, be likely to have here, making her way alone to her nephew in

[28] R. G. Scott, 'The Development of Tourism in Fiji since 1923.' Suva: Fiji Visitors' Bureau, 12 May 1970.

Opposite above: The uncommercialised Pacific the tourist dreams of but, nowadays, rarely finds, in spite of the travel agents' posters.

Opposite below: The realities of 'solarism'.

Charles de Gaulle airport, Paris. The passenger tubes.

Toronto?' It is not, 'How well does a Pan American pilot coming on or off duty at Kennedy manage?' or, for that matter, 'Do the Board members of Air France find Charles de Gaulle convenient?'

There are bound, of course, to be some passengers who will have special problems, and no airport, however efficient and well planned, can be expected to forecast and provide for every difficulty that might arise. But some are common enough to be reckoned with, and yet they receive no official attention. There are, for instance, a lot of deaf people about, but until very recently airports have expected them to hear the announcements broadcast over loudspeakers, just as if their hearing had been normal. The information staff at Heathrow now attend courses put on by the Royal National Institute for the Deaf to help understand the difficulties of deaf people when travelling. Among the cases presented to students on these courses is that of the deaf man who caught a flight from London to Glasgow. Because of fog, the plane was diverted to Edinburgh. He waited for some time at Edinburgh, expecting to be picked up by a relative, because he had not heard the announcement about the diversion.

There are, of course, plenty of people with good hearing who fail to hear announcements and the fault is not always theirs. The quality of reproduction offered by the public address systems at some airports is abominable and that inside aircraft is often so bad as to be virtually unintelligible.

The lesson is, of course, that very small airports can smile and muddle their way through, often with remarkable success, but large airports have to

226

function perfectly in all their details. If one item in a complicated system fails to work properly, the result all too often is chaos.

The biggest problems are faced by airports which handle a great deal of international traffic.[29] Here there are likely to be more friends and relations meeting passengers and seeing them off, more language difficulties, more misunderstandings, longer delays, greater tensions, worse frustrations. Some airports – Chicago O'Hare is a good example – recognise this and go to a lot of trouble to ease the path of non-American passengers, for example by means of well-displayed airport guides in foreign languages, but many others, perhaps most, give the impression of simply not understanding or caring what it is like to travel 5000 miles and arrive at a big, strange foreign airport for the first time. And it is not, alas, true that everybody who travels by air speaks English, comforting as the pretence may be for airport authorities.

If there were an international prize for the ugliest urban landscape, some of the leading contenders would certainly be the areas around a number of the world's airports. Even when planners have gone to great pains to prevent the familiar industrial and domestic sprawl that grows up haphazardly around most terminals, the result has usually been depressing and vacant. This is partly because airports have to be situated on flat land which does nothing to hide the acres of concrete, and partly because, for safety reasons, tall trees or any other obstructions that might soften the skyline are not tolerated. As the more affluent homeowners flee from the aircraft nuisance, a nuisance which affects eyes, ears and nose, neighbourhoods decline and take on that unloved appearance. What we finish up with all too frequently is an unappealing wasteland of warehouses, car parks and poor housing. Anyone who has had the misfortune to spend time around, say, the airports of Paris, London or Chicago will recognise the picture all too well. In this urban wilderness the only oases are a number of airport hotels doing what they can to refresh the traveller, which is often rather little. There can be few voyagers by air who have not on occasion been deeply cast down by spending a night in one of these hostelries. Of course, it is not entirely the fault of the hotels. They are victims of their location, of the very transient nature of their patrons and of the need to provide something reasonably acceptable to people of many nationalities, cultures and incomes. They must offer a standard product whether they be in Dakar or Dubai or South Dakota, and that is exactly what

[29] Heathrow is the outstanding example. Its passenger traffic currently ranks it as the world's fourth busiest airport, after Chicago O'Hare, Atlanta and Los Angeles, all of which have a high content of US domestic traffic, and substantially higher than Kennedy Airport, New York.
But O'Hare has a relatively easy life, with thirty-one scheduled carriers against Heathrow's seventy-three, and only two million international passengers compared with Heathrow's twenty million. Half of O'Hare's passengers transfer from one flight to another and do not, as the airlines put it, 'terminate'. The comparable figure for Atlanta is seventy per cent and for Heathrow fifteen per cent. Each transfer passenger is counted as one arrival and one departure. If they counted as only one movement, i.e. as one passenger, Heathrow would move into second place after Chicago.

Dallas/Fort Worth, Texas, under construction: one of the world's largest and most advanced airports.

they do. The task does little to invite imaginative or distinctive innkeeping. Which frequent traveller has not been awakened, either by the scream of a jet or by over-cooling or over-heating, in a pitch-dark room in such a hotel, and experienced a sense of panic because he had no idea where he was? Who, even worse, has fumbled for and eventually found the light switch, and then has desperately searched the room for evidence of his whereabouts and failed to find it? Who, like one of your authors, has even stumbled down to demand of a startled night porter in what part of the world he was, only to find that the man spoke no English? That particular nightmare ended in the hotel car park when Turkish registration plates helped place the hotel in Izmir.

This, however, has to do with the faceless anonymity of airports, not with their efficiency. The Kennedys and the Heathrows are inefficient, exhausting nightmares, begun in one age and struggling desperately to function in another. They can only point backwards.

One guess would be that the future will lie either with airports like Atlanta, Georgia, with its 104 gates, able to take 130 wide-bodied aircraft simultaneously and designed specifically to allow passengers to change aircraft with a minimum of time and effort, or with well-planned regional airports, like those at Cologne or Düsseldorf, which are not to be allowed to grow. If and when Cologne shows signs of becoming too small, then a new airport of the same size will be built at, say, Mainz or Koblenz. Airports which have grown piecemeal and which are being strangled by the increased traffic they have to handle year by year cannot survive. They will probably decline and moulder away, rather than shut.

But, meanwhile, these sprawling, exhausting, inefficient giants employ a very large number of people. They are not so much airports as occupational towns, commuter centres, factory estates, where thousands of men and women work, eat, but rarely sleep. However unsatisfactory such places may be from the passengers' point of view, they represent a much-prized source of wages, salaries, perks and, in some instances, alas, loot, to people who have built their way of life around them. The social history of aviation includes them just as much as passengers. A major airport is a broadly-based community, with its skilled and unskilled members, its middle and its working class, its honest citizens and its criminal fringe, its own peculiar language and ethics.

An analysis of the staff employed at Heathrow in 1976–7 tells us something about the nature of the aviation community. In that year there were:

British Airports Authority employees	2,564
Government employees	2,710
Airline employees	40,213
Concessionaires' employees	7,115
Contractors' employees	316
	52,918

Given a fresh start and new buildings planned specifically to meet the needs of the 1980s, there is no doubt that these numbers could be considerably reduced, although such a step would certainly meet with powerful opposition from the trade unions concerned. But it seems likely, even so, that by 1990 airports will be employing considerably fewer people and considerably more electronic and automatic equipment for every million passengers they handle. The check-in desk in particular is most unlikely to survive the 1980s, except at very small airports.

As airline profit margins narrow, management is increasingly thinking about self-service as a way of keeping down costs. 'We have to use the cheapest source of labour available to us and that is of course the passenger,' says a British Airways executive. In future, as we load our own baggage, print-out our own tickets on automatic dispensers and unpack our own sandwiches, we may even look back with regret to the days in the Seventies when the elegant 747s were staffed by a full complement of stewards who served pretty plastic meals on pretty plastic trays.

One would also hope that much earlier than the end of the 1980s the mutilation and loss, temporary or otherwise, of passengers' luggage, a torment so common nowadays, will have become a thing of the past, together with the fearsome delays involved in the arrival of baggage at the point where the owners are waiting more or less patiently for it. The wretchedly inadequate methods of baggage handling nowadays have become an international scandal which the travelling public is unlikely to be willing to tolerate much longer.

But, with airports as with everything else, the impossible and totally illogical can always happen, confounding all prophecy and common sense.

Diamonds in The Sky

The new airport in Saudi Arabia is a case in point. Built in the desert, it covers an area of twenty-one square miles along the Red Sea, twelve miles from Jeddah. It is easily the largest and most expensive airport in the world. One building, covering a hundred acres, is to be used during only one month of the year, to handle three million Muslims arriving for the pilgrimage to nearby Mecca.

The commercial terminal is placed to handle 16,000 passengers a day, although until fairly recently Jeddah had practically no air traffic at all except for pilgrim traffic. There is a Royal Pavilion for the Saudi ruling family and visiting heads of state, seven mosques, a hotel, a hospital and a town to house airport staff and troops for the military air base associated with the airport. The airport buildings are air conditioned throughout – the temperature at Jeddah often reaches 120° F in the shade – and marble extensively used for facing. A nuclear power station generates the electricity required and runs the large desalination plant which treats water from the Red Sea at the rate of 883,000 cubic feet a day.

If anyone had prophesied at the beginning of the 1970s that by the end of the decade the world's biggest airport would be at Jeddah, he would have been told, perfectly correctly, that what he was producing was a wild fantasy, not a prophecy. What the world would have forgotten was that unlimited money combined with an autocratic ruler has a way of turning fantasies into reality. In this respect, Jeddah airport is remarkably like the Pyramids.

But, keeping one's imagination under control and one's feet a little more firmly on the ground, another forecast must be that the disruption brought about by bad weather will have to end. Aircraft and airports without the equipment to cope with poor visibility will simply be pushed into the background. With such a huge investment in modern aircraft, these expensive planes will have to keep much more strictly to time and place.

Helicopters should not be left out of our forecasts. During the Sixties, there was much talk about the rosy future for helicopters but, great as their advantages might be, it was impossible to brush aside certain real economic disadvantages. It was obviously wonderful to be able to avoid the increasingly dreadful traffic congestion on the ground and to take off and land on the lawn of the White House or the roof of a department store, and very important people, to whom cost was no object, did this sort of thing regularly. There were also in the Sixties, and even more in the Seventies, helicopter links between nearby airports such as Heathrow and Gatwick and Kennedy and Newark and, in one or two cases, an air taxi service from the centre of the city to the airport ten or twenty miles away. But the cost of this kind of service has remained high and the proportion of passengers making use of it consequently very small.

Helicopters, for all their usefulness, suffer from two major drawbacks: one is that a really big helicopter, built to take fifty or a hundred people and their baggage, has not yet been developed, and the other is that the peculiar construction, with overhead rotors and considerable vibration, involves heavy maintenance cost. Yet, even with helicopters still in what one has to regard as a primitive phase, the extremely successful experience of British Airways with their Penzance/Scilly service shows that on suitable routes helicopters can be a very good financial proposition. With low on-the-ground overheads and excellent, all-year-round bookings, Penzance/Scilly is at the top of British Airways profitability league. The machines are idle for an absolute minimum of time. Ten minutes between landing and take-off is normal, passengers and baggage being unloaded and loaded perfectly comfortably in this brief period.

Given the right aircraft, which at the moment do not exist, London/Paris or London/Brussels might well show similar results. To be able to fly direct from city centre to city centre would be a very attractive thought to most passengers. The airlines and the airport authorities would like to experiment with such services but permission has so far been refused in the belief that the noise level would not be acceptable to people living and working in the area of the heliports. This situation could well change, however, with the arrival of bigger, quieter helicopters and the use of rivers as heliport sites.

Airports, safety, fares, speed and reliability – all these things are fundamental. Whether an aircraft has an air-to-ground telephone service, flying secretaries, a tea room in the air, Elizabethan meals or two bars is not really very important. If a general criticism has to be made of airlines in the 1970s, it should probably be that they have continued the bad old habit of the 1960s, to concentrate too much on the frills and too little on the basics. The 'basics', however, can be interpreted in two quite different ways. It may mean getting the whole flying operation technically and physically right – an end to delays and disruptions, far more attention to the genuine comfort and convenience of passengers, a radical simplification of the fare structure – or it could, alternatively, mean acknowledging, with appropriate guilt and humility, the profound damage the aeroplane, like the motorcar, has inflicted on the quality and variety of human life. Following this act of confession, it may mean taking decisions which could at least mitigate the harm that has already been done and, with luck, prevent even worse happening in the future.

TEN

'The Age of Mass Mobility'?

The aviation industry, like most others, has brought both benefits and catastrophes to humanity. Technical historians are in a world of their own, but the authors of a social history of air travel are necessarily involved in values. They have a clear duty to spell out the pros and cons to the best of their ability. To dwell only on the benefits is to be content to remain in effect unpaid public relations officers for both the airlines and the aircraft manufacturers and to adopt an uncritical and irresponsible view. So we shall end with a piece of social accounting.

On one side of the balance sheet we have to place the series of remarkable technical achievements, spanning roughly the whole of the present century, which have brought powered flight to a stage of development undreamed of in Victorian times. We might perhaps summarise this by saying that now it is possible to put more than 300 people in an aeroplane and to take them high above the weather from Europe to Australia in, barring mishaps, less than twenty-four hours, feeding them constantly on the way and diverting them with films and recorded music en route. The stages by which this miracle has been accomplished are indicated in the previous pages. On a somewhat lesser scale, one can make a holiday trip from London or Frankfurt to anywhere around the Mediterranean in three and a half hours and cross America from coast to coast in four. If one has a deep enough pocket, one can cross the Atlantic by Concorde in the absurdly short time of three and a half hours. Above all, flying today is outstandingly good value: in an age of inflation the real cost of air travel has declined enough to enable families of moderate means on different sides of the world to be occasionally reunited. This is the nature of the achievement and it is certainly not to be denigrated.

But there are a number of disturbing factors to be set against it. Encouraged by prodigious government subsidies and by decades of cheap and abundant oil, the airline operators have caused enormous areas of fertile, level land to be sterilised by airports, whose appetite has grown steadily more insatiable over the years, and the noise of whose aeroplanes has made life at best miserable and at worst almost intolerable for the millions of people all over the world who are unfortunate enough to live within a radius of five miles and even more of the runways.

Perhaps, however, we should be more concerned about the alliance between aviation and tourism. As we have explained earlier, the aviation industry created mass tourism, willingly or unwillingly, in order to cope with the problem of having too many empty seats on the aircraft. The prime aim of the modern tourist industry is economic – to fill seats and beds and, if this is the only measure of success, it has succeeded admirably. But its success contains the seeds of its destruction. Destinations draw closer each year, but they may become less and less worth visiting. What the tourist finds increasingly is a global uniformity, a fantasy life-style of huge and what he is persuaded to think of as 'luxury' hotels, marinas, swimming pools and another standard product known as 'night-life', all of which have no relevance to the culture of the country he is supposed to be visiting.

A high proportion of Europeans bearing the flattering label of tourists do not, in fact, engage in anything at all that could reasonably be called tourism. They go straight from the airport to their hotel–shopping–café complex in the sun and they stay there for two weeks, or whatever the length of their holiday may be. They are there because they have bought guaranteed sun, the only commodity they cannot get at home in Bradford or Oberhausen or Lille. This is not tourism at all. It is, to coin a word, solarism.

Tourism is a mixed blessing, especially when the host countries belong to the developing world. Sooner or later the natives may come to resent the visitors, especially when the resulting inflation hits their economies hard and all but a very small minority of hotel-keepers, shopkeepers and bus-proprietors find themselves worse off than they were before. Meanwhile, however, the life style of the invaders has rubbed off on them. They begin to demand it for themselves and in a short time their governments have a major and unsolvable socio-economic problem on their hands. There is also the very real danger that a country may become economically dependent on tourism, making it highly vulnerable to the whimsical and unpredictable decisions of tourists to transfer their patronage elsewhere or, if money should become short, to stay at home.

The airlines, in short, have made it possible for millions of people all over the world to find a much-needed fantasy world for two or three weeks in the year and to forget temporarily the real problems of boring jobs, ugly surroundings and urban tension. What the tourist industry, aided and abetted by its aviation colleagues and the media, has done is to provide the masses with cut-price and therapeutic escapism.

But the impact of aviation must be looked at as a whole, and it is consoling to find the leading figures in the industry are thinking deeply about the implications of this new nomadism. One of them is the President of the Boeing Corporation, Tex Boullioun:

Diamonds in The Sky

The world's population is spreading over this earth at a rate today that makes all past migrations pale in comparison.

And the impact on earthbound portions of our societies is awesome – traumatic – profound – immense.

The Eskimo on the ice, the Bedouin in the desert, the Bantu in the forest and the Polynesian on the sea are not beyond the reach of the jet which swirls cultural patterns, products and politics together in its wake around the world.

While many people extol the jet's benefits, others decry its noise, its use of land and fuel, and its disruption of established life-styles. The jet's inevitability is being fought by farmers and students in Japan, by conservationists in Florida, and by landowners in a hundred other places.[1]

That was in 1978. Would Mr Boullioun be so convinced of the 'inevitability' of the jet now, as the petroleum supply position worsens daily? And fuel is only one problem.

In the early summer of 1979, the media were again filled with reports of delays and cancellations and of passengers stranded in airports, and it is interesting to examine the causes of three days of chaos at London's Heathrow in mid-June. The trouble started with a one-day strike by a small number of key scientists and engineers whose absence was enough to reduce traffic by seventy-five per cent. The following day, when things should have been back to normal, the computer that processes information for Air Traffic Control was out of action and this brought flying to a complete halt. Even when the computer service was restored after some hours, the airlines were unable to clear the back-log of passengers because of a go-slow by air traffic controllers in Spain. Additional difficulties arose when the Italian Government temporarily cancelled all charter flights from Britain in retaliation against an oil company that refused to sell Alitalia more than its UK quota of fuel. All this demonstrates the extreme vulnerability of air transportation; its operation can so easily be halted by economic, technical, political and above all by human factors.

On the technical side, the industry is now so dependent on its computers that United Airlines insists that we do not reveal the exact whereabouts of its Apollo Computer, which is housed in a fortress-like installation 'somewhere in Colorado' and without which 'the airline simply would not function'. Computers can be sabotaged and they can go wrong but far more distress to airline passengers is likely to be caused by human failures. In the words of Tex Boullioun: 'Passenger security and comfort is affected greatly by the interlocking relationship of international services. Therefore, there is a need to minimise the impacts of strikes and showdowns upon the entire system. I can think of no other business that can be adversely affected so rapidly in several nations by the events in a single city.' How very true and how clearly demonstrated by recent events in Europe! But to solve the problem, all Mr

[1] 'The Age of Mass Mobility', F.T. World Aerospace Conference, August 1978.

Boullioun can suggest is that 'work rules which meet the peculiar problems of air transportation and yet allow for meaningful redress for all parties must be promulgated'. It is unclear what the President of Boeing has in mind but it is good to know that at least he realises that while things remain as they are 'the benefits and appeal of air travel are being lost in the discomfort of the ordeal'.

Mr Boullioun was making those remarks in the summer of 1978 when the de-regulation boom was at its zenith and he drew attention to the cyclical nature of the airline industry; he noted that newspapers were currently full of headlines like: 'Blue Skies Ahead for the Airlines', 'Airlines Take-off', 'Record Earnings', 'Record Air Traffic', 'The New Jets Are Coming', and so forth, and he went on: 'Four years ago . . . no such headlines were appearing; there was little to smile about. Four years from now the same could be true again.'

Less than one year after that confident speech the outlook for the airlines is once more filled with uncertainties and dangers. The immediate consequences of the fuel crisis are bad enough, but if general recession follows how much disposable income will there be for air travel? Within twelve months, the Jumbos could again be travelling half-empty across the Atlantic, and for those who can still afford to fly, things might perhaps be that much more agreeable. If a slump does come, just because the problems of mass mobility will seem less urgent, they will probably be pigeon-holed and there they will stay, waiting to pop out and torment us the next time we hit a high point in the aviation cycle.

At the time of writing, all this is speculative, but not so unlikely that the President of Boeing is not thinking about it.

Air transportation will remain cyclical, we cannot eliminate the effects of the general economy, but we can ameliorate them. We can avoid the cycles of waste created by continuing system disturbance and delays. We can manage the cycles of technical improvement, of market expansion, of passenger service or safety increase. Let us not fritter away our current success, nor let others do it for us.

And so say all of us.

Books for Further Reading

This is in no sense a bibliography of aviation. It is rather a list of publications which have been read or consulted and found useful during the preparation of the present book.

Few of the books mentioned have much, if anything, to say about passengers and the way they have been handled or treated at different periods. For this and much other indispensable information, we have relied to a great extent on periodical and newspaper articles and on the personal reminiscences of passengers and airline staff.

General works on aviation history

Brooks, Peter W., *The Modern Airliner: its Origins and Development* (1961)
Davies, R. E. G., *A History of the World's Airlines* (1964)
Duval, G. R., *British Flying-Boats and Amphibians, 1902–52* (1966)
Elkins, H. R., *Round the World in Eighty Days* (1934)
Falconer, B. L., *Flying Around the World* (1937)
Gibbs-Smith, Charles H., *Aviation: an Historical Survey from its Origins to the End of World War II* (1970)
Jackson, A. J., *British Civil Aircraft, 1919–52*, 2 vols (1959–60)
Penrose, H. J., *British Aviation: the Pioneer Years* (1967)
Penrose, H. J., *British Aviation: the Adventuring Years* (1973)
Rivers, Patrick, *The Restless Generation* (1978)
Serling, Robert J., *Wrights to Wide Bodies: the first 75 years* (1978)
Stroud, John, *Annals of British and Commonwealth Air Transport, 1919–60* (1962)
Stroud, John, *European Transport Aircraft since 1910* (1966)

Airships

Eckner, H., *My Airships* (1958)
Lehmann, E. A., *Zeppelin* (1937)
Nielsen, T., *The Zeppelin Story* (1955)
Robinson, Douglas H., *LZ 129 'Hindenburg'* (1964)
Shute, Nevil, *Slide Rule* (1968)
Valth, J. G., *Graf Zeppelin* (1959)

Particular manufacturers

Andrews, C. F., *Vickers Aircraft since 1908* (1969)
Barnes, C. H., *Short Aircraft since 1900* (1967)
Bowers, Peter M., *Boeing Aircraft since 1916* (1966)
Handley Page Ltd, *Forty Years On* (1949)
Weyl, A. R., *Fokker: the Creative Years* (1965)

Airline operations and policy

Cooper, M. H. and Maynard, A. K., *The Price of Air Travel* (1971)
Grumbridge, Jack L., *Marketing Management in Air Transport* (1966)
McFarlane, R. A., *Human Factors in Relation to the Development of Pressurised Cabins* (1971)
Road, Alan, *The Facts about an Airline* (1978)
Wheatcroft, Stephen, *Air Transport Policy* (1964)
Williams, J. E. D., *The Operation of Airlines* (1964)
Young, M., *Civil Aviation* (1944)

Particular airlines and routes

Affleck, Arthur, *The Wandering Years* (1962)
Baldwin, N. C., *Imperial Airways* (1950)
Fysh, Sir Hudson, *Qantas Rising* (1965)
Fysh, Sir Hudson, *Qantas at War* (1968)
Laile, Henry, *Les Transports Aériens Air France* (1963)
Ministry of Information, *Atlantic Bridge* (1945)
Munday, E., *A Report of a Flight Made to London from Mpika* (1932)
Qantas Empire Airways: 40th anniversary (1960)
Rusman, E., *Wings Across Continents* (1935)
Salt, A. E. W., *Imperial Air Routes* (1930)
Sherman, Arnold, *To the Skies: the El Al Story* (1972)
Wachtel, Joachim, *The History of Lufthansa* (1975)
Western Airlines, *Oh How We Flew* (1976)
Wilson, Mike and Scagell, Robin, *Jet Journey* (1978)

Accidents, insurance

Insurance Institute of London, *A Short History of Aviation Insurance in the United Kingdom* (2nd ed., 1968)
Johnson, George, *The Abominable Airlines* (1964)
Launay, A. J., *Historic Air Disasters* (1967)

Airports

Los Angeles Department of Airports, *50th Anniversary* (1977)

Index

ACKNOWLEDGEMENTS

The authors would like to thank the many private individuals, airlines, travel companies, libraries, museums and other organisations which have helped them with information, advice and facilities during the preparation of *Diamonds in the Sky*, and particularly the following: British Airports Authority; British Airways, especially the extremely knowledgeable and always kind and helpful Ron Wilson; El Al; IATA; KLM; Lufthansa; National Air and Space Museum, Washington DC; Pilkingtons, St Helens; Qantas; TWA; United Airlines; Air France; and John Stroud for his expert advice throughout. This is, of course, in addition to the assistance provided in the course of filming the television series presented by Julian Pettifer, acknowledged by the BBC at the end of each programme.

Thanks are due to the following for supplying black and white photographs: Caroline Rogers, page 8; Sir Alan Cobham, page 11; British Airways, pages 13, 47, 71, 75, 81, 83, 100, 123, 126, 127, 132, 137, 147, 149, 202, 205; Air France, pages 16, 21, 22, 89, 143, 226; *Flight International*, page 24; National Air and Space Museum, Washington DC, pages 26, 85, 87, 94; *Punch*, pages 28, 112; Qantas and Harry Hastings, pages 30, 34, 36; KLM, pages 39, 40, 50, 66, 69, 78; Lufthansa, pages 42, 48, 59, 60, 65, 105, 125; United Airlines, page 53; Canadian Pacific, page 56; Musée de l'Air, Paris, page 63; Popperfoto, pages 92, 154, 156, 214; Aer Lingus, page 102; Port Authority of New York and New Jersey, page 110; John Stroud, pages 116, 120, 122, 129, 145; Cincinnati Preservation Society, pages 107, 109; Boeing Aircraft Company, pages 114, 194; the Trustees of the Imperial War Museum, page 118; Pan American World

Airways, page 135; South African Airways, page 140; Shannon Free Airport Development Co. Ltd, pages 151, 152; SAS, pages 159, 168; Krupp, page 161; TAP, page 163; Air-India, page 165; Richard Adam, pages 172, 175, 177, 178, 183; Harry Hastings, page 190; Mervyn Broadway, pages 185, 187, 192; *The Times*, page 196; *Chicago Tribune*, page 200; Cox Photography, page 207; British Airports Authority, page 216; Thomas Cook Group Limited, page 219; Dallas/Fort Worth Regional Airport, page 228.

Thanks for supplying colour material are due to: Musée de l'Air, Paris, facing pages 48 and 49; Imperial Tobacco Company and Mardon Son & Hall Limited, facing pages 64 and 65; Mervyn Broadway, facing pages 144 *top*, 192, 193 *top* and *bottom*; Boeing Aircraft Company, facing page 144 *bottom*; John Stroud, facing pages 145, 160 *top* and *bottom*; Lufthansa, facing page 161 *top*; Ann Nicholls, facing pages 161 *bottom* and 209 *bottom*; Air France, facing pages 176 and 209 *top*; El Al, facing page 177; Canadian Pacific, facing page 208 *top*; British Airways, facing pages 208 *bottom*, 224 *top*, 255 *top*; Japan Air Lines, facing page 224 *bottom*; Tor Eigeland/*Daily Telegraph* Colour Library, facing page 225 *bottom*.

Thanks are also due to Secker & Warburg for permission to quote material from *My Farce From My Elbow* by Brian Rix on page 146, to *Harpers & Queen* and Betty Kenward for permission to quote the material on pages 202–3, to *Punch* and Fay Maschler for permission to quote the material on pages 208–10, and to Jonathan Cape for permission to quote the lines by George Seferis on page ii taken from *Collected Poems 1924–1955* translated by Edmund Keeley and Philip Sherrard.